THE NATIONAL MUSEUM

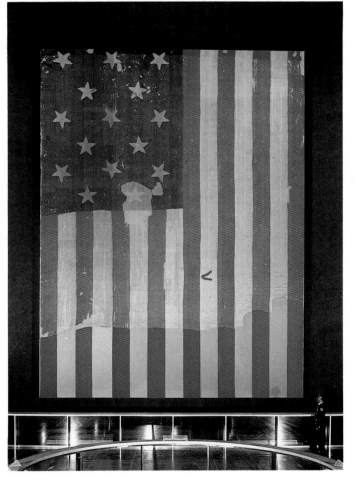

OF AMERICAN HISTORY

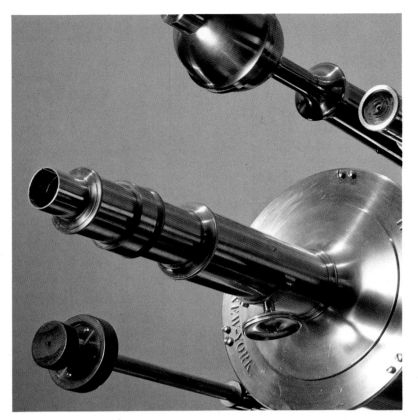

THE NATIONAL MUSEUM

by Shirley Abbott

OF AMERICAN HISTORY

Harry N. Abrams, Inc., Publishers, New York

Page 1: *Francis Scott Key's Star Spangled Banner that flew at Fort McHenry in 1814.*

Pages 2-3 and 13: *This freeswinging pendulum—the centerpiece of the Museum—was devised originally in 1851 by French physicist Jean Foucault. It is not (as many visitors suppose) a perpetual motion machine but a demonstration of the earth's rotation.*

Right: *A detail of the "Winton Bullet," an eight-cylinder racing car of 1903.*

Pages 8-9: *This American drugstore of about 1890 reflects the past of the apothecary trade.*

Page 10: *Detail of a locomotive.*

Editor: Edith M. Pavese

Photography art directed by David Larkin
Photography (except where noted) by
    Michael Freeman and Robert Golden

Library of Congress Cataloging in Publication Data
Abbott, Shirley.
    The National Museum of American History.

    Bibliography: p. 389
    Includes index.
    1. United States—Civilization.   2. National Museum
of American History (U. S.) I. Title.
E169.1.A117   973   81-5032
ISBN 0-8109-1363-1   AACR2

First Edition

Printed and bound in Japan

CONTENTS

FOREWORD

This is not an introduction to a Museum, but an introduction to a book about a Museum. The book was not written by "a Museum historian," but by a gifted professional writer who loves museums and who takes you around ours, telling you how she feels about the objects she finds there, and about some of the Great Persons associated with those objects.

She has identified those objects in ways that she felt would be most interesting to you. We, on the Museum staff, have watched with wonder and admiration as she has illuminated the places and the things that are familiar to us in her often unfamiliar ways.

In this Foreword I want to add just a word of my own, which is intended to convey some sense of the difference between what happens when you try to make a Museum, which is our occupation, and what happens in the equally difficult but quite different process of trying to make an illustrated book. I imagine you sitting there, in your own living room, leafing through this volume, looking first at the shimmering pictures, filling these beguiling images with your own imagination so as to expand their two dimensions into three.

Any photographic image invites us to move it around, turn it upside down, stretch it out. On the other hand, we are properly diffident about manhandling objects too much. Each one has, after much earnest scholarship, an "orient." It has been assigned a place. Unless we are very bold indeed we are likely to defer to that scholarship in telling us where our imaginations can dare to place them. I want to exhort you not to be too deferential. Feel free to play with these images. You can't break them or hurt their feelings. And all scholars are fallible.

You can do anything with the images in this book that amuses you. You can put them together to make jokes, or to compose a set of images which come together just because they are pretty. In the Museum itself we have to be more careful than that, because the way we exhibit things provides six or seven million visitors a year with their sense of what history was. In a very real sense, the Museum guards our nation's memory. We work, in the interest of generations that will come after us, to store up and recall the objects that are important witnesses of our past. And while we will never know enough about the past to be absolutely sure of everything we do, we know that the objects themselves have their own certainty, their *own* confidence.

Each of the things you see pictured here, and each thing you find in the Museum itself, was chosen. Nothing in these collections just happened to be left over, nor was anything forgotten in some cupboard and thoughtlessly left there. Our predecessors and we have had to try to choose, and then to preserve, everything you see.

Please look closely at the objects in these pictures, and at the things themselves when you come into the Museum. You should feel free to ask why it is there, if it is being kept the way it really was, if it is placed as it should be, in the right company (or, perhaps, without any company at all if it is a better solo performer than ensemble artifact). Check what we have done against what you yourself do as you pick up and move about, in imagination, the objects which you have created in your mind out of the images you found in this book. Turn them over in your mind. Put them against the light where their contours are distinct. Let these objects speak to you, privately, first. Then come to us and tell us if you agree with the ways in which we have tried to let them speak.

I am inviting you to become a participant in a Museum, not just a consumer of its messages, a visitor to its halls. Each of us has favorite objects. These are the ones that draw from our unconscious the electricity that builds up there, awaiting a powerful symbol to which it can arc. In that moment, a recognition—a knowing again—occurs, which helps us see in that symbol an old friend. Through it we then feel less estranged from the world.

We require such favorite objecst if we are to avoid a dangerous accumulation of "potential" empathy, a condition that we call loneliness. The best class of objects to palliate that condition, are, I think, animate objects, and, among animate objects, the best class is composed of those of the same species as ourselves. But there is considerable virtue in placing, between our intense moments of incandescence with real people, lower-intensity encounters with objects, and lower still, with images of objects.

Now let me tell you just a little about the way we feel about the Museum out of which these pictured objects are taken. It is the nation's memory, made tangible in collections of objects. It is also an assembly of people, whose job it is to collect, protect, and place before you, those objects. The first museum, that established by Ptolemy in Alexandria, probably had no inanimate objects in it at all; it was a university. In the English-speaking world we tend not to think of picture galleries or of libraries as "museums," though we would think less of any museum that had neither within it. Our Museum has people who study and write and teach within it, nearly three hundred of them, including those people who help other people do all those things. It also has many libraries, some of which are just a few books or sheets of computations, and it has hundreds of thousands of pictures, though perhaps only a few thousand actually displayed at one time. (I suppose that if one counted those tiny pictures, called "postage stamps," we should raise that number to something over twelve million.)

In the Museum building we have, therefore, innumerable two-dimensional objects, some of them masterpieces of design, as fine as those to be found in any gallery in the world. We have huge brawny machines and fragile crystals. We have some objects, like the Star Spangled Banner, which anyone can recognize, together with some things so tiny and esoteric that only two or three people in the world know what they really are. But all of them are there because they matter to the American people, because they have been selected by some American to be more significant than objects discarded. And they all tell us something important about our national experience.

What they tell us changes with every person who sees them, because there is no such thing as a truly "inanimate" object except when it languishes unnoticed. Each of our objects comes to life in the presence of an attentive visitor. It begins to glow, its cheeks to flush, its joints to move, when you come by. The animation of an object is a miracle so common as generally to go unnoticed, but it happens all day, every day, in our Museum. So we invite you to anticipate that experience by playing with the pictures in this book, reading about them in Shirley Abbott's eloquent prose, and then, full of your own ideas about them, coming to awaken them in the National Museum of American History.

—Roger G. Kennedy
Director, The National
Museum of American History

13

THE AMERICAN EXPERIENCE
as seen in the
National Museum of American History

We held it certain that going toward the sunset we would find what we desired.

—Cabeza de Vaca*

The history of America, brief as it is, is the record of a thousand confrontations and antagonisms, some of which have been destructive, others fruitful in amazing ways. The basic problem of American politics, it has been said, is to reconcile liberty with order—a noble and quite magnificent undertaking that has produced, among other things, our Constitution. It has also produced some spectacular pratfalls. Perhaps more than the history of other nations, ours has proceeded by paradox and been colored by irony. Even as set forth in the standard textbooks, the story of the United States bears a definite familial resemblance to a fast-paced movie plot, full of hairpin turns and twists, tragi-comic episodes, and conflicts that upon being resolved simply produce other conflicts. If the long saga of human life on earth could be made into a film, the last four hundred years of action on the North American continent would move along at the frenzied pace of a Buster Keaton silent—and with some of the same kinds of heroes and villains and some of the same lunatic flavor.

America was "discovered" more than once, of course: first by the hardy and inventive people who crossed the Bering Strait around 25,000 B.C. (the date is guesswork) and slowly took possession of the two continents; and later by the Vikings, who settled in Greenland around A.D. 1000 and in some place called Vinland the Good. For all we know there were other

landfalls too by seagoing Irish, Polynesians, Africans, or Japanese. But western Europe knew little or nothing of all this. The real discovery was made in 1492 by a Genoese navigator sailing under Spanish colors. He had calculated to land in Japan, but it might be China, or India. Who could be certain? Among his papers he carried a letter from Ferdinand and Isabella to the Great Khan, whoever that might prove to be, as well as some pro-forma greetings which could be used for any ruler found in the new land.

On the islands of San Salvador and Hispaniola he found no emperors, only an amiable population that smoked tobacco and mostly went naked. Nevertheless, having collected some gold dust and six brown people whom he enslaved, Columbus sailed east once more and duly reported to his backers that he had found Asia. This was wishful thinking. Like most of his contemporaries Columbus was unable to comprehend that he had come upon something more terrifying in its potentiality even than the edge of the western sea and its mythical dragon. He had found half the world, and this half was inexplicably *new*—two vast continents, as it turned out, that the Bible had never mentioned, the Pope had never heard of, and that had gone undreamed of in the philosophies of Plato, Aristotle, and Saint Augustine. It took at least fifteen years before the first map was made and before even the intelligentsia of Europe began to grasp what Columbus had done, and much longer for them to understand what antique knowledge he had undone, what new forces he had released.

The American adventure got underway fairly slowly at first, compared with the growth rate that was soon to set in. The first serious settlers, one hundred and twenty Englishmen in three

* Spanish explorer who, beginning in 1528, walked from Florida to Arizona.

ships, arrived at the mouth of the James River in Virginia in 1607. They were cityfolks utterly unaccustomed to camping in the wilderness and unacquainted with the basic techniques of survival, and they did not do well. Having used up all their provisions, they tried to barter with and then to steal from the Indians, who had hardly been happy to see them in the first place and reacted ferociously. The English would surely have died of hunger and exposure had it not been for their remarkably tough leader, Captain John Smith. He formulated the basic commandment of the American frontier and made it stick: "He that will not work, shall not eat."

A few years later, a group almost as ill-equipped but with a higher sense of purpose disembarked far to the north of Virginia and went into the "hideous and desolate wilderness full of wild beasts and wild men," as their chronicler William Bradford described it afterward in his history *Of Plymoth Plantation*. They had come expecting martyrdom, realizing that they were

> liable to famine and nakedness and the want, in a manner of all things. The change of air, diet, and drinking of water would infect their bodies with sore sicknesses and grievous diseases. And also those which should escape and overcome these difficulties should yet be in continual danger of the savage people, who are cruel, barbarous, and most treacherous, being most furious in their rage, and merciless where they overcome, not being content only to kill and take away life, but delight to torment men in the most bloody manner . . . .

The Wampanoag Indians whom these pioneers met turned out, on the contrary, to be both courteous and helpful, at least for the first few years. But the landscape was just as savage as William Bradford had predicted, and the mortality rate as high. How many immigrants from Columbus's time onward have not arrived on American shores trembling at what might await them, and already half-dead from fear?

Nevertheless, by 1710 this new land had a European population of 300,000 on its Atlantic perimeter. (In what is now the United States and Canada there were possibly about a million Indians at that time.) Most of the Europeans

Page 14: *Horsedrawn passenger and mail wagons like the one* opposite *carried many an immigrant westward. In front of the coach, from left to right, are the cherished possessions that various newcomers brought along from the Old World: a piece of linen sheeting used as a bag, a blue woolen dress and coat, a Slovene apron, a reed hamper, a Swedish dress, a Scottish chest, and a Russian furniture scarf of embroidered linen damask.*

I think the true discovery of America is before us. I think the true fulfillment of our spirit, of our people, of our mighty and immortal land is yet to come.

—*Thomas Wolfe,*
You Can't Go Home Again, *1940*

were English, Scots, Scotch-Irish, mingling with a few French, Dutch, and German. And there were black men and women, too. No one knows how many, precisely, had arrived by this date. Possibly one of the most fateful events of American history had occurred one August day in 1619 when a Dutch man-of-war put in at Jamestown and sold its cargo: twenty "Negars." These twenty may have been regarded as indentured servants rather than outright chattels. But the distinction between white bondservant and black slave was soon made in colonial lawbooks and in the minds of the colonists.

Of course if the casual transaction of slave trafficking had not taken place at Jamestown in 1619, it would have happened in another port or another year. From Columbus's first voyage onward, slavery was a persistent enterprise in the New World. Queen Elizabeth's famous privateer, Sir John Hawkins, was a slave dealer, as were innumerable other English, Dutch, Spanish, and Portuguese captains. Any Indian or African was fair game and scarcely any seagoing nationality of Europe kept aloof from the traffic. The first black slaves came to New England in 1638 in the Salem ship, Desire. By 1700 there were slaves, both black and red, in every American colony, including Plymouth and the Massachusetts Bay.

By all logic, these 300,000 European settlers of 1710, who hardly thought of themselves as Americans, whatever their condition of servitude, should have diminished in numbers and died out. They were confronted by an impenetrable forest that edged right up to the coastline and by increasingly hostile resistance from the original inhabitants of that forest, who had already had some harsh lessons as to the challenge they faced from the newcomers. The climate was often horrendous, ranging from stifling to chilling right on the same spot: malaria in July, pneumonia in January. But the settlers did not die out, and, along the course of the eighteenth century, history took one of its extraordinary turns—something as momentous in its way as the invention of agriculture thousands of years earlier. By 1770, the original 300,000 had multiplied to 1,700,000. Only one fourth of this unprecedented increase came from immigration; the birthrate among the colonists

averaged thirty percent per decade, which was twice what England's was at the same period. By 1790, the year of the first census, the population was 3,900,000. It was a population explosion unequalled before or since in any country even in our own explosive century, and the staggering birthrate was accompanied by low infant mortality. To judge from numbers alone there had never been an environment so hospitable to the human species.

Part of the reason for this upsurge must have lain in the sheer richness of the land and the purity of its air and water. The forest might be untamed and uncivilized, inhumanly lonely, lacking even a road or a trail, but in one sense it was paradise. Fish of all varieties swarmed chock-a-block in the rivers. Mussels, oysters, and clams abounded in the bays and estuaries. Lobsters were often stacked up on the Massachusetts beaches—the Puritans scorned them. "The abundance of seafish are almost beyond believing, and sure I would scarce have believed it except I had seen it with mine own Eyes," wrote an Englishman named Francis Higginson on Cape Cod in 1630. All along the Atlantic coast, and inland, fruits, berries, herbs, and nuts grew plentifully in the wild. Apple, peach, and cherry trees sprang up and bore in record time.

And there was game—deer, rabbits, turkeys, razorback hogs, squirrels, and possums running in the woods; ducks, swans, and geese flocking on every river and bay. And not a bird or a deer was the property of any baron or earl or the subject of any game law. The game laws of England were notoriously harsh—even as late as the eighteenth century poachers could be fined, mutilated, or even put to death, depending upon the circumstances and the whim of the county magistrate. But in America a family could revert to the condition of Cro-Magnons, if they wished, and live the year round by hunting and gathering. They would not go hungry, nor would they be hauled off by the sheriff for summary judgment on the village green.

As soon as the colonists were able to master its techniques and learn to cook and preserve its products, they discovered that native American agriculture was productive and nourishing. Most settlers knew some of its fruits already—white potatoes, for example, had already become a staple of the European diet. Indeed by the end of the sixteenth century more than fifty Indian foods had been taken back to Europe and adopted—corn, turkey, pumpkins, squash, and new kinds of beans, among others. Yams and peanuts had become dietary staples in Africa. (Tomatoes are also a native American wild fruit but for many years were thought to be poisonous.) Half the crops the world eats today were originally grown by American Indians. Their famous triad of corn, beans, and squash, supplemented by game, makes a reliably balanced diet. Indian farming was the job of the women, and their skill in planting and fertilizing was impressive to the Europeans. These women also knew miraculous ways of drying and preserving—turning beef into jerky, pork into ham, corn into hominy.

But to change one's eating habits is perhaps the most revolutionary act of all, and the hardest. The colonists at first disdained the native bounty and did not want to abandon barley in favor of corn or mutton in favor of pork. As Stephen Vincent Benét wrote in *Western Star,* the change came, nevertheless:

> . . . those who came were resolved to be
>   Englishmen,
> Gone to world's end, but English every one,
> And they ate the white corn-kernels, parched
>   in the sun,
> And they knew it not, but they'd not be
>   English again.

There, oddly, is perhaps the most persuasive explanation of the population upsurge in the eighteenth century. For it must have come in part from that very sense of a new identity—the death of the Englishman (or whatever other nationality) and the birth of the American—and from the sense of mission in a landscape where a man and woman could support twelve, fifteen, twenty children, if they wished, on farms that yielded more when there were plenty of hands to work them. "O my America, my new-found land, My Kingdome . . . My Myne of precious stones," the poet John Donne had written, far away in England. He was not speaking of

geography but of his own joy at beholding the body of his mistress, yet the metaphor was exact and prophetic, in both the private and the public sense. For the limitless possibilities of life in the new-found land clearly provided colonial Americans with an energy that expressed itself procreatively.

Travelers to even the most dangerous and primitive parts of the backcountry in the mid-eighteenth century could hardly keep from noticing America's most plentiful and dependable crop. In 1767 an Anglican priest named Charles Woodmason, attempting to bring God's word to the Carolina frontier, observed, half-astonished, half-resigned:

> In many places they have naught but a Gourd to drink out off, Not a Plate, Knife, or Spoon . . . . They are so burthen'd with Young Children that the Women cannot attend both House and Field. . . . There's not a Cabbin but has 10 or 12 Young Children in it. When the Boys are 19 and the Girls 14 they marry, so that in many Cabbins You will see 10 or 15 Children. Children and Grand Children of one size, and the Mother looking as young as the Daughter. Yet these poor People enjoy good health. . . .

Poor people out in the backwoods were not the only segment to display a generative ebullience. In 1747 Benjamin Franklin, who himself was one of ten children and had five half-siblings besides, published a piece of whimsey called the "Speech of Polly Baker." It exemplifies the exuberance of the times. A young woman who had been hauled before a Connecticut court for having given birth to her fifth illegitimate child rebukes her judges as follows:

> Can it be a crime . . . to add to the King's subjects, in a new country that really wants people? . . . How can it be believed that heaven is angry at my having children . . . ? The duty of the first and great command of nature and nature's God, increase and multiply; a duty from the steady performance of which nothing has been able to deter me, but for its sake I have hazarded the loss of the public esteem and have frequently endured public disgrace and punishment; and therefore ought, in my humble opinion, instead of a whipping to have a statue erected to my memory.

And even the black population, working under often appalling conditions and with far less apparent incentive than the Polly Bakers, increased and multiplied. Statistics on American blacks are less than reliable before 1790, but the census of that year counted 757,000, of whom ninety-two percent were slaves. By 1860 this population had increased sixfold to 4,400,000, with a birthrate only slightly lower than that of whites. All this occurred in the teeth of all the evils of the slave system and, according to the best recent scholarship, with imports not greatly affecting the total (the trade was closed in 1808). Indeed the United States was the only slave power in this hemisphere where the black population did increase.

No one knows, of course, how many blacks died of malnutrition or abuse during slavery and after (more, probably, than the pro-slavery factions would have said and fewer than the abolitionists thought), or with what added force the nineteenth-century perils of puerperal fever and other infectious diseases fell upon them. And yet in spite of everything that worked against them, even this most set-upon group of Americans survived their ordeal as a people.

What made the nation was partly numbers, but partly human will. By the 1770s there was a core of people in America who looked upon themselves as Americans. They drew their sense of identity from a hundred sources—from their own sense of independence and power, from the width of the Atlantic Ocean, from their success at getting the Stamp Act repealed in 1766. They drew it from such leaders as John and Samuel Adams, George Washington, and Benjamin Franklin, who was the first American to achieve international fame. The nation's charter, or what we now perceive to have been its charter (celebrating its signing on July 4, though that is not when it actually was signed), was written out by hand on a lap-desk by Thomas Jefferson, an Enlightenment aristocrat and Virginia slaveholder. Each generation since 1776 has argued about the nature of this complex and mystifying man—about what kind of radical he was, if he was a radical, and about what he meant, exactly, when he set forth his

Overleaf: *George Washington, eleven feet high, in the guise of Zeus. Horatio Greenough's neo-classical marble sculpture was installed in the Capitol Rotunda in 1844 and acquired by the Smithsonian in 1908.*

stunning doctrines in the Declaration of Independence.

> We hold these truths to be self-evident, that all men are created equal; that they are endowed by their creator with certain [Jefferson had originally inserted "inherent and"] inalienable rights; that among these are life, liberty & the pursuit of happiness: that to secure these rights, governments are instituted among men, deriving their just powers from the consent of the governed. . . .

As if this were not sufficient, he went on to say that if any government denied these rights, the people had the right to abolish it and set up a new government as they saw fit. The Declaration was for one thing a piece of peerlessly wrought propaganda, designed to win support and enrage the King of England. But it has outlasted its original purpose, and each new generation has had to ask, "Should we take that literally?" Even today surely no one can read the Declaration, really read it, without feeling momentarily shaken by what it says. It is as clear as the Sermon on the Mount and has some of the same religious force. It has given rise to some of the more amazing paradoxes in American history.

All men equal? When Thomas Jefferson came to attend the second Continental Congress in Philadelphia in 1775, he brought his bodyservants with him—two black slaves named Jesse and Richard. Of whom were Jesse and Richard the equals, and how were they to go about the pursuit of happiness? Some interpreters have argued that obviously Mr. Jefferson was a slaveholder and Virginia gentleman and therefore what he intended to say was that free white men who owned property (and only they) were created equal. Yet that is not what he wrote, and surely a stylist of his caliber would have bothered to make the distinction. A number of "thinkers" have labored to prove that Jefferson did not mean what he said, or was crazy if he did. In 1826, a few days before he died, Jefferson wrote of the Declaration,

> May it be to the world what I believe it will be (to some parts sooner, to others later, but finally to all), the signal of arousing men to burst the chains under which monkish ignorance and superstition had persuaded them to bind themselves, and to assume the blessings and security of self-government.

In the imaginations of Americans and other revolutionaries, the notion of equality and inalienable rights has gone marching on (limping severely at times) and has come to include poor men, black men, women, and children. In the 1830s one of the most radical of American reform movements—abolition—sprang straight from the principles of the Declaration. Certain women who served the cause of abolition (for example, Sarah and Angelina Grimké of Charleston, South Carolina, and Elizabeth Cady Stanton of Seneca Falls, New York) concluded that if black men must be freed and enfranchised, then surely so must women. It took Abraham Lincoln most of his life to conclude that Jefferson's "men" might conceivably include blacks—and even then he was completely opposed to a mixed society. But when he went to speak at Gettysburg it was not the Constitution he invoked as his rallying cry for the Union but the Declaration of Independence: ". . . conceived in liberty and dedicated to the proposition that all men are created equal."

The rationale of almost every drive for social and economic reform—Civil Rights, the labor movement, populism, feminism—has harked back to the notion that all are created equal and are therefore entitled to an equal share. Jefferson's words are self-renewing. As Bruce Catton wrote in 1978, "Men are still acting on those words, and they always will. The idea has lost none of its power." The apparent impossibility of living up to the spirit of the Declaration has only acted as a spur to those who keep insisting that we try.

At the moment the charter was signed, the signers realized that they stood every chance of being hanged as traitors or of being transported to the Tower of London and then hanged. They lacked the military power to back up their writ of rebellion. Nevertheless the story of the Revolutionary War, although being sober fact, ranks with the sagas and the epics of Anglo-Saxon England and Carolingian France, as well as the celluloid ones of our own times. In a comparatively few years, an ad-hoc army of

A silver chalice (center) and tankard, designed and made in Massachusetts in the 1760s. At far right, a pewter teapot of 1735.

In America the taste for physical well-being is not always exclusive but it is general; and though all do not feel it in the same manner, yet it is felt by all. Everyone is preoccupied caring for the slightest needs of the body and the trivial conveniences of life.

—*Alexis de Tocqueville,*
Democracy in America, 1835–40

farmers, sharpshooters, and self-made guerrillas defeated the most disciplined professional fighting force of its day.

The amateurs' side had, of course, an enormous geographical and psychological advantage to offset its military shortcomings. With men like George Washington, Benedict Arnold (until he betrayed the cause), and Nathanial Greene the rebels also had a quality of generalship that would not be seen again until Robert E. Lee, Stonewall Jackson, and Albert Sidney Johnston took command of the Confederate forces eighty years after. And on the part of the professional army, there was much amateurish blundering: General John Burgoyne, bogging down in the lavishness of his own supply trains, unable to control the Indian warriors he had recruited, naively issuing muskets to a contingent of Vermonters called the Green Mountain Boys, who proceeded to turn expertly on Burgoyne and massacre all his Hessians. Or Lord Cornwallis allowing the Americans to close in on him at Yorktown while the French destroyed his supply ships at sea. Not all the blunders were British, of course. But the story of the war, even when told in the most objective language, takes on the mythic dimensions of a tableau that has always been dear to American hearts: Pomposity Undone.

And if this were not enough, French and Prussian noblemen came to aid the new nation— the Marquis de Lafayette, and the Count de Rochambeau, and the Baron von Steuben, donating their pedigrees and their ancient prestige, as well as their services. As if to balance off the grandeur of such names—as well as the dignity of General Washington and the aristocratic panache of such Southerners as Light Horse Harry Lee and Banastre Tarleton— there was a corps of independent backwoodsmen who had a new weapon called the Kentucky (or the Pennsylvania) rifle and knew how to use it. They were herders and farmers, mostly, but a far cry from Thomas Jefferson's beloved law-abiding yeomen. They were also ferocious fighters, and their grandsons would emerge from the woods again when the Civil War broke out.

For though we love to invoke the mythology of the town meeting and the orderly, well-governed New England village, one basic political strain in the land has always been an entrenched anarchism. Many observers sensed this. William Byrd II, a Virginia grandee of early colonial times who had firsthand acquaintance with the backwoods people, knew well enough that what had brought most of them here was hatred of all governments whatever. "Besides the hopes of being safe from Persecution in this Retreat," Byrd wrote in 1728, "the new Proprietors . . . inveigled many over by this tempting account of the Country: that it was a place free from those 3 great Scourges of Mankind, Priests, Lawyers, and Physicians." For a long time it was as free from Law as from lawyers. When these men came forth as American soldiers in the Continental Army, it was not the principles of Jefferson or Locke they fought for, or the desire to be equitably represented in the legislature. What they wanted was a piece of land (and they knew that as veterans they would get it), a plow, a mule, and a husky woman. And a government that would cling to the east coast, levying no taxes and raising no armies. Thousands of such men drew lots for land after the war was over and lit out from the Pennsylvania, Virginia, and Carolina backcountry. They crossed the hills into Georgia, Tennessee, and Kentucky, putting as much distance as they could between themselves and civilization, picking up and moving a hundred miles or so onward when society got too close to them.

Paradox and irony have continued to infuse the story at all levels. The Declaration of Independence, with its absolutist defense of individual liberty, was followed by the Constitution, that most intelligent, workable, logical, expandable of blueprints out of which grew our whole ponderous system of government. And the American Revolution, which was fought to secure a gain that would surely have evolved anyway, gave way to another kind of revolution, deeper than any political one. The late Jacob Bronowski wrote that "Revolutions are not made by fate but by men. Sometimes they are solitary men of genius. But the great revolutions in the eighteenth century were made by many lesser men banded together. What drove them was the conviction that every man is master of his own salvation." He was speaking of the Industrial Revolution in England, and the dozens of inventors and capitalists who made it, but his equation, if multiplied to the next power, also applies to the Industrial Revolution in America. Of all revolutions it was made not by a few solitary geniuses or even by "lesser men banded together" but by an entire people.

The United States in the nineteenth century remains a most awesome example of human expansiveness. Anything one says about it would probably prove true. But two things are inescapable. First, it was a century of work. Not all Americans earned a decent wage or lived in a decent house or had a chance to go to school, nor was there any such thing as medical care in the sense that we construe it. But everybody worked—men, women, and children. Horses, dogs, and mules worked; even cats were expected to perform a useful function. And now in the 1980s we still profit from, even sometimes suffer from, the results of all this nineteenth-century work. In 1800 there had been only one city with more than 50,000 inhabitants—Philadelphia—and only thirty-three "urban places," as the United States Census calls them, meaning that they had populations of 2,500 or more. By 1900 there were thirty-eight cities with populations larger than 100,000 and a total of 1,737 urban places. And cities were only one of a hundred nineteenth-century enterprises.

The railroads present perhaps the most characteristic example of what American energies could do when harnessed. In 1800 there was no such thing as a railroad. By 1900 there were 190,000 miles of track, spanning the nation. (By 1916, mileage had increased to 254,067, which was its greatest extent.) As Oliver Jensen wrote in his *American Heritage History of American Railroads,* "The railroad was the biggest business of nineteenth-century America, and it made nearly all other businesses possible." In recent days the railroads have fallen on terrible times, but those 254,067 miles of track were the foundation of the modern American economy.

If ever there was an instance of "lesser men banded together" (thousands of them) making a revolution it is in the building of railroads in the United States. A bill authorizing a transcontinental link had been signed by President Lincoln in 1862. That was about all he had to do with it. The job itself was done by the unlikeliest assortment of politicians, schemers, gamblers, and common laborers ever assembled for one purpose. The Central Pacific, whose responsibility it was to lay track from California eastward, was controlled by four tough businessmen, including Leland Stanford (the governor of California) and Charles Crocker, an organizer and manager whose inspired idea it was to hire Chinese labor. The Chinese performed prodigies—and for nearly no pay. As Mr. Jensen writes, "They proved . . . industrious, chipping away by hand at tunnels . . . , laboring under vast falls of snow, hanging over precipices in baskets to drill holes for explosives, and erecting the long snowsheds without which the line could not have made it over the Sierras to the plateau country of Nevada and Utah."

The Union Pacific, working its way westward from Council Bluffs on the Missouri River, was under the control of a crowd of promoters and sharks, most of them with good friends in Congress (a useful mechanism which both the Union Pacific and Central Pacific kept well oiled). The UP construction company, called the Crédit Mobilier, was a complicated, fraudulent edifice that eventually collapsed in scandal. "In Washington they vote the subsidies, in New York they receive them, upon the plains they expend them," said Charles Francis Adams, Jr., in 1869. The man out on the prairies doing the expending was one Grenville Dodge, whose crews were composed mainly of Irish immigrants. "The greatest sight on the Union Pacific," writes Mr. Jensen, "was the tracklaying."

Little flatcars, pulled by a horse and usually driven by some urchin, would load up, and move up on the last finished rails. Out ahead the ties went down, five to a twenty-eight-foot length of rail. Then the "iron men," five to a rail on each side of the track, would pull on command, hefting the five-hundred-

25

In 1840 the campaign headquarters of the Whig party, vigorously promoting the "log-cabin" candidacy of William Henry Harrison, looked like this.

Montesquieu says, "Countries are well cultivated not as they are fertile, but as they are free"; and the remark holds not less but more true of the culture of men than of the tillage of the land. And the highest proof of civility is that the whole public action of the State is directed on securing the greatest good of the greatest number.

—Ralph Waldo Emerson, "Civilization," 1862

Page 29: *Detail of a flatbed printing press, invented by George Clymer in Philadelphia in 1813.*

You tell me that law is above freedom of utterance. And I reply that you can have no wise laws until there is free expression of the wisdom of the people—and, alas, their folly with it. But if there is freedom, folly will die of its own poison .... You say that freedom of utterance is not for time of stress, and I reply with the sad truth that only in time of stress is freedom of utterance in danger.

—William Allen White, Editorial, Emporia Gazette, *1922*

to seven-hundred-pound iron forward and, at the word "Down!," dropping it right in place or so close that it was soon "lined" to the gauge. The little car would already be moving forward on it while clampers and spikers were fastening it down—three strokes to the spike, ten spikes to a rail, four hundred rails to a mile. . . . By late spring of 1866 the work became so precise and efficient that laying a mile a day became the rule, later stepped up to two and three.

On one famous day, working against a bet, the crew actually laid ten miles of track. As nation-builders go, they were not the sort of crowd to delight the civic-minded. In addition to gun-toting Confederate and Union veterans, according to Mr. Jensen:

> There were also freed slaves, hordes of tough Irishmen from the eastern cities, Germans, English adventurers, and that usual miscellany of tight-lipped characters who tend to join foreign legions. . . . As the base camps moved westward, setting up shop at places like Fort Kearney, North Platte, Julesburg in Colorado Territory, Cheyenne, and at other locations long since forgotten, a movable city accompanied them, a Gomorrah of gamblers, saloonkeepers, and painted women who went to work almost as the first train appeared. "Hell-on-wheels" it was called. . . .

And on May 10, 1869, two locomotives stood nose to nose at Promontory, Utah, and the telegraph tapped out its message for the East: ALL READY NOW. THE SPIKE WILL SOON BE DRIVEN. Somehow, and in record time, the job had been done.

Next to the almost terrifying industriousness of the nineteenth century in America, its second salient quality is inventiveness. Everybody in the nation seems to have turned inventor. Large problems, of course, always attract plenty of volunteer intelligence. But almost no problem in the nineteenth century was so small as to be ignored. In fact, one of the most ingenious aspects of nineteenth-century American culture was that people seemed determined to invent problems. They needed things that people had not previously needed. Sweeping westward, they needed a fast, cheap way to build a decent house. And so in Chicago in 1833, someone invented the balloon-frame method of construction, which simply employs a frame of two-by-fours nailed together. Fortunately someone else had already invented a machine that turned out good cheap nails.

Another most urgent need was for information. If working people are to educate themselves, they have to be able to sit up and read at night. For perhaps the first time in history, poor people were interested in having an inexpensive, reliable light. Eventually, after putting up with whale oil and kerosene, they got their light. In order to invent a functional kitchen, women had first to grow impatient with kitchen drudgery and secondly need some free time to do other things. Catherine Beecher and Harriet Beecher Stowe (both of whom cooked but had better things to do) devised a scheme for a workable kitchen and in 1869 published a book about it, *The American Woman's Home*. They proposed a compact kitchen efficiently arranged, with plenty of storage space, enough light, and a water pump near the sink. It all sounds obvious because all their suggestions, and many more, have long ago been adopted. Their work brought about an important change in American homes—and sparked an important industry.

Between 1865 and 1900 the U.S. Patent Office issued nearly 600,000 patents, catering to an orgy of inventiveness that had no prior parallel. Better paper clips. Better machine-made tacks. Improved sawmill equipment and lathes. Lead pencils and faster ways of producing them. Cheap watches that kept better time than cheap watches were supposed to keep. Rotary egg-beaters. Plows that sliced through the tough roots of the Great Plains grasses. The numbers of things that Americans decided they could use—could not, in fact, do without—in the nineteenth century is astonishing. The whole population seemed to have got the habit of looking critically at every object that came into their hands—could it not be made better, or at least different? Was not some new tool or notion needed to improve performance in kitchen or barn or factory, or on the fields of war? Canned milk? Sliced, prepackaged cheese? Guns that fired six bullets without reloading? The nineteenth century, from one point of view, was an on-going festival of Things.

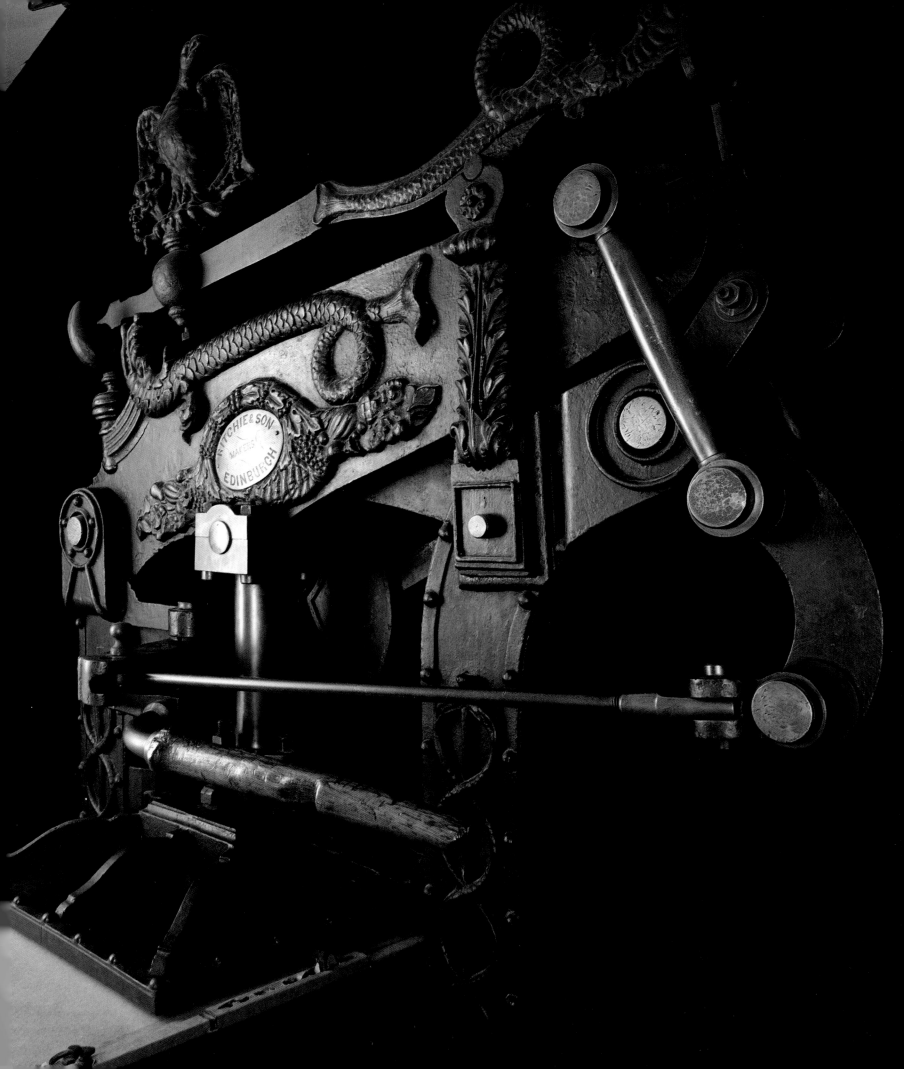

Critics of American society have often pointed to our materialism: our greed, our practicality, our obsession with machines and, worse, with unnecessary machines, which are known as gadgets. They speak of our robber barons, our sweatshops, the sharp business practices of our large and small capitalists, the fatuity and dishonesty of some of our commercial sloganeering, the frequency with which such sloganeering sloshes over into our political and even religious life. Our defenders point to our national piety, our lofty principles, our numberless universities, colleges, junior colleges, and our billions spent in foreign aid.

Yet somehow it is the interplay of spirituality and greed, grubby practicality and lofty principle that has provided our basic source of energy. If Americans are a believing people, some of the things they have most earnestly believed in are iron and steel, steam engines, electric generators, and publicity. From the first the country was full of inventors, schemers, gamblers, investors trying to figure out the shortest route from capital through labor to the ultimate goal of profit. Mechanics trying to figure out machines and invent new things to do with them. The inventiveness of the nineteenth century had its roots in the noblest exponents of Enlightenment philosophy. And, all along, our materialism has had some oddly spiritual components.

That archetypical founding father, Benjamin Franklin, was an experimenter and inventor of the first rank. But unlike Sir Isaac Newton or other great scientific minds, he did not seek the design of the universe. He craved the functional. Among other things, he designed a practical (and beautiful) woodburning stove and he sold it by means of a printed pamphlet. Madison Avenue has never done any better than his *Account of the New-Invented Pennsylvanian Fireplaces.* Franklin warned his prospective female purchasers that sitting beside an open hearth (as they all did) would give them "colds, rheums, and defluxions," which had been known (alas) to descend to the "jaws and gums, and have destroyed many a fine set of teeth in these northern colonies. Great and bright fires do also very much contribute to damage the eyes, dry and shrivel the skin, and bring on early the

appearances of old age." No doubt he believed every word he wrote, but it may be just as well that this distinguished American scientist and diplomat was operating before the Federal Trade Commission came into being.

Thomas Jefferson, too, was an inventor and a scientist in the practical sense (though he never went out into the marketplace, as Franklin did). In *Inventing America,* a brilliant examination of the intellectual background of Jefferson's Declaration, Garry Wills describes the love of the mechanical that was so large a part of the cultivated mentality in Jefferson's day.

"In the Enlightenment," writes Mr. Wills, "the mechanic became the very model of utilitarian ingenuity. Plate after plate in the supplementary columns of the *Encyclopédie* gives us, in lovingly engraved detail, each ratchet and spring of the most complex machines. One is watching the birth, in august surroundings, of *Popular Mechanics.* . . . " Furthermore, the man whom Jefferson admired above all others was David Rittenhouse, who according to Wills was "America's supreme mechanic." Rittenhouse was a celebrated astronomer and clock-maker, and the designer of an orrery, or moving mechanical model of the solar system. (He built two orreries, in fact, both of them famous throughout the colonies.) Wills continues: "Jefferson loved not only the Rittenhouse machine, but the whole mechanical vision of the universe it opened up for him. . . . America, born in the age of science, should be able to achieve an unparalleled precision in her way of doing business. Jefferson wanted all that and something more: he was determined to measure things by a machine."

If that is so, then Jefferson would have been dazzled and astounded had he been able to watch the progress of the nation he helped to found, and to measure that progress by its machines. He would have been astounded not only by American inventiveness—one contraption following another in rampant, exultant profusion—but by how the spirit of the people literally demanded these machines. The machines not only fostered productivity and efficiency and profitability (qualities Mr. Jefferson valued) but altered the fabric of society and spawned the most complex political and ethical questions.

The Constitution had scarcely been ratified before a bright young New Englander named Eli Whitney went to Georgia for a visit to a large plantation. While there, he invented the cotton gin, a little box with a wheel inside that separated short staple cotton from cotton seed. As much as any other single factor, it also locked the South into a cotton-and-slave economy: ginned it neatly out from the rest of the nation and made its interests different from those of other sections. The South would remain a fugitive, agrarian nation-within-a-nation until the 1940s, when other agricultural machines— cotton pickers, for example—and other crops erased the need for common labor on the land.

A century after Whitney's cotton gin came into wide use, Henry Ford, using the principle of the assembly line, came up with the Model T. It turned the whole nation into a commonwealth of consumers and transformed the economy into something inextricably involved with automobiles, petroleum, and asphalt. Between 1908 and 1927, fifteen million Model T's were sold. Now the farmers had fast, reliable transportation to town. Now young men and women had a private place to wage a courtship in, miles from Mama's horsehair sofa and Papa's watchful eyes. The Model T was not the first car, or even the first cheap, good car, but it might as well have been. It was the first cheap, good car to reach a mass market. The first edition in 1908 sold for $850 and by 1925 the price was down to $290. The Model T on view at the National Museum of American History today is polished to a high gloss and in prime condition. If we had a pantheon of machines, it ought to occupy Jupiter's place.

For not only did it cause a social revolution, it demonstrated a profound quality of the American machine age, and of the preferences of Americans. In the 1830s Alexis de Tocqueville— the most prescient of all the early analysts of American culture—had worried about the moral and aesthetic effects of American mass production, which he knew was sure to come. "Quantity increases, quality goes down," he wrote. "When only the rich wore watches, they

were almost all excellent. Now few are made that are more than mediocre, but we all have one." From the point of view of a French aristocrat like de Tocqueville, this was truly a dilemma, but this time he was at least half wrong.

For another paradox of American commerce has been that the quality of manufactured goods has been generally high, rather than generally low. With due allowance for Murphy's Law (which states that anything that can go wrong, will) American automobiles, TV sets, radios, diesel engines, zippers, rainslickers, blue jeans, and the lot have worked well and lasted longer than might reasonably have been expected. But in any case, one aspect of the American mentality has been to prefer the Model T to the Daimler or the Rolls-Royce, and ready-made trousers to the bespoke suit, no matter what the differences in quality and durability. The Model T (and its equivalents in other categories) serves its purposes well enough, and it can be guiltlessly junked after a few years. By this very fact, it serves as the engine of our economic system. More people will have to be employed to make more Model T's, and the same people that make them will also buy and drive them and then throw them away. Like the car itself, the system is full of flaws, and, like the American auto industry itself, is prophesied to perish. But whatever its perils, it is still our *modus operandi,* and as the latest inflation statistics show, nobody has yet figured out anything better.

Another theme of American inventiveness that might have interested Thomas Jefferson (who took careful note of every bird, flower, and leaf he saw, and wrote everything down) has been to see the great possibilities of small and apparently inconsequential things. Thomas Edison labored to invent a filament for an incandescent light bulb, one purpose of which was merely to enable ordinary people to stay up and read after dark. Even though they were regarded as dangerous lunatics, Edwin Drake and Uncle Billy Smith drove a pipe into an underground pool in Pennsylvania and pumped out the petroleum: surely, they thought, there was some use for this greasy substance, which hitherto had been allowed to seep out in small

Opposite: *Henry Ford's Model T (detail of headlight and hood).*

It would seem as if in the United States every man's power of invention was on the stretch to find new ways of increasing the wealth and satisfying the needs of the public. The best brains in every neighborhood are constantly employed in searching for new secrets to increase the general prosperity, and any that they find are at once at the service of the crowd.

—*Alexis de Tocqueville,*
Democracy in America, *1835–40*

quantities and had been sold in bottles as a cure-all. The television screen began as one end of an electronic tube set into a hulking, free-standing cabinet—a 1940s radio with a window in it. It was an amusing novelty for the few who could afford it and who also happened to live close enough to the one or two broadcasting stations. When *Life* published the first photos of a TV set, did its editors realize that in only a few years this freakish miniature would put them out of business as a news magazine?

It is no accident, either, that people with the gift to see the potential in small, commonplace, practical things not only saw the potential of the smallest thing of all but also became the first to set up a crash program, on taxpayers' money, to investigate that potential. (And what else but a crash program—the most money and the best brains combined with the least possible amount of time?) With its navy nearly destroyed and little in its arsenal in 1941, the United States had by 1945 cranked up its industrial machine to full speed and had also, in two brutal, swift flashes, destroyed a pair of medium-sized Japanese cities. Of all technological feats, this one was and is the most terrifying. In 1750, experimenting with lightning rods and later, perhaps, with a kite and a key, Franklin proved that lightning in the clouds and static electricity were the same. Now a braintrust had proved that matter and energy were the same. Only one hundred ninety-three years separated the two events, which is as sobering as any other fact about the nuclear age.

Something of all this, and much else besides, filters through to even the youngest or most casual visitor to the National Museum of American History. Because it houses and preserves so many American paradoxes in such a multiplicity of forms, the Museum is the place above all others where Americans aspire to bring their young. (There are a few other such pilgrimage places: the National Air and Space Museum, the White House, Disneyworld, and perhaps one or two more with an irresistible magnetism for the parent in search of instructive entertainment for his offspring.) With or without children in tow, people come to the Museum looking for knowledge about America. The quest is practical and utilitarian. How do things work,

Opposite: *This sleek engine, designed in 1901 by Anton Riedler, pumped oil to the main turbine governors in the first hydroelectric station at Niagara Falls, New York.*

... America, where people do not inquire concerning a stranger: What is he? *but:* What can he do? ... *The husbandman is in honor there, and even the mechanic, because their employments are useful. The people have a saying that God Almighty is himself a mechanic, the greatest in the universe; and he is respected and admired more for the variety, ingenuity, and utility of his handwork than for the antiquity of his family.*

—*Benjamin Franklin,*
Information to Those Who Would Remove
to America, *1782*

what do they look like, sound like, smell like? What is a linotype? How can a machine make pencils? How does a camera make pictures?

But they also want a kind of knowledge that is thoroughly impractical and idealistic. Whether they voice it or not, the question people ask of the Museum is the one J. Hector St. John de Crèvecoeur asked two centuries ago, "Who is this American, this new man?" Modern attitudes have of course undone the primeval simplicity of the query. Now some of us want to know whether there was a new woman along with the "new man." And who are we, all we Americans, now in the 1980s? Are we really one people? Have we any future? Have we any valid connections with our own past?

The answer the Museum gives is complicated and paradoxical, multi-layered, inconclusive, light-hearted and solemn at the same time. American history, we learn, *is* technology to a very great extent. American history is things. It is an enormous, much-mended flag. It is a satin-finish diesel engine, the embodiment of efficiency and success. A machine shop all ready to roll, smelling cleanly of metal and oil, capable of machining other machines. A whaleboat, shallow as a skiff amidships, which hardly looks seaworthy for a rough lake, much less the Pacific Ocean. A dazzling red cotton-picking machine with the appeal of a nursery toy. A green locomotive of magnificent dimensions, its drive rods ready to move, its noble hoot recorded on tape and played back to an appreciative audience every ten minutes in the Railroad Hall.

Who are we Americans and what have we prized? Not just Benjamin Franklin's suit and George Washington's false teeth, but a Bible quilt, designed and sewn in 1885 by Harriet Powers of Georgia—an otherwise unknown black woman. A comfortable dining room in a turn-of-the-century Brooklyn home, ornamented with all the mass-produced finery of its time, from the lace tablecloth to the knick-knacks on the shelves. The chairs that Robert E. Lee and Ulysses S. Grant sat in while talking terms at Appomattox. (The Southerner, elegantly jacketed and sashed, had to ask a favor: "There is one thing I would like to mention. The cavalrymen and artillerists

Harpoon from an American whaling boat, about 1860.

A short rushing sound leaped out of the boat; it was the darted iron of Queequeg. Then all in one welded commotion came an invisible push from astern, while forward the boat seemed striking on a ledge; the sail collapsed and exploded; a gush of scalding vapor shot up nearby; something rolled and tumbled like an earthquake beneath us. The whole crew were half suffocated as they were tossed helter-skelter into the white curdling cream of the squall. Squall, whale, and harpoon had all blended together. . . .

—*Herman Melville,* Moby Dick, *1851*

own their own horses in our army. . . . I would like to understand whether these men will be permitted to retain their horses." Grant was slovenly but magnanimous. "Well, the subject is quite new to me. . . . I take it that most of the men in the ranks are small farmers, and as the country has been so raided by the two armies it is doubtful whether they will be able to put in a crop. . . . Let all the men who claim to own a horse or a mule take the animals home with them to work their little farms.") A film clip of Jackie Robinson rounding third in an easy lope. The unabashedly dowdy dress Bess Truman wore to a White House dinner. Chet Huntley's face on the screen of an old Zenith, his voice hopelessly intoning, "The President fell in a blaze of gunfire this afternoon in Dallas, Texas." (The children watching the broadcast on a recent afternoon were not yet born when the event took place in 1963. They are disbelieving. "Did he really die?" one of them asks, and another answers, "No.")

Defining the culture of a people is a difficult task. Pendulums and carbon molecules may behave in predictable ways, but human artifacts seldom link up neatly all by themselves. But by some miracle a thousand diverse objects at the Museum of American History fall into place, and the visitor goes away elated at the end of the day, full of a sense of accomplishment, sure of his personal connection with what he has seen. "Oh God, does that bring it all back," men say as they look at the Army barracks from World War II. "Oh, that is just like my grade school classroom, we even had those same two pictures on the wall."

This experience—of connecting—may be what sets the Museum apart from all others. For while it contains sacred relics like Jefferson's lap-desk and the Star Spangled Banner and many other completely unique treasures, it is also rich in the touchable and the commonplace. And even such items as the lap-desk are, after all, perfectly ordinary possessions that were later deemed extraordinary. No one, no matter how poor or deprived his background may have been, can venture through the Museum without seeing things that he himself has owned. One of the kitchens will resemble his great-aunt's. One of the television sets will remind him of the first one he ever had. Yet all those objects must surely have some intrinsic historic and social meaning—else they would not be in the Smithsonian. How exhilarating this experience is, to feel a part of American history. It is an entirely different experience from spending an afternoon, say, in the National Gallery. Few of us can wander through a fine arts museum saying, "Yes, my grandmother had one of those," or "That reminds me very much of my Renoir at home."

There are other lessons, too. We learn that there is something to history and politics beside what was contained in the five-hundred-odd pages of the sixth-grade history textbook. Such categories as football and baseball have histories, too, just as much as governments. Babe Ruth can be as important a part of history as William H. Seward. On one floor of the Museum, George Washington presides in classical (and some would say improbable) marble splendor, but in another place we find a photo of the elegantly bearded countenance of Wilt Chamberlain. In a 1940s film clip of a World Series game, some anonymous outfielder drops the ball—a day that shall live in ignominy. "They were just as bad as we are," a child observes with some satisfaction.

Nearby a crowd of twenty or so watches a rapidfire montage of historic American films. Charlie Chaplin battles his way down an up escalator, only to be hoisted aloft once more. (Here is a man, we realize, with a truly profound understanding of machines.) A well-upholstered, outraged couple confront Groucho Marx, who has, of course, been giving them the business. "Sir," exclaims the stuffed shirt. "This lady is my wife. You should be ashamed." "If this lady is your wife," replies Groucho, *"you* should be ashamed." The film and the gag are repeated some twenty-five times in a Museum day. It always gets a laugh. The audience is pleased, relieved, to be reminded that this nation has always had a sense of humor. And has one still. Dolley Madison's silk gown may be a national treasure, but so is the madness in Harpo's eyes.

The Museum itself has a sense of humor, a thoroughly commendable respect for nuttiness,

and an unerring affinity for the poignant—perhaps the only museum in the world that does have. On a recent day in a special exhibition, "The Nation's Attic," the following items were on view:

1. The blue toothbrush shared by Colonel Frank Borman and Captain James Lovell during their journey around the moon.

2. A silk purse made from a sow's ear: neither the purse nor the process of any conceivable use but, as the label points out, "a triumph of chemistry over conventional wisdom."

3. A vast (size 18) pair of shoes handmade for a Norwegian Goliath in the Union Army. He died in action (presumably barefoot) before the shoes arrived.

4. The simple wood cross that marked Casey Jones's grave.

5. A nose-thumbing machine used in Warren G. Harding's 1920 presidential campaign.

6. A plug of tobacco taken to the South Pole by Commander Robert Peary.

7. A lock of Millard Fillmore's hair.

Frivolous and inconsequential it all may be, but for the casual student of cultural anthropology it beats body counts and hydrogen bombs, the class struggle, the Great Depression, and other reminders of our unpleasanter adventures as a species. Casey Jones, that brave engineer, at least died for a cause that everybody can understand: "getting her there on time." The whistle of the Cannonball Express called out in the Mississippi night as Casey leaned out the cabin window, opened the throttle, and hollered over the boiler head to the fireman (or so the fireman reported after Casey died in the crash), "The old girl's got her high-heeled slippers on tonight!" But rounding the curve at top speed, he suddenly saw a stalled train down the line. "Jump," he shouted to the fireman. To see the grave marker of such a man is worth the trip to Washington. One could say that Casey Jones was in love with a steam engine.

In fact, throughout the Museum one can discern that many people are in love with engines. Critics of American life used to delight in pillorying the United States as a

In the last two decades the jet plane, as much as television, has revolutionized presidential campaigning. This is the interior of the Caroline, John F. Kennedy's campaign plane in 1960. He and his staff, and select members of the press, virtually made their home in it in the months before the election. Kennedy's pilot commented, "He never worries about flying or tries to second-guess me about the weather. He just climbs aboard and relaxes." The notebook in the foreground holds aircraft-use and inspection reports.

Overleaf: Detail of the Harlan and Hollingsworth steam engine from Machinery Hall.

I am the farmer, bondsman to the soil.
I am the worker sold to the machine.
I am the Negro, servant to you all.
I am the people, humble, hungry, mean—
Hungry yet today despite the dream.
Beaten yet today—O, Pioneers!
I am the man who never got ahead,
The poorest worker bartered through the
    years.

Yet I'm the one who dreamt our basic
    dream . . . .

—Langston Hughes,
"Let America Be America Again," 1938

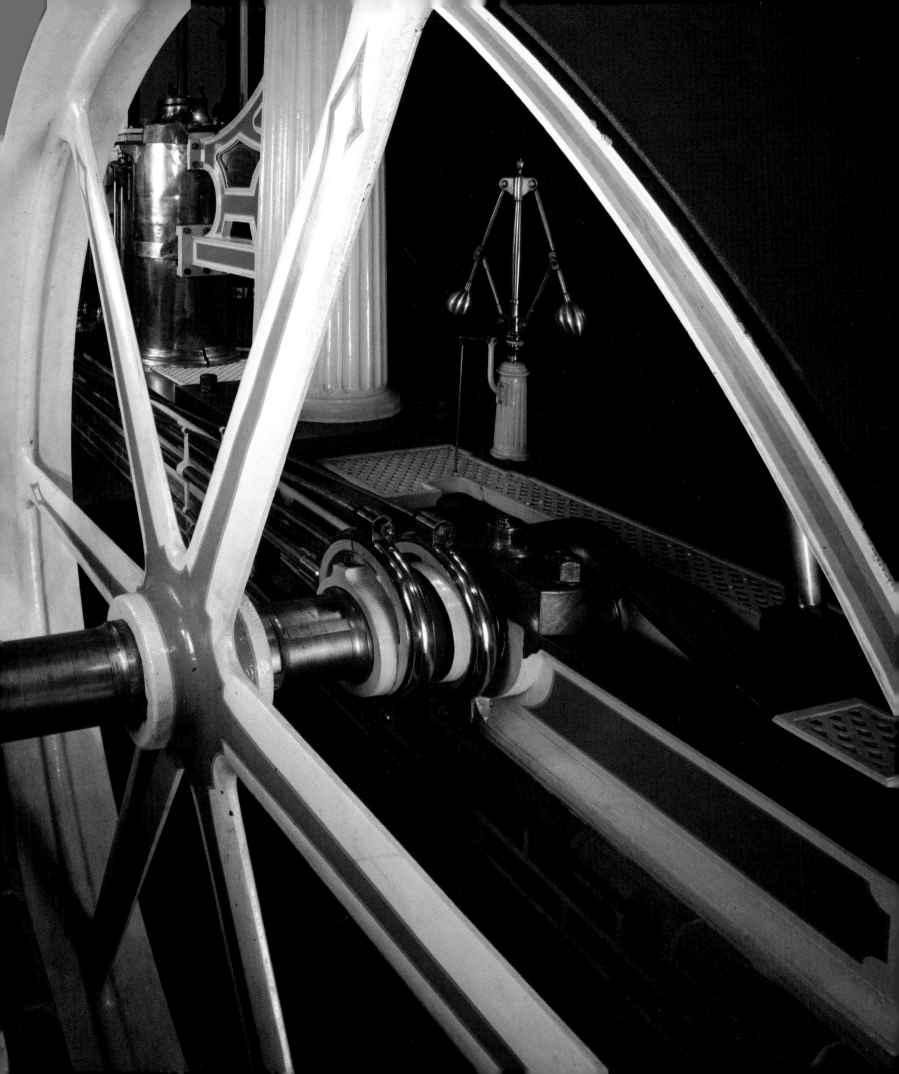

cultural desert presided over by Babbitts, the bastion of mindless materialism. But they surely never took a look at the Harlan and Hollingsworth mill steam engine in full swing. In the Power Hall at 10 A.M. on some mornings a Museum docent opens a valve, and the Harlan and Hollingsworth, room-sized and with a stately architectural quality, comes up to operating speed. Its ivory paint and green trim are impeccable, its steel parts shine like the moon. Belts, shafts, pulleys, and a governor with rotating flyballs whirl in silent and inexpressible grace. In the center, an imposing yellow Doric column supports the walking beam, which rocks with a majestic cadence. An orchestral accompaniment (a Haydn symphony) would be appropriate.

The docent, who apparently loves and understands this machine as a choreographer might understand dancers, explains that the Harlan and Hollingsworth once powered the machine shop of the Southern Railway in Charleston, South Carolina. As steam engines go, this one, whatever its aesthetic virtues, is not particularly efficient but Southern Railway kept it in service until 1927, long after it might have been replaced. Ralph Waldo Emerson wrote that beauty is its own excuse for being. He was speaking of a flower, but the beauty of a steam engine is also something that our culture prepares us to savor. The audience at the Harlan and Hollingsworth performance is often reverentially happy. Machines, we expect, should be dirty, noisy, and dangerous. Yet here is one that is graceful, silent, and dignified. What more poignant artifact of American fantasies than this?

Not many nations are willing to measure their identity by such ephemera as old toothbrushes and unused army boots, or to admit freely that their historic spirit resides in walking-beam steam engines, combine-reapers, calculators, permanent-wave machines, and atom-smashers. In no other capital city is there any such institution as this Museum. For according to the conventional view of things, it isn't history and technology that are mates but science and technology. History is married to politics.

And yet history here has been machine-made, at least in part. Anyone who doubts this might spend an hour amid the farm machinery, thinking of wheat tonnage and the changes in the balance of power that wheat brings about these days. Probably there is no other national museum that is filled with such an apparently random collection of objects, few of which are works of art in any conventional sense. Some of them are not even the first or the best of their kind but simply "examples of" or "models of." But it is the randomness that we admire, and the ordinariness. Where else can we see clothespins, license plates, gas meters, and street-drain covers on display? All these things add up to a statement both poetic and political about the American character. They reflect not only the tensions of our history—its accidents, strokes of luck, grandeur, and failures—but our own mentality. We are random and ordinary, too.

The relationship of the American people with the Smithsonian Institution and in particular with the National Museum of American History, which is only one component of it, has been characterized by an almost boundless faith. (If the Smithsonian, as most people call it, displays a thing, it is automatically worthy and authentic; if the Smithsonian says a thing, it is true.) In 1980, five million visitors came to the Museum. Apart from official correspondence the Smithsonian receives some 30,000 pieces of mail annually directed to "Washington Museum," or "Museum on the Mall." Much of this is intended, it turns out, for this Museum. All of it is answered, up to and including such scholastic pleas as "I need some information about the Civil War. Send me everything you have." A batch of letters that arrived in a recent week reflect the varying expectations that Americans have of their national attic:

"Enclosed, herewith, is a copy of an American Artifice that I believe may be of interest to you. . . . "

"I have a watch that was my grandfather's and have been trying to find some information about it. . . . The face of the watch states: Weill and Harbourg. . . . "

"I have been told that my Great Great Grandfather has on display at the Smithsonian

James Smithson, an English eighteenth-century amateur scientist and out-of-wedlock son of the Earl of Northumberland, although he never visited America nor had any American connections, left his entire fortune to the United States for the purpose of setting up "the Smithsonian institution, an establishment for the increase & diffusion of knowledge among men."

Institute a pair of FORCEPS. . . . I would like to find out if this is so."

"I am looking for information about the tools needed for sharpening shears, knives, and small tools."

"I am attempting to identify which company first sold mens trousers with zippers in the New England area."

All this curiosity would surely have seemed legitimate to the Englishman who established the Smithsonian in the first place. How he did it is well known, though his motivation has never been fully explained. His name was James Smithson. He was an eighteenth-century amateur scientist and the out-of-wedlock son of the Earl of Northumberland and a' rich heiress named Elizabeth Macie. He grew up as a gentleman and was educated as such at Oxford, but perhaps because of the circumstances of his birth he never married or had children. When the time came to draw up his will, he left his fortune to a nephew and then—for unknown reasons—specified that if this nephew died without issue, the money should be given to the United States and used to set up "the Smithsonian institution, an establishment for the increase & diffusion of knowledge among men." Smithson had never visited the United States, nor did he have any American friends or connections. But clearly he wanted the world to remember him, and perhaps thought that fame was more easily come by in a raw new nation than in England.

In 1835 the nephew died without heirs, eleven years after James Smithson. The American envoy in London, learning that his country had inherited £100,000 from an obscure English bachelor, suspected the donor of lunacy. President Andrew Jackson, and most of Congress, regarded the gift as an affront and a nuisance. Nevertheless, an emissary was finally dispatched to collect the money. It was before the days of the bank transfer: the man converted the legacy into gold coins, packed it up in one hundred and five sacks, and shipped it back to Washington. It was worth about half a million dollars, and nobody had any idea what to found, whether library, laboratory, museum, or observatory. The cause of increasing American knowledge was hardly helped along when

Congress risked most of the money in bad investments: Arkansas state bonds, for example, which never paid a pennyworth of interest.

But in 1846, largely because of the efforts of John Quincy Adams, Congress voted to appoint a Board of Regents for the Smithsonian and agreed to pay an annual interest of six percent on the original bequest. The Regents engaged an architect named James Renwick to design the first building. His specialty was the medieval style—he later built St. Patrick's Cathedral in New York—and for the new institution he re-created a twelfth-century Norman castle and set it on the Mall: an incongruously feudal home for what was essentially a legacy of the English Enlightenment to a nation where everything was, perforce, modern. Today it houses some administrative offices of the Institution and has become its symbol and landmark.

The next building was Arts and Industries, completed in 1881 to contain the exhibitions that the Smithsonian had inherited from the Centennial Exposition in Philadelphia in 1876. This was the real beginning of the Museum of American History. And in the second century of the nation's life, the Smithsonian Institution took shape as the enormous, worldwide cultural enterprise that it now is: a complex of museums (American History, Air and Space, Natural History, and six fine arts museums), the National Zoological Park, biologic and oceanographic laboratories, the John F. Kennedy Center for the Performing Arts, the Woodrow Wilson International Center for Scholars, and a network of research centers. Its publications and traveling exhibitions are known throughout the world. For half a million dollars—and an idea—James Smithson and the cause of knowledge have truly been well served.

When people say "the Smithsonian Museum" what they usually have in mind is the National Museum of American History. As a wide-angle mirror of American culture, the Museum is far from perfect. But in spite of, or even because of, its gaps and omissions, the Museum does accomplish a most necessary purpose, and an oddly spiritual one, given the down-to-earth quality of its collections. And this purpose is perhaps even more vital now than it was in

1876, when the Museum acquired forty-two carloads from the great Philadelphia Centennial, which had proved, once and for all, that America was an industrial nation. For taken all together, the collection of this Museum affirms a principle that all citizens of a democracy must believe in. It is the idea that common people have sense enough to run their own governments and that over the long haul they will do it better than any professional elite or committee of experts. And that furthermore, in even the most ordinary person may lie reserves of inventiveness, determination, courage, and good humor.

Look at the row of typewriters, the first one literally useless (you can write longhand much faster than it types) but each one along the line getting a little better. Who remembers the names of each tinkerer or has any idea what motives drove him onward? Look at the wooden carousel horses, carved with the kind of craftsmanship once spent on cathedral portals. What kind of artisan would take so much care with a gimcrack intended for an amusement park? Look at the "Jailed for Freedom" pin. The cause of suffrage did matter enough to American women that a few were willing to go to jail for it. Listen to a visitor reading aloud from an Abraham Lincoln memorial ribbon: "I have said nothing but what I am willing to live by, and if it be the pleasure of almighty God, to die by." Lincoln, who could make such an utterance, started life in the backwoods, in the most brutal and degraded circumstances. Look at the photograph of Bessie Smith, listen to her recorded song. By what miracle did this black orphan girl turn herself into one of our finest singers?

Persistence, skill, and talent are by no means peculiar to Americans; nor do all Americans possess even one of these qualities. Our thoughts about our national character have grown darker of late; and yet perhaps we have not entirely disgraced our original charter. The National Museum of American History tells us who we are. It is useful to have one institution whose job it is to confirm us as a people and to remind us that our history, in whatever curious vessels we may find it, is our strength.

Visitors view mementoes of 1600 political campaigns.

It is told that such are the aerodynamics and wing-loading of the bumblebee that, in principle, it cannot fly. . . . If all this be true . . . life among bumblebees must bear a remarkable resemblance to life in the United States.

—John Kenneth Galbraith,
American Capitalism, *1952*

AT HOME IN AMERICA

This kitchen from Malden, Massachusetts, as it might have been about 1776, was a world to itself. Here the family cooked and ate, did their indoor labors, prayed, and improved their minds. An edifying work, Religion of Nature Delineated, is opened to a passage on happiness. Hand-made spectacles are out of their case. The wooden tankard will soon be foaming over with beer—in those days everybody drank, even small children. An apple pie has just come from the oven; in the kettle might be a heavy stew.

A Nation of Homebodies

The true character of Americans is mirrored in their homes.

—Moreau de Saint-Méry, French revolutionary and emigré, describing Philadelphia in the 1790s

Perhaps no culture has ever been so home-centered as the American. It is a national trait that existed before there was a nation. In all climates people of course live under roofs, and splendid houses are a sign of power and a source of pride. But "home" in America means not only the roof we sleep and eat under. It is the place where we are most ourselves, where we are comfortable, where we entertain our friends and set up "entertainment centers" for ourselves. Until this century home might also be a place to earn a living, the locus of public as well as private life. Throughout American history, home has been the material evidence of the true inner nature of the owner, evidence to be cheerfully and frequently put on display. "Come sit in the kitchen and watch me cook," we say to our guests. But American visitors to France or England, even today, are invariably astonished and a little hurt that few people they meet ever seem to invite *them* home and certainly not into the kitchen.

On his celebrated visit to the United States in 1831, Alexis de Tocqueville quickly perceived that we are a nation of homebodies:

The Americans, who mix so easily in the sphere of law and politics are, on the contrary, very careful to break up into small and very distinct groups to taste the pleasures of private life. . . . Instead of dancing gaily in the public square as many people of the same social status in Europe still delight to do, an American may prefer to spend his leisure hours quietly drinking in his own house. Such a man enjoys two pleasures at once: he thinks about business affairs and gets decently drunk at home.

De Tocqueville put this lightheartedly but as usual he went to the essence of things. For he knew as well as anyone that he was witnessing a momentous development in social history, a development that might be called the end of peasantry. If people of low social status were no longer cavorting in the public square, it was because they had—by the simple expedient of being independent homeowners—taken possession of their free time. They owned more than their houses, they owned themselves.

In the most famous of his *Letters from an American Farmer,* written about 1780, J. Hector St. John de Crèvecoeur, a French-born American author and agriculturalist, commented on the new architecture that accompanied this trend. The traveler in rural America, he wrote, "views not the hostile castle, and the haughty mansion, contrasted with the clay-built hut and miserable cabbin, where cattle and men help to keep each other warm, and dwell in meanness, smoke, and indigence. A pleasing uniformity of decent competence appears throughout our habitations."

In Crèvecoeur's century, and for centuries previously, the great majority of the English peasantry had lived in just such miserable cabins, filled with smoke and evil smells and even with livestock. They owned no land and had no homes, except whatever dirty and uncomfortable shelter their landlords might provide. And by the seventeenth century the squalid security of this world had fallen apart as the English and Irish countryside was transformed by the inexorable process known as Enclosure. The gentry laid claim to open lands that had for centuries been common pasturage,

Page 48: *This section of a timber-frame house with its massive central chimney was built about 1698 in Ipswich, Massachusetts, for a cooper, George Hart. A larger room, not visible here, was added on the opposite side of the chimney in about 1750. The framing methods were those of medieval England: heavy timbers held together by laboriously carved joints. (The original house was covered with weatherboards and clapboards; here it has been left unenclosed.) Compact as it is, the house was warm and serviceable. By 1752 parts of three families lived here—Hart, his widowed sister, and his son, who no doubt also had a family.*

Left: *One of the oldest rooms in the Museum is this upper chamber from the Seth Story house in Essex, Massachusetts, built about 1684. It is utterly forthright—the beams, plaster walls, and floors are bare and undisguised. The furniture is chiefly oak. The armchair is for the head of the household; lesser mortals could sit on stools. Like the house, the furnishings are sturdier than necessary. The chest beneath the casement window was the main storage piece, for neither closets nor the idea of privacy was yet construed as a necessity in domestic life.*

Overleaf: *This heavy oak table-chair, exhibited in the Story chamber, is an excellent example of early American (or medieval English) practicality and thrift. It was made about 1670.*

so that such independent herdsmen and farmers and villagers as there were, were shut off entirely from any chance to make a living. Throughout the seventeenth and eighteenth centuries the roads of England and eventually the city streets teemed with the dispossessed—men, women, and children driven off the land, an excess and starving population.

There were at least half a dozen complex reasons why the idea of home took on an implacable sanctity among American settlers. Shelter from the elements was an obvious and immediate necessity. Of the 102 people who landed at Plymouth in December, 1620, fifty-one were dead by the next spring, chiefly from exposure to the icy Massachusetts winter. But at Plymouth and elsewhere, settlers had yearnings that went beyond shelter. Before he set sail to America and founded the Massachusetts Bay Colony, John Winthrop had written, "Why then should we stand striving here for places of habitation . . . & in the meane time suffer a whole continent as fruitfull & convenient for the use of man to lie waste without improvement?" If God's work were to be done in the New World and the fruitful continent filled with people and material improvements, the workers had to have houses—the best they could devise. The God of the Puritans most definitely did not require his servants to live in hovels, or not for long. They needed a warm hearth, thick walls, glass windows, and good beer in the cellar.

To the homeless of England and Ireland, the penniless Scotch-Irish immigrants, the laborers who had but recently been tramping the roads or sitting in prison, a house certainly was shelter and greatly needed for that. It may even have represented godliness and a token of one's willing participation in the divine scheme. But it transcended even holiness. John Winthrop might quote Scripture as he liked and remind his flock that they were the chosen people, but other pioneers came with other Bible verses in their minds, perhaps this one from Isaiah: "And they shall build houses, and inhabit them; and they shall plant vineyards and eat the fruit of them. They shall not build, and another inhabit; they shall not plant, and another eat."

My house, my land. From which I shall not be evicted, where I shall not be oppressed. The idea is still palpable in America today. The pulse of the nation's economy is measured by a thing called housing starts. Bank rates on home mortgages make front-page news. And when the decennial questionnaire arrives from the U.S. Bureau of the Census, it does not inquire after our health, education, or state of grace but our houses. How many rooms for how many people? Own or rent? Is the plumbing adequate?

J. Hector St. John de Crèvecoeur's "pleasing uniformity of decent competence" did not appear all at once. In its beginnings American domestic architecture tended decidedly to the indecent and the incompetent. Jamestown was settled by gentlefolk who committed almost every conceivable blunder, and predictably they were not very skillful builders. They had landed in the spring of 1607; eight months afterward, when winter had already set in, they were still living in lean-to's, make-do's, and even holes in the ground. The houses that they did manage to erect were shoddy, usually with more potential as firewood than shelter. Even after the colony had been established for several years, a visitor remarked that "ther Howses are generally the worst yet that ever I sawe."

Though the Pilgrims were more industrious and purposeful than their feckless Virginia brethren, they were not at first much better off. On Christmas Day, 1620, nine days after arriving at Plymouth, they began building the first house for "commone use." A few weeks later it caught fire and burned, leaving the colony in the snow once more. (Communal housing, which might have seemed the most logical and economical solution for the early colonists, apparently did not appeal to them. From Massachusetts to Georgia people put up single-family dwellings the minute they had timber and time and skill enough.)

When the first lasting structures finally emerged in Massachusetts, they were often little better than huts. In 1631 Lt.-Governor Thomas Dudley of the Bay Colony, reporting a recent fire, spoke of them as "English wigwams." But if they were wigwams, they had been patterned after the turf or mud huts of the mother country rather than the shelters of American

Indians. One of the remarkable and consistent features of American houses was that they were as old-fashioned as the new settlers knew how to make them. But the ancient forms they copied were often poor and primitive. The architectural historian Fiske Kimball has pointed out that while the first American houses were far beneath the dignity of the leaders and chroniclers among the settlers, "to many farm servants and poor people the rude shelters meant no more than a perpetuation of conditions at home."

The huts of old England dotted the New World landscape for some time, but frame houses appeared alongside them early in the seventeenth century. In 1627 a Dutch trader, Isaac de Raisiers, wrote that at "New Plymouth . . . with a broad street about a cannon shot of 800 feet long leading down the hill . . . the houses are constructed of clapboards, so that their houses and courtyards are arranged in very good order, with a stockade against sudden attack." And at Salem in 1629 a contemporary witness counted ten small frame houses besides a "fair house newly built for the Governor." In England by this date, wood was already disappearing as an architectural material—the deep forests of medieval and Roman Britain had been cut down and not replenished. But in America timber existed in apparently inexhaustible supply. And thus the typical house of the colonies and of the new nation was made of wood. Even today most American houses are built on wood frames.

The basic colonial house was copied by memory from the late medieval houses of England. There was a chimney around which a simple rectangular room was constructed. If there was a second story, it was overhanging. It might be an unfinished loft. In the South, the chimney was placed on an outside wall, and when expansion was necessary, it was made by adding rooms horizontally, not vertically. Roofs were long and sloping and usually thatched. But there were innovations. English houses had often been half-timbered, with plaster walls between the timbering. The bitter climate of Massachusetts quickly persuaded the colonists to alter this design: only the interior walls were plaster; outside walls were tightly finished with clapboard. The earliest surviving specifications for a New England frame house are for the dwelling of one William Rix in Boston in 1640:

one framed house 16 foot long and 14 wide a chamber floare finish summer and joysts a cellar floare with joysts finisht the roofe and walles clapboarded on the outside the chimney framed without dawbing to be done with hewn timber. . . .

That is, one room and an unfinished loft, framed with a heavy sill, laid on masonry foundations. The large chimney stood at one end of the main room, and next to it a staircase. The house had a side door and a few small windows.

Had the folktale about the three little pigs originated in America, William Rix's house could have been the wolf-proof cottage finally devised by the third little pig. If ever there was a demonstration of hard-won achievement, proceeding by trial and error, one step at a time, it is the history of colonial architecture. This may explain the fascination of Hart House, the fine example of a New England frame house at the Museum of American History. Here, at last, is a solid American home just as it ought to be. It has been left in an unfinished state for us by the Museum, so that we can see how skillfully and methodically things were being done by this time. It is a "late" house, built for a prosperous cooper of Ipswich, Massachusetts, in 1698— about fifty years past the "pure" English medieval stage of American architecture. Hart House is already creeping into the Georgian period, with such stylish and sophisticated details as decorative paneling, an open balustraded stairway, molded cornices, high ceilings encased in plaster. This is no pioneer lean-to. There is nothing makeshift about it.

Two fundamental American dwellings came into being in the colonial period: the saltbox of New England and the log cabin of the frontier. Neither was, at first, American. The frame house was English, the log cabin Swedish. To the modern imagination no house is more characteristic of the colonial period than the log cabin. Enthusiasts have even built "reconstructions" of Puritan settlements featuring log cabins. But the Puritans graduated from huts to frame houses and never

Left: *The stoneware flask with the large "R" is one of the few known eighteenth-century American stoneware pieces that is dated and signed. As the inscription says, it was made by Henry Remmey, New York, June 18, 1789. Remmey was probably an apprentice at that time in the family pottery. The mug, dated 1773 and decorated with spiral "watch springs" comes from New Jersey or Connecticut.*

Overleaf: *A bell-metal posnet—a three-footed saucepan to set above hot coals. The long-handled ladle is made of brass and marked "WK."*

Below: *These sturdy-looking ceramics—a mug, an ovoid jug, and a vase—were made in Massachusetts in the mid- and late-eighteenth century. Pottery was one of the earliest New England industries. By 1800 at least three hundred potters were turning out functional kitchenwares.*

built log cabins at all. The log house was the development of a farther frontier.

The first of them was built very early—in 1638 by the first Swedish pioneers in Delaware. A log cabin is ugly and thoroughly practical. Nothing but an axe is required to build one; if the logs are carefully fitted at the corners and the chinks well daubed with clay, the log house is a cheap, quick way to shelter from the rain and the snow. But the English did not like it; it was the Scotch-Irish who first began to use it on the frontier. During the eighteenth century, according to one scholar, "it spread rapidly through the English colonies, and by the American Revolution had become the typical American frontier dwelling from Maine to Tennessee."

Even more than the stark New England frame house (the very simplicity of which calls up the virtues of the original inhabitants), the log cabin is a fixture of American mythology. So straightforward is its design that it is hard to believe the Puritans did *not* live in log cabins. Historians who see the frontier and the Indian in a romantic light have credited the Indian with inventing the log house and bestowing it upon the pioneers. The Southern Indians, particularly the Cherokee, the Creeks, and the Choctaws, did live in log houses. Undoubtedly they got the idea from white settlers. (And yet the Scotch-Irish who poured into the Cherokee country of Georgia and Alabama after the Revolutionary War may well, in their turn, have picked up some techniques from the Indians—in the same way that they learned how to grow Indian corn and beans and to make hominy and hoecake.) After 1840, the strongest possible political advantage for a political aspirant was a log cabin as a birthplace. Of all the men claiming the distinction Abraham Lincoln was probably the only President who actually *was* born in one.

The log cabin lasted into the twentieth century. Many are still standing today, some still in use as barns or perhaps in some remote rural poverty pocket as houses. American domestic architecture never has proceeded in a straight line. While a Tidewater farmer like William Ely was building a respectable imitation of a Georgian mansion, another family in the Carolina backcountry was setting up a lean-to, hoping to build a log house before winter came on. The Museum's log cabin was built by an English carpenter in Delaware a hundred years after the Swedish pioneers had made the first one.

At any time or place, the houses of early America reflected both the ambitions and limitations of their owners: perhaps the ambitions more so. The first effort might be crude: a one-room cabin with a hearth. But there was always a way to enlarge it. Knock out a wall, divide the rooms, add an upper story, build a lean-to at the back, extend the roof. In such a way did the saltbox evolve—it is merely a two-room house with additions. In the South, as well, many a thing that had begun as a cabin ended up, after a coat of paint and much alteration, as a "mansion." No structure was necessarily regarded as final.

The log cabin too was a way station. The pioneer family, as soon as they were able, turned it into an outbuilding. In the South, if and when a dirt farmer finally elevated himself to the status of planter, he would build himself a frame house with a verandah and turn his cabin into slave quarters. There was, of course, always a subclass (which included all blacks and some whites as well) brutally exempt from the opportunity for upward mobility that characterized the American frontier. No one, of course, was ever exempt from its hardships and labors.

Upward mobility, if only in dreams, has been an abiding feature of American life. No wonder that early American houses mirror the ideal. But there is another trait they mirror that is less distinct in our time. With the exception of bondservants and a few others, white colonial Americans owned their own plots and built their own houses. Perhaps never before in history had Europeans come so close to an equitable distribution of property. Land was everywhere and it was free; it was also the basis of wealth. The Royal Governor of Massachusetts remarked in 1764 that "Property is more equally distributed in the colonies, especially those to the northward of Maryland than in any nation in Europe."

It would be foolish to look back upon colonial America as an egalitarian paradise. Poverty and

riches existed side by side along with slavery, as they always had. But the gulf between was not nearly so wide as in London or Glasgow. Wealth was fluid, not fixed. Industrialism had not yet arrived; neither had the day of the expert. The family in need of a house did not consult an architect or contractor nor look at a developer's prospectus. As Marshall Davidson writes in his *History of Notable American Houses,* "There was no such thing as a professionally trained architect in America throughout the seventeenth century or for scores of years to come." In need of a house, you built what you could, and the neighbors helped. If you were lucky, some of them might be craftsmen. But if so, they were part-time craftsmen, amateurs. It is this quality of inventiveness —at ground level—that shines so strongly in the early colonial rooms at the National Museum of American History. "And they shall build houses, and inhabit them; and they shall plant vineyards and eat the fruit of them."

On the other side of the world from Canaan, millenniums later, the prophecy came true.

Give to pots and trays and pans, grace and glimmer of romance.

—Ralph Waldo Emerson, "Self-Reliance"

Metal was scarce—and cooking utensils were prized in colonial America. Pots and kettles had to be adaptable and long-lasting; these have a simplicity of design that has overwhelming appeal to modern eyes.

Right: *A copper coffeepot with a wooden handle and a copper teakettle of the late eighteenth century.*

*T*he main room of this mid-eighteenth century
Delaware house, which comes from Mill Creek
Hundred, near Wilmington, looks too finely
finished to twentieth-century eyes to be what it
is—the inside of a log house. The first American
log houses were built in Delaware about 1638 by
Swedish settlers and, like the later log cabins of
the nineteenth-century frontier, were intended as
make-do shelter until the family could build a
frame house. But this log house, possibly made
for a miller around 1740, was clearly built to last.
The mantel is used to display a plate, a
candlestick, a glass bottle and other objects of
daily use. The clock on the wall was truly a
luxury for its day. On the pine-top table an apple
pie is under construction. A potentially deadly
feature of the commodious fireplace is that the
ovens are in the back wall. The housewife, wearing
long skirts and apron, would have to lean over the
blaze to retrieve her pie. (Deaths from burns
were not uncommon in the colonial household.)
The yellow chair with its arched slats was made
in the Delaware Valley.

This red earthenware punch bowl, inscribed "I F 1769" has a clear lead glaze—not likely to improve the health or increase the longevity of those who drank punch from it. It is a homely piece, yet it shows the efforts of a traditional potter to make a more refined kind of tableware.

For all its pioneer simplicity, the bedchamber of the log house from Delaware (see main room on preceding page) exhibits many niceties. The chest of drawers, an example of the William and Mary style, has brass drawer pulls imported from England. The cradle blanket is plain, but on the big bed the quilted counterpane, which has been dyed a light green, perhaps with a combination of indigo and goldenrod, is painstakingly stitched.

Opposite: *"To my son William Dole and heirs forever my Dwelling house that I now live in, together with my barn. . . ."* *Such was the bequest in 1705 by Richard Dole of Newbury, Massachusetts, who had built his dwelling some thirty-five years previously. In 1723 his grandson inherited the ancestral home and decided to remodel it. In the second-story room, opposite, he replaced the old casement windows with modern sashes, enclosed the beams, installed wood panelling on the fireplace wall, and added paint (an unthinkable extravagance and even vulgarity to the original Puritans). The chest of drawers is also newfangled, being an improvement over the traditional lidded storage chest. But the austere spirit remains: the floors bare, the windows uncurtained, and the chairs built for ramrod spines.*

Above: *This canvas work picture, "The Queen of Sheba admiring the wisdom of Solomon," was stitched in 1744 by one Mary Williams—a Massachusetts girl and possibly a wealthy one, since she had the time and skill for the elaborate embroidery taught in young ladies' needlework classes. Under a canopy, Sheba admires Solomon in his gray frock coat. The couple are flanked by merrymakers and musicians. The horse-drawn carriages in the upper register are fanciful but the houses might have been straight from New England. The Reuben Bliss parlor (following page) could have been in one of them.*

*T*his parlor from Springfield, Massachusetts, is (and was intended to be) a showplace of American decorative skill. Reuben Bliss, who created it, was a master joiner. He did not build the house but bought it in 1753 and began remodeling it. He had just taken a wife, Elizabeth Hitchcock, and was setting up in business. Possibly he wanted their home to be a kind of advertisement to the trade. He made and installed the fine Georgian-style panelling on all four walls—an unusual exercise of taste. The landscape over the mantel offers a panorama of the Connecticut River Valley with Mt. Tom and Mt. Holyoke. In the corner at left is a cherry highboy made in the area in about 1750. The rush-seated chairs include features of the Queen Anne style, and the ladderbacks by the fireplace are of imposing height and solidity. Reuben Bliss was too old to soldier in the Revolutionary War, so he stockpiled guns in his dwelling and served on a quartermaster committee. Bliss House stood until 1925, and the parlor was thereafter acquired by the Museum.

The classic American chairs opposite and at left are embodiments of the Englishness of colonial taste as well as its concomitant Americanness. The Windsor chair became popular in England during the early eighteenth century, and by the middle of the eighteenth century craftsmen in Philadelphia were producing them. They transformed the original heavy English design into something light and daring. They also devised a way to mass-produce the chair, turning out the parts in large numbers and then assembling the product. Its engineering is superb—the chair is held together without a single screw or nail. The example at left, with a bow back and bamboo turnings on its spindles, was made in Philadelphia in the late eighteenth century. (The Second Continental Congress, voting independence, did so sitting on Windsor chairs.)

The Queen Anne chair, opposite, is all graceful curve. It has a shell on the top rail, a shaped splat, a horseshoe-shaped seat, cabriole legs, and ball-and-claw feet. It was made in New York around 1750. The style originated in England but was adapted with great diversity and elegance here. It represented a softening of the harsh seventeenth-century styles. Sensuous and fashionable, it was a sure sign that at least a few colonial Americans had both leisure and discernment.

This somewhat comfortless-looking parlor was finished in 1808 for Edmund and Deliverance Crowell of Holmes' Hole (now Vineyard Haven), Martha's Vineyard, Massachusetts. It was a seafaring community with about seventy houses, but Crowell, so far as is known, was not a sailor but a tailor. For its time, the house and the decor were typical of modest dwellings. The comb-back Windsor rocking chair was an up-to-date but not necessarily expensive parlor fixture. The woodwork and mantel are carved with the neo-classical fretwork—fans, diamonds, ovals, intertwining circles—that were the height of fashion in the new nation. The townscape over the mantel, which has three-story houses in it, may have been the work of a local teacher, Jane Norton.

*F*ar from Massachusetts and Virginia, new
settlers who had not come from the British
Isles built homes in America and struggled to
survive in alien circumstances. By 1800 Spaniards
had already been living in New Mexico for some
two centuries, and this room is typical of the
homes they made. The thick adobe walls (an
Iberian and North African tradition) and deep-set
windows helped deflect the heat. The plain pine
chest was for storage, as was the cupboard behind
it; there are also plenty of niches and shelves. The
walls were regularly whitewashed. And because
sheep farming was important in the area, the
owner of this relatively modest house could cover
the packed earth floor with a wool rug.

*T*he gentility of the colonial South has probably been over-emphasized. For every William F. Byrd II with a private library, a mansion, and a regiment of slaves, there were a thousand simpler souls living in modest circumstances. Still, this parlor from a rural Tidewater house built about 1770 has an authentic air of Palladian elegance. It belonged to William Eley of Isle of Wight County, Virginia, who raised livestock and tobacco and was an active Revolutionary. The house had only two rooms on the first floor, but the parlor has extraordinarily fine woodwork that would have been a credit to a far larger Georgian-style house. The corner cupboard and the paneled fireplace wall are also impressive touches. The red velvet suit on the manikin was not Eley's but is quite in keeping with the room. Its lattice design has black floral sprigs; it was probably tailored in France for an English nobleman. The upholstered chair, in the Chippendale style, is another unusual luxury for this day. The table is set for tea—by now Americans of the middle class were addicted to the beverage.

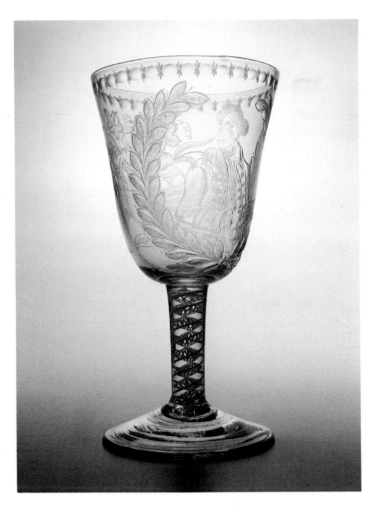

Left: *During the colonial period most fine glassware had to be imported. This English commemorative goblet, probably manufactured about 1760, has a round funnel bowl engraved with a portrait of John Wilkes, an English reformer and member of Parliament, flanked by garlands and holding a scroll inscribed "Bill of Rights." The stem contains a white glass opaque lace twist inside a single spiral thread.*

Opposite: *This sweetmeat dish features three shells at the bottom and a central cup supported by a shell-encrusted stem. It was made about 1771 by Bonnin and Morris in Philadelphia, probably the first American porcelain manufactory. Copying English styles, Bonnin and Morris struggled, without success, to compete with the Chinese and English porcelains that were flooding the American market.*

Overleaf: *These six particularly fine early pieces of engraved American glassware were made by a German craftsman, John Frederick Amelung, who opened the New Bremen Glass Manufactory near Frederick, Maryland about 1785. The case bottle, far left, is engraved "B. Johnson, 1788." Three pieces bear the monogram "WAG."*

Left: *This decanter, an early attempt to produce lead glass, was made by George Ravenscroft in England about 1676. Though intended to be clear, due to imperfections in the glass formula the decanter is "crizzled" (clouded by a network of fine internal cracks).*

Opposite: *White has not always been* de rigueur *for a formal wedding gown. According to family tradition this was the bridal dress of Catherine Livingston, daughter of the Revolutionary patriot Philip Livingston, when she married Stephen van Rensselaer on January 23, 1764, in New York City. The gown is yellow silk brocaded in a trellis pattern overlaid by polychrome chrysanthemums and roses. The front is trimmed with applied serpentine bands of ruching, and the style is "à la française," meaning that the back hangs freely in pleats from the neck. The skirt has side hoops and a train.*

Right: *This "freedom suit," homemade of cotton nankeen lined with linen, was so called because it marked the end of the wearer's apprenticeship. It was given to one Jonathon Sheldon in 1775 and thought to have been made by his master's wife. Kindly though her intentions may have been, the suit is clearly ill-fitting. On loan from the Wahwenawasigh Chapter of the Daughters of the American Revolution.*

Above, right: *This pear-shaped English guitar—cittern, as it is also called—was used in America. A descendant of a more elegant Italian ancestor, the guitar has fewer frets; the neck of this one terminates in a sickle head with machine screws. The ornamental rose (detail,* above) *covering the sound hole has no acoustical function.*

Opposite: *Many men needed shoe and knee buckles in the eighteenth century—if not of silver, then of less costly materials. The large silver shoe buckles at top were presumably worn by a colonel of the Seventh Virginia Regiment in the Revolutionary War. The silver ones at lower left were, according to tradition, the property of Major General Richard Montgomery, who fell at the Battle of Quebec in 1775. The other shoe buckles and the knee buckles at lower right are set with paste.*

In good old colony times,
When we lived under the King,
Three roguish chaps fell into mishaps
Because they could not sing.

—American-English ballad

The cello, opposite, *is a piece of folk art—and craftsmanship—from Lebanon, Maine. The heart-shaped tail piece is marked on one side* "Pamela/1794, J. Jewett Fecit," *and on the other,* "George Jewett, AD 1795." *The peg box,* above, *is carved in the shape of a young girl's head.*

Step and prop-iron, bolt and screw,
Spring, tire, axle, and linchpin too,
Steel of the finest, bright and blue;
Thoroughbrace bison-skin, thick and wide;
Boot, top, dasher, from tough old hide
Found in the pit when the tanner died.
That was the way he "put her through."
"There!" said the Deacon, "naow she'll
    dew."

—Oliver Wendell Holmes

"The Deacon's Masterpiece," which Holmes describes in his famous poem, was a one-horse shay (or chaise) like this one. It was found in 1904 in an old barn in Portsmouth, New Hampshire, still in running condition, although it had been built about 1770. The Deacon's shay had been so wonderfully constructed that it ran for a whole century and then fell to pieces all at once. This masterpiece was obviously even sturdier. It carried two passengers as well as a driver, who sat precariously on the three-legged iron stool in front of the wheels. A chaise was one of the lightest and fastest of eighteenth-century carriages, if less impressive than the larger phaetons and landaus. The 5-foot-6-inch wheels are built to keep mud from splashing upward, but passengers must have had a rough ride, all the same. The section of cobblestone pavement at lower right was typical for its day: likely to develop potholes, destructive of wheels, hooves, and boots, not to mention noisy and almost impossible to keep clean.

Above: *According to Henry Ward Beecher, "a tool is but the extension of a man's hand," and early American tools often have the individuality of the creator. Above is an eighteenth-century Pennsylvania Dutch "goosewing" hewing axe resting on the bed of a nineteenth-century planer. Both tools were used for squaring timbers.*

Above: *The American felling axe had its own evolution. Its European ancestor at upper left is poll-less—that is, it is all "bit" or cutting edge, with no extension opposite the cutting edge. In the seventeenth century the French and English used such tools for trading with the Indians, who patterned their tomahawks after them. The two belt-axes in the center show how, in the eighteenth century, a weighted poll was added to the long, unbalanced bit, and the typical American axehead (as at right) took on a squarish shape.*

Opposite: *The axe had myriad uses, as these eight examples prove. In the top left corner is a mortising axe (for making square holes in a block of wood) and to the right of it a hewing axe. Below them, left to right, a cooper's side axe (for shaping barrel staves), a felling axe, a turpentine axe (for chipping the bark of pines), a sod axe, and a shingling hatchet with a long poll.*

Preceding pages: *Wood was the pre-eminent building material in colonial and nineteenth-century America, and builders and artisans used a variety of distinctive woodworking planes, many of them beautiful as well as practical. Reading from lower right, here are a cabinetmaker's plow and a carriagemaker's router (both for cutting grooves); at center, a carpenter's jointer (eighteenth-century European). Behind it is a patternmaker's spoon plane and, standing on its heel, a joiner's molding plane.*

Right: *Along with the axe and the adze, the brace is one of the fundamental hand tools and has been used since the fifteenth century by such craftsmen as armorers, chairmakers, carriage builders, and cabinetmakers. These braces were made in the eighteenth and nineteenth centuries.*

Tools, guns, nails, and horseshoes were all vital to the colonists, who made iron production an early priority. In 1641 the "Company of Undertakers for the Iron Works in New England" was formed. These three models show a blast furnace, a forge, and a rolling and slitting mill as they looked in 1650 at Saugus, Massachusetts.

Above: *Iron is present in the earth's surface mixed with other minerals and with oxygen. A blast furnace such as this is needed to heat the ore to the point that slag forms and molten iron runs into troughs at the bottom of the furnace. Charcoal was the fuel here, and the blast came from a bellows that was operated by a water wheel.*

Opposite, top: *Pig iron as it comes from a blast furnace is too brittle for making tools. A forge like this one is needed to remelt the iron into a pasty mass called a bloom, which is then hammered to rid it of impurities and make it malleable.*

Opposite, bottom: *This is a rolling and slitting mill—an innovation in its day—where small iron bars were heated and then slit into small rods, which were finally converted into iron nails.*

The Long Rifle

*But Jackson he was wide awake and wasn't
    scar'd at trifles
For well he knew what aim we take, with
    our Kentucky rifles,
So he led us down to Cypress Swamp, the
    ground was low and Mucky,
There stood John Bull in martial pomp but
    here was old Kentucky.*

—American ballad from the Battle of New
Orleans, 1815

Radical advances in weaponry are often at
first more devastating psychologically
than militarily. Gunpowder itself was of
limited usefulness on the battlefield in its early
days, but those who possessed it seemed also to
command the powers of the devil. New weapons
also have a way of causing unpredictable events
off the battlefield. Gunpowder put the knight-in-
armor—and hence feudal society—out of
business.

The American long rifle is just such an
advance in weaponry: at first of limited use but
of profound psychological effect. The rifle did
have real ballistic advantages over the musket:
it offered some hope of hitting a target. But
what the rifle achieved was more important than
ballistics. In the American mind, and in that of
the British, it helped create the heroic figure of
the American backwoodsman—the marksman
firing relentlessly from between the chinks of his
log cabin, the invincible scout in coonskin.

What makes a rifle better than a musket is
the relatively simple matter of a spiraling groove.
A musket has a smooth bore—that is, the inside
of the barrel is smooth. The musket ball,
propelled by a charge of powder, caromed
down the barrel (usually wide bore, about .80
caliber) and fell to earth one knew not

where. There was no use in taking aim, or not
much use. And the range was short. Even the
famous "Brown Bess" flintlock, which was the
standard weapon of the British Army in the
eighteenth century and later, was so inaccurate
as to seem almost harmless. One officer
complained, "A soldier must be very unfortunate
indeed who shall be wounded by a common
musket at 150 yards, provided his antagonist
aims at him; and, as to firing at a man at 200
yards, with a common musket, you might just
as well fire at the moon."

The ignition system of the musket posed yet
another problem. The flintlock was the most
advanced method: pulling the trigger caused a
hammer carrying a flint to strike a steel plate
and send a shower of sparks into the priming
charge, which then ignited the main charge and
blasted the missile out in a cloud of smoke and
powder. The gun that the first American colonists
brought with them, however, was a primitive
predecessor of the flintlock, the matchlock. It
was so heavy that it had to be propped up on a
stand. No man could hold it up and at the same
time execute the fifteen or so steps needed to fire
it. A powder charge and a ball had to be rammed
into the barrel, and another charge of powder
placed in a pan at the gun breech. This was set
off by means of hot ash from a slow-burning
rope, "the match," which had to be kept ignited.
If all went well and it did not begin to rain, the
powder in the barrel would catch and the bullet
would exit.

By that time one's intended prey might well
have ambled off into the forest or filled one's
hide full of arrows. (If the prospective victim
stood still, it must have been from sheer
curiosity.) But the matchlock could be lethal,
as the experience of Captain John Smith
demonstrates. One day at Jamestown as he

Page 96: *This long rifle of 1760 is an early and transitional type of Pennsylvania or Kentucky rifle. Unlike a musket, a gun with a rifled bore can be accurately aimed. Among the first American inventions were usable rifles like this one. They later became a major factor in the development of the frontier.*

Right: *This hunting gun is a dog lock long fowler— that is, a smoothbore, .75 caliber weapon with a rare kind of flintlock ignition system. It was brought to Spencer Hill (now East Hartford), Connecticut, in 1654 by an exiled Scottish officer named James Forbes, who undoubtedly used it for Indian fighting as well as birdhunting.*

attempted to set off his matchlock, the charge backfired and almost burned him to death. Clearly, the matchlock was no instrument to conquer the continent with. As Lee Kennett and James Anderson point out in their recent study, *The Gun in America,* the weapons of Captain Smith and Miles Standish were not destined to be those of the American frontier.

And then, sometime early in the eighteenth century, perhaps around 1720, settlers of German descent in western Pennsylvania began to craft a new kind of weapon. Strictly speaking it was not new. Since the middle of the sixteenth century European gunsmiths had known that "rifling" had great advantages. That is, they knew that if a spiraling groove were cut into a gun bore, it would cause the bullet to spin, not carom, and thus the gun could be aimed. The problem was that unless the bullet fit tightly, it would fail to catch in the groove and spin. And if it did fit the bore, it had to be hammered down the barrel with a mallet—as tedious a process as firing a matchlock.

But the Pennsylvania craftsmen were able to solve these problems, and a few others as well. Practical men and born toolmakers, they gave up trying to create the perfect bullet and instead wrapped the lead ball in a patch of greased leather. This not only gave a tight fit against the grooves, it also simplified loading. They also lengthened the barrel to four feet and sharply reduced the caliber to about .40. This Kentucky rifle, as it came to be called, was accurate at ranges up to 300 yards. Not only that, it was lightweight and portable—nine pounds. With its small caliber it took smaller shot and less powder—economy as well as convenience.

It was the ideal weapon for a hunter. (The edge it gave the settlers over the Indians was quickly dissipated when the Indians got rifles themselves.) Deadly and beautiful, it was one of the earliest examples of functionalism in an American art. It had some of the mystique of the samurai sword. Those who owned Kentucky rifles prized them. Some rifles were cheap and shoddy, of course, but most smiths chose fine woods and brass fittings for the stocks and reveled in the leanness and simplicity of this new firearm. The only effective use for a musket was in pitched battle—many muskets in an impregnable line. The rifle was meant for the hands of a lone marksman at a distance.

The idea that the Kentucky rifle won the Revolutionary War is pure myth, as historians have been patiently explaining for many years. The flintlock musket was the preferred weapon on both sides; yet the American long rifle was already in use and the average British soldier was unnerved by the mere notion of the American sharpshooter. George Washington knew that this was so, and played brilliantly upon the situation. He would set up exhibitions of marksmanship, in hope that spies would carry reports of them to British headquarters, and he also encouraged the "use of Hunting Shirts, with long breeches made of the same cloth . . . it is a dress justly supposed to carry no small terror to the enemy. . . . " In other words, pose as a rifleman whether you own a rifle or not.

One stunning American victory in which the rifle played a part was the battle of Kings Mountain in North Carolina on October 6, 1780. The British contingent, consisting of about 1,200 American Tories, was led by Major Patrick Ferguson. One of the great ironies of the war is that Ferguson, an Englishman and a crack shot, had in 1776 patented a rifle of his own invention, one of the first breech-loaders. Attempting to clear the backwoods of hostile pioneers while Lord Cornwallis advanced northward up to the coast, Ferguson ran into some 3,000 rifle-wielding rebels. His own men carried smoothbores of the most indifferent quality. The Americans annihilated the Tories and killed the Major as well, with few casualties of their own. But whether it was marksmanship or simply superior numbers that won the day at Kings Mountain is arguable. The first American battle where rifles were clearly decisive was the Battle of New Orleans in 1815, in which Andrew Jackson led 2,000 redoubtable backwoodsmen against the British lines.

The real place of this gun was on the frontier. Without it there might have been no Daniel Boone at Cumberland Gap. Yet the rifle transcends ordnance. It is not an object, it is an idea. It is the essential element in an American image and dilemma that lingers into our own day. The rifle was the hardwon possession—almost the double—of a classic American character, skinny and angular as his gun, more like an Indian than an Englishman:

> He was tall, and so meager as to make him seem above even the six feet that he actually stood in his stockings. On his head, which was thinly covered with lank, sandy hair, he wore a cap made of foxskin. . . . His face was skinny and thin almost to emaciation; but yet it bore no signs of disease;—on the contrary it had every indication of the most robust and enduring health. The cold and the exposure had, together, given it a color of uniform red. His gray eyes were glancing under a pair of shaggy brows . . . his scraggy neck was bare, and burnt to the same tint with his face; though a small part of a shirt collar, made of the country check, was to be seen above the overdress he wore. A kind of coat, made of dressed deerskin, with the hair on, was belted close to his lank body. . . . On his feet were deerskin moccasins, ornamented with porcupines' quills, after the manner of the Indians, and his limbs were guarded with long leggings of the same material as the moccasins, which, gartering over the knees of his tarnished buckskin breeches, had obtained for him, among the settlers, the nickname of Leatherstocking. . . . A leathern pouch hung before him, from which, as he concluded his last speech, he took a small measure, and filling it accurately with powder, he commenced reloading the rifle, which, as its butt rested on the snow before him reached nearly to the top of his foxskin cap.

This was the deerslayer, the pathfinder, hawkeye—Natty Bumppo—as described by James Fenimore Cooper in *The Pioneers*. Long Rifle was another of his nicknames. He was the first grand creation of American fiction and, after the cowboy, perhaps a key myth of American history. (John Wayne and Gary Cooper, as screen personalities, are only two of Natty's descendants.) His hold on the world's imagination comes precisely from that long rifle, reaching "nearly to the top of his foxskin cap." The rifle itself was new but newer still for being in the hands of a man like Natty. If he was a free and wild American, it was because he had a gun and a powder horn.

The idea that freedom comes out of the barrel of a gun—or to state the matter another way, that to disarm a man is to render him powerless—is an old one in the western world. Perhaps the most radical development on the American continent, quite apart from any claims for inalienable rights, was the contention that the citizenry should be armed. The rulers of most European countries felt strongly that the citizenry must certainly not be armed. Arms, and in particular firearms, were for professional soldiers or the aristocratic officers who commanded them, or for wealthy sportsmen.

In France the weapons trade was strictly controlled, and the people had no weapons. What need had a poor man for a weapon? He was forbidden to hunt, he had no call to defend his honor, and there was a standing army to defend his country for him. Guns were for soldiers, swords for gentlemen. Citizens with guns could only be plotting insurrection. England in the Middle Ages had had a tradition of a popular militia but it had died out, and by the eighteenth century the situation was much the same as in France. Apart from soldiers, great lords, and highwaymen, the mass of people had no arms and would hardly have known how to use them in any case.

But in the American colonies, things were different. There were few gentlemen and no standing army. Anyone who left his defense in the hands of another would end up dead. And defense was not the only concern. The woods were full of game—often the only source of meat. Furs and deerskins were important exports. And if all these motivations had not sufficed, the British wanted the colonists to be armed. They had no intention of sending the British Army over here.

Similarly, in the early eighteenth century as the coastal colonies became somewhat more secure, the gentry in such ports as Charleston and Baltimore realized that it was in their interest to keep the frontier armed: let the uncouth Scotch-Irish, who were beginning to arrive by the tens of thousands from 1710 onward, go out into the wilderness and fight Indians. But to fight, they had to have guns. Supply responded to demand and in a few years the Pennsylvania Germans perfected the long rifle. Everything, including technology, conspired to put a gun in every colonial household.

Realizing just what kind of power they now possessed, these new Americans hastily enacted laws designed to keep weapons out of the hands of slaves and Indians: the democratization of weapons could go only so far. In 1792 Congress prohibited slaves, freedmen, and Indians from joining state militias.

Thus it was that when a Bill of Rights was added to the Constitution, the right of the citizenry to bear arms, unhampered by Congress, was listed second after freedom of speech. Alone among civilized nations today the United States still guarantees this right, which is unlimited in any effective way even in states with presumably limiting legislation. Of late one segment of the public, pointing to assassinations and homicides and gun accidents, has come to favor abrogating the Second Amendment. But the outcry against abridgment has been almost as vociferous. The root of it all goes back to the hero in his foxskin cap. His long rifle, a relatively simple invention, a spare and handsome mechanism designed by anonymous hands, did more than just shoot straight. For better or worse it made an American hero out of the man who carries a gun.

Overleaf: *Both these rifles are fine examples of early breechloaders in which the bullets and powder were inserted into the rear of the barrel, rather than having to be rammed down the muzzle. Although this method was a great technological improvement over muskets and Kentucky rifles, it was nevertheless slow to be adopted. The rifle at top was invented by Major Patrick Ferguson, a British army officer, in 1776. A small number of his troops were armed with such weapons during the Revolutionary War. An American army captain named John H. Hall designed and patented the rifle at bottom in 1811. His innovation was the hinged breech, which made loading very fast. Like all rifles in the days before metal cartridges, it had a powerful flashback, capable of removing one's eyebrows and lashes. The Hall rifle saw service as late as the Civil War. This one was made in 1824.*

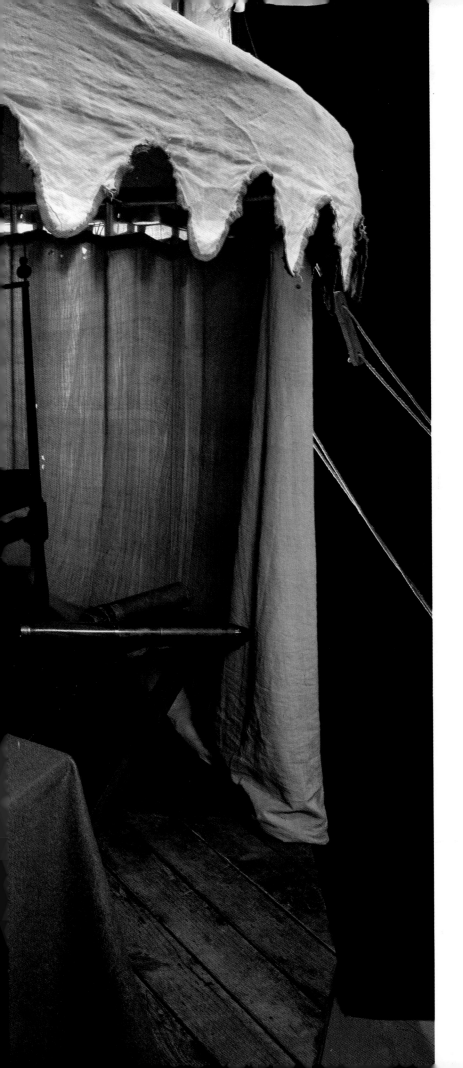

I have the Honor to inform Congress, that a Reduction of the British Army under the Command of Lord Cornwallis, is most happily effected. The unremitting Ardor which actuated every Officer and Soldier in the combined Army in this Occasion, has principally led to this Important Event. . . .

*T*hus, blandly, on October 19, 1781, did General Washington inform his countrymen that the Americans had won the war and that Lord Cornwallis had surrendered at Yorktown. It is likely that he signed the dispatch in this marquee tent, which he had used on the field occasionally during the war for staff meetings, officers' conferences, and finally, on this evening, as a banquet hall. The stiff-necked Cornwallis had not come to the surrender himself but had sent a deputy, General Charles O'Hara. Washington magnanimously invited the man to dinner—a nice military courtesy. The mess chest on the table, with its tin plates, platters, utensils, and tankard, was for field use only. At headquarters Washington dined off china. The military bed in the background is covered with a woolen blanket that Washington actually used. The bed folds up for easy transport. The camp stool, covered in leather, is one of a set of eighteen that Washington ordered in 1776. His brass field telescope, imported from England, lies atop it with its original case of russet leather.

This bell-metal mortar and pestle was used at the Battle of Monmouth in 1777.

...the Superiority in a naval force on this lake is an Object of the first moment—it has been hitherto shamefully neglected—but now we have Information for 100 Carpenters from the Eastward and 50 from Philadelphia...all at Work in building Gondelows...

—Letter from General Anthony Wayne to Benjamin Franklin, *July 29, 1776*

*T*he model, opposite, *single-masted and square-rigged, is exactly the sort of "Gondelow," ("gondola" or gunboat) that "Mad" Anthony Wayne was waiting for. It is the* Philadelphia *(see also next page), built by American ship carpenters and launched on Lake Champlain in August, 1776—a reminder that the Revolutionary War was fought with axes and adzes as well as muskets. The* Philadelphia—*a massive, cumbersome oaken hulk fifty-four feet long—was one of eight gunboats built for a remarkably ragtag flotilla under the command of Brigadier General Benedict Arnold. His objective was to halt the British advance southward, under Sir Guy Carleton, from Canada toward Fort Ticonderoga. The two "navies" met at Valcour Island on October 11, 1776; after six hours of desperate fighting, the* Philadelphia *went down with her crew of forty-four and her three main battery guns. Arnold lost the battle, in spite of his skill as a naval leader, but he had sufficiently hindered Carleton's advance so that the British withdrew northward and did not attempt to capture Fort Ticonderoga that autumn.*

This is the bow of the Continental gondola Philadelphia *with her 12–pounder gun in its original slide carriage. In 1935, almost 159 years after she sank, the gunboat was raised intact from the bottom of Lake Champlain with much of her equipment and nearly a hundred other artifacts. The hole in her starboard bow, made by a 24-pound shot, is the one that finally sank her. A rugged and uncomfortable man-of-war, the* Philadelphia *nevertheless bespeaks the courage of the crew who manned her, fighting against virtually hopeless odds and yet somehow managing to carry the day.*

This sword, which belonged to a now almost
forgotten military hero, General Jacob Brown,
is one of the more splendid relics of the War of
1812. The Senate and Assembly of New York
State presented the sword to Brown in recognition
of his successful campaigns against the British
along the Niagara frontier, particularly at Fort
Erie. The scabbard bears scenes of the battle of
Niagara, and the straight blade of the sword
is decorated in gold and silver chasing on a dark
blue background. The pommel is in the shape of
an eagle's head—a fitting symbol of a nation that
had just established itself as the supreme power
of the Western Hemisphere.

Above: *(Left to right) This bronze howitzer, or hand cannon (the ball is in the foreground), is similar to the ones used against the Miami Indians on the Northwest frontier in 1794. Led by General Anthony Wayne, American regulars won the Battle of Fallen Timbers (near what is now Toledo, Ohio), opening the area to settlers. The canteen was probably made about the same period for army use. The blue knapsack, decorated with a frog-legged eagle, was used by a militiaman in the early 1800s.*

The gold-mounted flintlock pistols, opposite, *the finest set of presentation arms of their time, were a gift of the State of Connecticut to Commodore Thomas MacDonough. MacDonough, a young, unseasoned officer, and his small fleet deployed short-range guns to advantage against the long-range British artillery, thus definitively routing the British from Lake Champlain during the Battle for Plattsburgh on September 11, 1814.*

Dr FRANKLIN'S REMARKS RELATIVE TO THIS PRESS MADE
WHEN HE CAME TO ENGLAND AS AGENT OF THE MASSACHU
-SETTS IN THE YEAR 1768 — THE Dr AT THIS TIME VISITED
THE PRINTING OFFICE OF Mr WATTS OF WILD STREET LIN-
COLNS INN FIELDS & GOING UP TO THIS PARTICULAR PRESS AF-
TERWARDS IN THE POSSESSION OF MESSrs COX & SON OF GREAT
QUEEN STREET IN THE POSSESSION OF MESSrs COX & SON OF GREAT
THE MEN WHO WERE WORKING AT IT COME MY FRIENDS WE WILL
DRINK TOGETHER IT IS NOW FORTY YEARS SINCE I WORKED LIKE
YOU AT THIS PRESS — AS A JOURNEYMAN PRINTER THEN SENT
FOR A GALLON OF PORTER & HE DRANK WITH THEM SUCCESS TO
PRINTING   FROM THE ABOVE IT WILL APPEAR THAT THIS
108 YEARS SINCE Dr FRANKLIN WORKED AT THIS IDENTICAL PRESS

JUNE 1833

The Most Insatiable Mind in America

When great men and women of history are transformed into legend—as inevitably they are transformed—they often double or triple in size. George Washington becomes the imperturbable hero in the bow of a rowboat, or the saintly youth of Parson Weems' fables. In the hands of the hagiographers, Thomas Jefferson becomes the Sage of Monticello: flawless and majestic. The popular legend of Benjamin Franklin, by contrast, has somehow diminished him from the vigorous, brilliant, complex character he really was into a bespectacled, elderly man, the author of a number of improving aphorisms: "Early to bed, early to rise. . . . " Yet anyone seeking a spiritual forefather for this nation and having a choice between George Washington and Benjamin Franklin might find Franklin a more congenial—even a more modern—ancestor. Before there was any such thing as the United States, he was the first American. Throughout the pre-Revolutionary period, almost to the day of his election to the Continental Congress, he thought of himself as a loyal subject of the King, but the English knew he was not English and the French knew he was not English. He was something new in the world.

He had a genius for playing a multitude of roles; he was comfortable in Parliament, at Versailles, or in a kitchen. He came from a plain, immigrant background. Born into a large family in Boston in 1706, Ben Franklin was self-educated and—apart from his apprenticeship in his older brother's printshop—self-made. His father Josiah was an immigrant and a poor man. His mother's mother had been an indentured servant. High as he rose in the world, Benjamin had no connections or advantages but those he created. At the age of seventeen he got tired of working for his brother and ran away to New

Preceding pages: *A wooden press that was made in England in the early eighteenth century and used by Ben Franklin as a journeyman printer in London, 1725–26. It is shown in the setting of a reconstructed shop of the period. At this kind of press a team of two men working hard could print up to 240 sheets of paper in an hour.*

Another view of the press used by Ben Franklin in "Watts" shop in Lincoln's Inn Fields, London. Forty years later Franklin, now a celebrated diplomat, returned to the printing shop where he greeted the old press, exhorted the printers to work hard and remain sober, and bought beer all round. From that moment the press became a mascot preserved with care and affection. In 1841 it was bought by public subscription and presented to the United States.

York to look for a job. Finding none, he went on to Philadelphia. In his *Autobiography* he relates that he got off the boat, bought himself "three great puffy rolls" at a bakery, and began knocking on doors. He was hired as a journeyman printer. The authors of schoolbooks have doted on that tale.

Franklin was a plain man but there is no point in pretending he was an average one. He was not one man at all but a myriad. In the grand-scale biography that he wrote of Franklin, Carl Van Doren defined him: "His mind was a federation of purposes working harmoniously together. Other philosophers might be dark and profound but Franklin moved serenely through the visible world, trying to understand it all. Other men of action might lay single plans and endlessly persist in them but Franklin met occasions as they arose and acted on them with a far-sighted opportunism. His mind grew as the world grew."

From journeyman, Franklin soon turned himself into one of the finest printers, and most successful publishers, in the colonies. He understood the value of information and had a head-on instinct for what people wanted to read. If his *Poor Richard* almanac was a huge, moneymaking success—and it was—it was because the colonies were starved for practical advice and daily amusement. For a genius Franklin was exceedingly hard-headed. He set up a system that we have lately rechristened "networking." He called his network the Junto. Twelve members (no more) met once a week and exchanged intelligence. Not gossip, but an agenda of concerns. What new laws were needed? What useful new books had appeared? Had any businesses failed lately and if so, why? Had any deserving stranger arrived in town? Later, as postmaster general of the colonies Franklin set up a model service—fast, efficient, and profitable. As much as any other thing he created, the postal service made the American Revolution possible. For the first time the colonists could communicate with one another and think of themselves as one people. It was all a matter of exchanging information.

In Franklin a hundred other famous Americans are foreshadowed. He had Andrew Carnegie's business sense, John D. Rockefeller's eye for the main chance, Abraham Lincoln's talent for making political capital out of humble origins and plain dress. (As American commissioner in Paris Franklin wore an old fur hat, which made him the toast of the town.) Of Thomas Edison it is said that his greatest invention was the method of inventing things, but his mentor in this was Franklin. He had no laboratory, no assistants, no grants, no university chair. He lived and worked in a small Philadelphia house with his wife, children, mother-in-law, and a shifting population of servants and houseguests. He ran a printing business and a retail shop. In this unlikely and undoubtedly chaotic setting he became one of the best-known scientists in the world—in fact the only well-known American scientist of his day.

His great discovery was the nature of electricity, and his famous experiments with the lightning rod and possibly with the kite (he may not actually have flown the kite in the rainstorm) demonstrated that lightning was electricity. Another experimenter in Europe, trying to replicate Franklin's experiment, was killed. What Franklin was doing was at least as dangerous as traveling in a spacecraft today. He seems not to have minded the risks, intent as he was on finding a practical use for what he had found out.

Attempting to electrocute a turkey two days before Christmas, he put two wires together and almost electrocuted himself. He later wrote that he was like "the Irishman . . . who, being about to steal powder, made a hole in the cask with a hot iron." But he went on to invent the lightning rod. He was curious about everything. Finding ants invading a molasses pot in the pantry, he devised an experiment to prove that the ants communicated with one another. Once when he had planned to watch a lunar eclipse, a storm blew up and obscured the view. Later he learned that in Boston the storm had hit after the eclipse, and he deduced that the clouds must have moved from west to east. So Franklin began gathering data on storms, and made the first accurate deductions about weather patterns in this hemisphere.

Later, as a colonial agent and then an American diplomat he made many transatlantic

crossings, during which he never failed to perform some oceanographic experiment. On at least two crossings he measured the temperature of the water in order to track the Gulf Stream. He was the first to study it. He knew, as most sea captains of the day did not, that a ship made better time by crossing the Gulf Stream directly than by running against it. Like Isaac Newton, he envisioned an ordered, knowable universe, and he wanted to discover its laws. But tracking the majestic swirl of the Gulf Stream did not distract his mind from the possibility of improving the speed of the mail packet from England. He spoke plainly and set down his findings in decent English. His writings on electricity are as clear today as they were then. Anybody who can read can understand him. A father of his country he may be, but he was definitely not a father of his country's scientific and bureaucratic jargon.

Women of all ages and types loved Franklin. What Carl Van Doren said of Franklin in 1938 has a nice resonance in 1981. "Always a person himself, Franklin treated every woman as if she were a person too, and made her feel more truly one than ever. Because he loved, valued, and studied women, they were no mystery to him, and he had no instinctive fear of them. Statesman and scientist, profoundly masculine, he took women into account as well as any other force of nature." At twenty-four he married Deborah Read of Philadelphia. To the marriage he brought an illegitimate son, whom Deborah adopted and raised. The marriage lasted happily for fifty years, until Deborah's death. "We are grown old together," Franklin wrote of her tenderly, "and if she has any faults, I am so used to 'em that I don't perceive 'em." Yet he was openly the friend and correspondent of many women. In America there was Catherine Ray, in England Polly Hewson and Georgiana Shipley—accomplished women whom Franklin appears to have loved for their minds.

As an aging widower and his country's emissary to France, he was as gallant as a thirty-year-old. He came to France in 1776 and served until 1784. Ironically, in the *haut monde* revolutionaries were all the rage. Franklin fell in love with a widow of sixty, Madame Helvetius, and wanted to marry her. The story goes that she once chided Franklin for not having visited her when she had expected him. He replied, "Madame, I am waiting till the nights are longer." When she turned down his proposal on the grounds that she wanted to be faithful to her dead husband, Franklin wrote a humorous piece for her. He claimed he had visited the Elysian Fields and had found M. Helvetius and Deborah Franklin married in the afterlife. "Here I am," he closed, "let us avenge ourselves." She still said no, but still they were friends. She was not the only great lady that he loved. Among others there was Madame de Forbach, who gave him an elegant walking stick, which he later gave to his good friend George Washington.

Franklin was no rake—it was not a case of no fool like an old fool. He was a fair and moral man, and a moralist as well. His behavior as he neared eighty recalls the piece he wrote secretly at the age of forty, advising a young friend on "the choice of a mistress." As much as anything he wrote, it reveals Franklin's nature.

His counsel was to get married instead of having a mistress.

> But if you will not take this counsel . . . you should prefer old women to young ones. Because they have more knowledge of the world, and their minds are better stored with observations, their conversation is more improving and most lastingly agreeable. . . . Because there is no hazard of children. . . . Because the sin is less. . . . The having made a young girl miserable may give you frequent bitter reflection; none of which can attend the making an old woman happy. . . . And lastly, they are so grateful!

Franklin is represented here by a printing press, a favorite suit, and the walking stick. No collection of objects could show the depth of the man or sum up what he did to ensure the birth and survival of the United States. But in this day when historians so often speak of social and economic "forces," these possessions of one founding father are reminders that people rather than blind forces make history. As his contemporaries knew, Benjamin Franklin was indispensable.

Among the few surviving relics of the Stamp Act of 1765 is this tooled leather box which held sheets of the hated stamps. It has the monogram of the British government—"GR" and a crown—as well as the inscription, "Stamp Act Pepd. March 8, 1766." The box belonged to Judge Benjamin Thomson of New Jersey, who remained loyal to the crown.

Opposite: *One of Franklin's many political talents was knowing when and how to play the plain republican in the plain republican coat. This suit of plum-colored silk (now faded to brown) may not strike the modern eye as particularly conservative, but in 1778 in Paris, where Franklin had gone to sign the Treaty of Alliance, it was a model of austerity, and it captivated the peruked and beruffled French. The coat has a narrow standing collar, self-covered buttons, and flap pockets. A waistcoat and breeches complete the costume. The suit is on loan to the Museum from the Massachusetts Historical Society.*

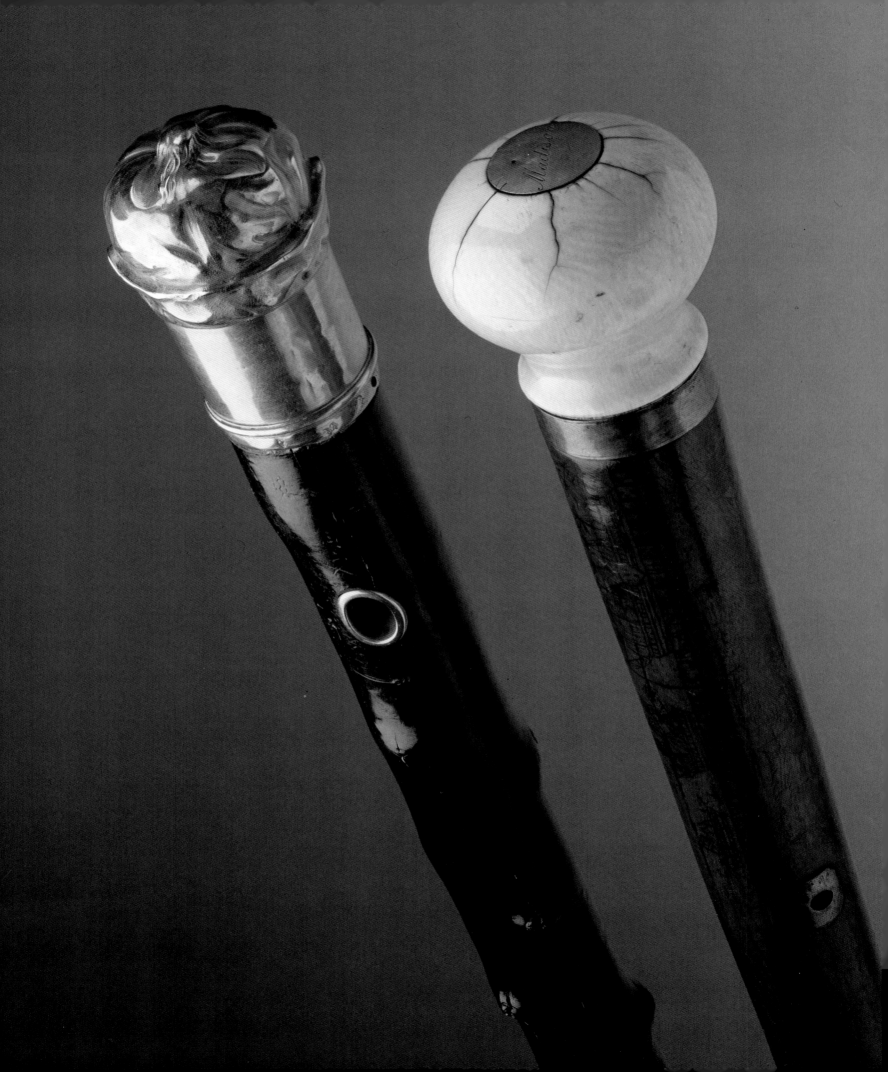

Above: *The unusual lightweight leather-upholstered armchair belonged to James Madison, the fourth president, who, it is believed, had it as a gift from Thomas Jefferson. The worktable, of mahogany, belonged to Dolley Madison, one of the most popular of American First Ladies.*

Opposite, left: *Franklin specified in his will that this "fine crab tree walking stick with a gold head curiously wrought in the form of a cap of liberty, I give to my friend and the friend of mankind, General Washington. If it were a sceptre he has merited it, and would become it. It was a present to me from that excellent woman, Madame de Forbach, the dowager duchess of Deuxponts. . . . "* The ivory-headed cane, *on the* right, *made from timber from the* U.S.S. Constitution, *and bearing an engraved likeness of that ship, was presented by Commodore J.D. Elliot to President James Madison, in recognition of the fact that he was called "Father of the Constitution."*

Above: *All that remains of George Washington's state coach is this copper panel from the door, decorated with three cupids and wreaths. The coach, originally made for Governor Richard Penn of Pennsylvania in 1771, was presented to Martha Washington by the State of Pennsylvania in 1777 and used by the President and First Lady in both New York and Philadelphia.*

Opposite: *John Trumbull painted this miniature portrait of George Washington (and a companion portrait of Martha) from life between 1792 and 1794, while Washington was president. Trumbull, the son of a governor of Connecticut, is famous for his portraits of the founding fathers.*

Above: *This writing case, or portfolio, used by George Washington during the Revolutionary War, consists of a mahogany box with a lid covered with black-grained leather and lined with paper. There are five compartments for paper, pens, pencils, and sealing wax. A folding leather pocket for manuscripts is attached to the case.*

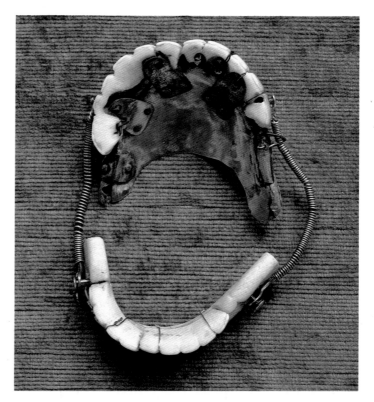

Right: *One persistent Washingtonian legend is that the great man's dentures were wooden. Fortunately, they were not. This pair (he had several sets) is of gold and ivory, with the lower denture made in three sections.*

Above: *A surveying compass owned by George Washington, who was a surveyor by profession. Made of cast brass, the compass is inscribed "Rittenhouse, Philadelphia," and the silvered dial is marked with an eight-pointed star.*

Left: *In 1776 the Philadelphia silversmith William Hollinshead made two dozen silver camp cups for Washington. All but this one were eventually melted down to make new items for the family. The cup is engraved with the Washington arms.*

Above: *The idealization—almost deification—of George Washington began in his lifetime and continued throughout the next century. This subscription box was one of hundreds used to collect funds for the Washington Monument—a marble-sheathed Egyptian obelisk in Washington, D.C. Construction began in 1848 and went on for another thirty-five years.*

Right: *Perhaps the most evocative of all the First Ladies exhibitions is this one, with its three figures in their fragile dresses. In the foreground is Martha Custis Washington [the manikin heads are not portraits, but the hairstyles are authentic] in a mob cap and a pink faille dress hand-painted with wild flowers. Behind her, Abigail Adams wears blue Canton crepe with a lace collar; Martha Jefferson Randolph, who occasionally served as White House hostess for her widowed father, wears a graceful Paisley shawl over a white gown. The room setting is based on the parlor in the Executive Mansion in Philadelphia at the time George Washington was president. John and Abigail Adams were the first presidential couple to live at what is now called the White House in Washington, D.C.*

Thomas Jefferson's enterprises were endless. One of them was a compilation, in four languages, entitled The Life and Morals of Jesus of Nazareth. *The clipped copies of the New Testament from which he took the text were sold with his library after his death, and eventually two of them were donated to the Museum.*

The

Life and Morals

of

Jesus of Nazareth

Extracted textually

from the Gospels

in

Greek, Latin

French & English.

MORALS OF JESUS

Humility recom...

S. LUKE.

...into your ears: for the
...Man shall be delivered in...
...hands of men.
45 But they understood not
...saying, and it was hid from
...that they perceived it not:
...feared to ask him of...

46 Then then...
...your names are written
...in heaven.
...that hour Jesus rejoiced

104 *The fruitless fig-tree.*

S. LUKE.

...saved thee.
43 And immediately he received
his sight, and followed him, glorify-
ing God: and all the people, when...

33 So likewise, whosoever he be
of you, that forsaketh not all that
he hath, he cannot be my disciple.
34 Salt *is* good: but if the salt
have lost his savour, wherewith
shall it be seasoned?
35 It is neither fit for the land,
nor yet for the dunghill; *but* men
cast it out. He that hath ears
to hear, let him hear.

CHAP. XV.
Parable of the lost sheep.
4 The baptism...
...from heaven...

The word "gin" is simply short for "engine," and no engine ever worked with more ironic social effects than the one opposite. It is Eli Whitney's own model of the device he patented in 1794. The crank-turned cylinder, equipped with circle-saw disks, efficiently separates short-staple cotton from its sticky green seeds. Just out of Yale in 1793, Whitney had gone to earn his living as a tutor on a Georgia plantation. The Old South was in decline. Cotton had once looked like a promising crop, but to de-seed one bale of it required an incredible two years of man labor. Consequently neither cotton nor slavery was a paying proposition. It can be argued that slavery might well have died out in the South of its own accord, as it was eventually to do in the North. But the cotton gin could produce up to fifteen bales of de-seeded cotton a day, and because mechanization had not yet come to planting, cultivating, and harvesting, the only way to raise cotton on a large scale was with slave labor. "I tremble for my country when I reflect that God is just," Jefferson had written, and now (as the cotton boom began) the course toward secession was set. A further irony was that Whitney's patent did him no good. The gin was so simple that almost any mechanic could copy it.

Above: *In 1803, in an unprecedented act, Jefferson bought "Louisiana" from France—about 828,000 square miles for some $15 million, an astounding bargain. He then dispatched Meriwether Lewis and William Clark to explore the uncharted domain. The compass above, bearing the name of the maker, "T. Whitney, PHILAD⁴.," is the one that belonged to Captain Clark.*

Right: *The Conestoga wagon, bright blue with a red underbody, originated in eastern Pennsylvania in the 1760s. For the next seventy years it was a frequent sight—laden with freight or migrating families—on the Cumberland-National Road, which was to have run all the way to the Mississippi but never made it. Covered wagons of other types carried homesteaders into the farther frontiers of the West.*

Above: *"Go ahead Crockett" is the engraving on the blade of this silver tomahawk. It was given to Davy Crockett in 1835 by some young men of Philadelphia—an appropriate memento for the Tennessee frontiersman, backwoodsman, and Indian scout. He died in 1836 at the Alamo.*

Above: *On July 8, 1853, the citizens of the coastal towns south of Tokyo were amazed to see strange vessels offshore. It was the fleet of Commodore Matthew Perry, come to "open" Japan and, not incidentally, impress that nation with American technology. Among Perry's ships was the steam frigate,* Mississippi, *which this model replicates. (The detail,* opposite, *is the paddle wheel and paddle box.) This bark-rigged steamer turned up at another famous occasion: she served with Admiral David G. Farragut in 1862 when his fleet captured New Orleans. The Union victory left the Confederacy in control of only Vicksburg and Port Hudson as river ports; while the Union besieged the latter town, the* Mississippi *was sunk.*

Nail to the mast her holy flag,
Set every threadbare sail,
And give her to the god of storms,
The lightning and the gale.

—*Oliver Wendell Holmes, 1830*

Except for Holmes' passionate rhetoric on her behalf, the Constitution—*perhaps the most famous of all American warships—might well have been dismantled in the 1830s, but the poem rallied such massive public support that the vessel has been preserved to this day. This model is of Old Ironsides as she looked during the War of 1812. Launched in Boston in 1797, the forty-four-gun frigate first saw action against privateers in the West Indies. In 1803 she became the flagship of Commodore Edward Preble's Mediterranean squadron, which blockaded Tripoli. But she rose to immortality during the War of 1812 when (under Commander Isaac Hull) she captured the British frigate* Guerriere, *and a number of other vessels later. Old Ironsides' armament consisted of thirty-two long 24-pounders, twenty-two 32-pound cannonades, and one long 18-pounder. The detail above is the starboard quarter, including at left the quarter-gallery, with some of the main armament.*

THE HEADLONG CENTURY

Machine shops like the one at left were the muscle, if not the soul, of American inventiveness in the last century. Reconstructed in part from a small factory in Harwinton, Connecticut, of about 1850, this machine shop holds tools powered by an overhead line shaft. At left is a metal planer built in 1839; at center (rear), a pulley lathe used for turning the rims and boring the hubs of pulleys; in the center (foreground) is a milling machine of 1852. At the far right is a standard lathe.

143

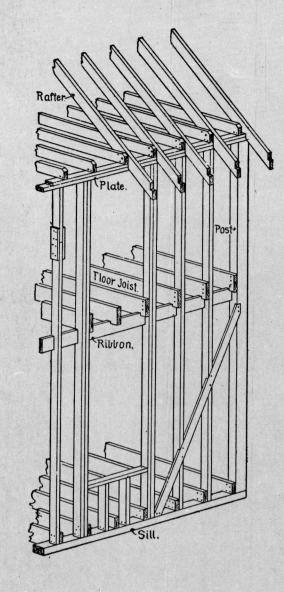

Rafter

Plate.

Post

Floor Joist.

Ribbon.

Sill.

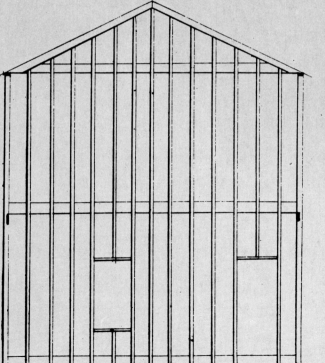

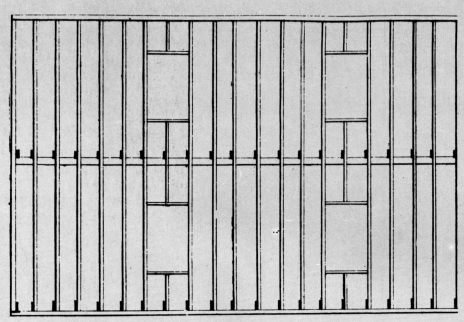

A House for the Millions

I was born close by a sawmill, was early left an orphan, was cradled in a sugar-trough, christened in a mill-pond, graduated at a log-school-house, and at fourteen fancied I could do anything I turned my hand to, and that nothing was impossible, and ever since, madame, I have been trying to prove it, and with some success.

—William B. Ogden, first mayor of Chicago, elected 1837

In the movie version of the winning of the West, it is the six-shooter that turns the tide. There is some truth in this. As it was used the six-gun was a far more lethal weapon than the rifle and certainly than the bow and arrow, which is what the opposition carried. No one piece of technology "won" the West, of course. But more than to the six-shooter or any piece of ordnance, credit should go to the two-by-four timber and the machine-made nail—and an ingenious new idea of how to put the planks and nails together.

In the early decades of the nineteenth century, the distance between the cutting edge of the frontier and the old settlements of the East grew wider, and the distance was more than geographical. If colonial Americans on the coast had set great store by their houses and had derived from them a sense of well-being, solidity, and self-respect (so palpable in the dwellings that survive), they were soon to be outnumbered by the galloping masses of the new century who had other kinds of demands to make of builders and far less genteel expectations of their housing.

The classic dwellings of New England, exemplified so handsomely by Hart House or the Reuben Bliss parlor from western Massachusetts, were virtual monuments to the families that built them. They were made to last, and they sheltered several generations of the same name. Such a room as the Bliss parlor shines with the love of tradition. The craftsman who carved the woodwork was just that—a craftsman, not an amateur trying to piece something together that would keep out the rain. But not all Americans could have such houses, or wanted them. The aspiring sawmill mechanic striking out in 1820 for boomtown Cleveland (pop. 1,000) was happy to live in something much flimsier. Who cared whether the house lasted for generations or was a credit to the family? The next generation might live in St. Louis. And when and if the mechanic could afford to live in luxury—maybe after twenty years or so—he would require considerably more flamboyance than the traditions of New England could supply.

One of our most persistent historical myths is that the westward movement was all rural, and that the migrants were inevitably homesteaders and farmers. We see the man and woman in a wagon, heading for a sod house on the prairie, and the shadow of the wagon train blots out everything else. But possibly the most important wave of westbound Americans was not agrarian at all but urban. They were cityfolks or were hoping to be. Shopkeepers, tailors, wheelwrights, dealers in furs, out-of-work road builders. And as one English visitor wrote, assaying the population of a wild young village named Chicago in 1833, "sharpers of every degree; peddlers, grog sellers, horse dealers and horse stealers . . . rogues of every description: white, black, brown, and red."

Whatever their spiritual shortcomings may have been by comparison with the presumably godfearing yeoman in his wagon, these people needed houses, too. They needed them fast and needed them cheap, and they lacked the time

Page 144: *Section of a "balloon-frame" farmhouse built in Illinois in 1855: a housing revolution engendered by the machine-made nail and the two-inch-thick sawn lumber.*

Right: *This Gothic-revival bedroom—"Gothic" chiefly in the eye of the beholder—was created in 1846 for Henry K. Harral, a wealthy businessman in Bridgeport, Connecticut. His architect was Alexander Jackson Davis, one of the foremost American purveyors of the medieval style. The woodwork is grained to look like oak; the bedstead, made of pine, poplar, and soft maple, were similarly painted and later grained to look like the walnut and maple of the dresser and night stand. Thrift was no object, nor comfort either at times, but as with clothing, elegance could not have too high a price.*

Page 149: *The fireplace is at one end of the Harral House Gothic bedroom. The gray and maroon silk gown could well have been worn by the mistress of such a house. Made in the fashionable silhouette of 1855, its combination of fabric and ornamentation is unique. With its lace collar and undersleeves and its precise cut, the gown could only have been the work of a professional dressmaker.*

and talent to build houses for themselves. Moreover they needed an astoundingly large number of houses. The first great western cities were Pittsburgh, Louisville, St. Louis, Cincinnati, Detroit and Chicago. They were not farming villages grown up. They had started out as commercial centers. And they grew at a rate to astound Boston and New York. Chicago, for example, had a population of about 100 in 1832. By 1835 there were 3,265 people in the town, increasing by 1,000 in just one year. In 1850, there were almost 30,000, and by 1870, 300,000. Houses weren't all they required, either—they had to have churches, schools, taverns, hotels, and most certainly jails.

But building for the cities, in 1830, was a problem with no satisfactory solution. Most of the immigrants were as bereft of carpentry skills as the first settlers at Jamestown had been. The traditional frame house of that day was a massive affair that needed many hands and some degree of know-how. Enormous timbers a foot thick had to be cut, squared, planed, and then joined together by mortices and tenons. Timbers bearing a pull as well as a thrust were often pegged as well. Pieced together on the ground, the frame needed half a dozen men to raise it. But except for the log cabin, this was the cheapest house that could be built. Log houses were of course the rule at first on the frontier. In 1830 a visitor to Illinois wrote back east, "I wandered down upon about a half dozen log houses and asked about Chicago. 'You're in it, stranger', they told me. " But even if there had been an endless supply of logs, a log house is not the ideal place to set up a land office or an inn or a retail store.

Then in 1833 in Chicago a new kind of house was devised—the balloon frame. Today, three-quarters of all American houses are built by a modification of this method. It is an invention that gained such widespread use as not to seem an invention at all. No one is sure whose idea the balloon frame was, but according to Lewis Mumford, the inventor was George W. Snow, a New Hampshire man who had come out to Chicago and gone into the lumber business. (Other historians have credited Augustine Deodat Taylor, a Connecticut carpenter whose name is as unfamiliar today as Snow's.) In any case, the first balloon-frame building was St. Mary's Church, built in July, 1833. It took three men three months to do the job. Before long the techniques had been simplified to the point that a house could be built in a week.

Balloon-framing consists simply of two-by-fours and other two-inch-thick members nailed together vertically and horizontally, like a basket. The strain goes in each case against the grain of the wood: the studs, nailed to the crosswise pieces, carry the weight of the roof. "Balloon-frame" was at first a term of derision, as if the whole thing would be blown away in the first strong wind.

From an engineer's point of view, however, the new frame was not only simpler but stronger than the old mortice-and-tenon method of joining. It was less likely to give way under stress than the laboriously made heavy-timber house. As one housing manual of a later period put it, "The Balloon Frame has passed through and survived the theory, ridicule, and abuse of all who have seen fit to attack it. . . . Its name was given in contempt by those old fogy mechanics who had been brought up to rob a stick of timber of all its strength and durability, by cutting it full of mortices, tenons, and auger holes, and then supposed it to be stronger than a far lighter stick differently applied, and with all its capabilities unimpaired."

What the Kentucky rifle was to the frontiersman, the balloon-frame house was to the city-dweller: an inventive advance that allowed an impoverished and ill-equipped people to move westward and survive. The Kentucky rifle, however, was no good without a marksman behind it. The balloon-frame house was so simple a notion as to require hardly any skill at all. A man and a boy, according to one contemporary observer, could now build a better house than twenty men formerly. Nevertheless technology played a critical part. Not only must the lumber be sawn accurately to size, but machine-made nails had to be cheap and plentiful. By the late eighteenth century, nail-making machines had been invented, and in 1807 one such machine was patented that could turn out 60,000 nails per day. By 1833 good nails

George Washington Arbaugh, the gold prospector-turned rancher to whom this simple kitchen belonged, did better than most. He never struck it rich, but possibly after wandering from one disappointing California gulch to the next, he settled near Mount Shasta in the late 1850s and built a log cabin and then a three-room, clapboard house, of which this is the kitchen. It never had any plumbing. Water was fetched in wooden buckets, like the one on the table. A yoke for carrying a pair of buckets hangs on the wall, at left. One modern convenience, on the edge of the table, is a hand-cranked apple parer.

cost only a nickel a pound. The price went
down another two cents a few years later.

George W. Snow, if indeed he is the right
man, was never elevated to the rank of Eli
Whitney or Cyrus McCormick, or Edison. Yet
as much as they, Snow invented America. And
so, possibly, did William Ogden, the ebullient
first mayor of Chicago, quoted above, who even
before he was mayor had taken an active role in
promoting such projects as church construction.
It was Ogden who presided over the phenomenal
Chicago land boom of the 1830s. If there is a
national house, the balloon-frame is it. It can be
small and ugly or it can be spacious and
distinguished. It can be used for almost any kind
of building, except a skyscraper. It is adaptable.
To it we undoubtedly owe a number of features
of modern American life—our comparatively
high standards of housing, our suburbs that seem
to materialize overnight, urban sprawl, and—
less directly—our high per capita consumption
of electricity and oil.

According to Henry Steele Commager, "The
American [he is speaking primarily of the
nineteenth-century American white male]
improvised jauntily, had little respect for custom,
and was willing to try anything. His reactions to
most situations was a practical one, and he was
happiest when he could find a mechanical solution
to problems: the cotton gin, the steamboat, the
harvester, the six-shooter, the sewing machine,
vulcanized rubber, the telegraph and telephone,
barbed wire fencing, the typewriter, and a
thousand other inventions. . . ."

Among those thousand others the balloon-
frame house must be counted. It was the basic
piece of technology for a nation that has
typically and temperamentally insisted that every
family must have its plot of land and its roof,
however shoddy, and that promotes home
ownership as a social ideal.

*The squat wood stove, the kettle, the teapot,
and other utensils may be similar to George
Washington Arbaugh's original furnishings
and all come from mid-nineteenth-century
California.*

This softly lighted library was an important addition, in about 1900, to the house of Benjamin B. Comegys, a Philadelphia banker. Few Americans required a separate library room at this epoch, but Comegys was clearly a man of erudition. The Minton tiles on the fireplace display scenes from Sir Walter Scott's novels; the leaded glass windows are another element in the romantic, pseudo-medieval atmosphere. Even the suit of armor, the vases, the expensive bindings of the books displays the cultivation of its owner, as well as his fashionable taste. The book in the foreground, opposite, *is* A Tour Round My Library, *a literary discourse on his books by Mr. Comegys.*

It is perpetually tea-time in this comfortable bedroom—clearly that of a little girl—in a suburban Boston house built toward the end of the nineteenth century. The table is set for two, and the guest-of-honor waits in her rocking chair. Doll clothes overflow a miniature trunk, and the neatly made doll bed is ready to receive its occupant.

Polly put the kettle on,
Polly put the kettle on,
Polly put the kettle on,
We'll all have tea.

Sukey take it off again,
Sukey take it off again,
Sukey take it off again,
They've all gone away.

—Nursery rhyme

Overleaf: As a bulwark against the projects of "ye ould deluder, Satan," the Massachusetts school law of 1647 required every community of more than fifty households to set up a public school. Thus began one of the greatest of all American social experiments. This Connecticut schoolroom of about 1863 exemplifies thousands of such one-room schoolhouses, with wood stove, splintery desks, portrait of George Washington, and religious motto.

Stay after
George Washington
is the father of his
Country
pre-cip-i-tate
pre-cip-i-tous
bark
pick
cord
cart
lost
farm
GOD IS LOVE

Stohlman's Confectionary Shop, with its spindles and fretwork, potted palms, and array of candy jars, purveyed ice cream and sweets in the Georgetown section of Washington, D.C., for almost a century—from 1865 to 1957. Ice cream has been an American passion at least since the time of George Washington, whose Mount Vernon inventory included ice cream pots and a "Cream Machine for Making Ice." The wholesale ice cream business got started in the 1850s in Baltimore, and shops like Stohlman's subsequently took their place in the urban landscape all over the country.

Left: *Designing infants' furniture that will outlast infancy is a problem not fully reckoned with even today. This Boston rocker of 1850 was a creative approach. Its seat extends, and the crest rail slots into one side of the seating area, creating a practical, if asymmetrical, cradle, which can later be used as furniture for an adult.*

Opposite: *This detail is from a red and white double-woven coverlet made for one Cynthia Walker of Oswego County, New York, in 1845. The eagle was the trademark of Harry Tyler, the weaver.*

Left: *With arms, feet, and stretchers made of pierced cast iron in the scroll design so dear to the period, this armchair on springs was patented in 1849 and manufactured in 1851 by the American Chair Company of Troy, New York.*

CYNTHIA. WALKER.

Nothing perhaps expresses the taste of an era so recognizably as what the people of that era choose to sit down on. The side chair, above left, was made by Gardner and Company of New York City in the 1870s or 1880s. It is made of perforated veneer with a painted floral ornament on the back. Above right is an upholstered side chair made in New York by Alexander Roux, a French emigrant cabinet-maker of the mid-nineteenth century. The chair opposite is one in a parlor set. It has a laminated wood back, pierced and carved, and in spite of its rococo curves, achieves a comfortable, mid-nineteenth-century stolidity.

Above: *The pressed-glass covered butter dish, vase, and sugar bowl were made by Gillinder & Sons, of Philadelphia in the late 1870s or in the 1880s. The pattern, featuring mountains, bison, deer, an Indian, and a log cabin, known as "Westward Ho!" well illustrates American fascination with the West.*

Opposite: *These two dainty "lotus ware" vases, decorated with floral reliefs, were made in 1893 by Knowles, Taylor & Knowles of East Liverpool, Ohio, and donated by them to the Smithsonian Institution in that year. Only in this late-nineteenth-century period did American potteries begin producing enough fine porcelain to offer some competition to the export wares of England, Europe, and China.*

Above: *This sugar bowl and the one at right are fine examples of nineteenth-century glass craftsmanship. The bowl above, ornamented with a lilypad decoration, probably was made in New York or New England. The blue bowl, with acanthus leaves, was made in the 1830s in Providence, Rhode Island. A type of early machine-pressed ware, "lacy-pressed" glass came to be so called because of its stippled and highly decorative surface, which could hide flaws that occurred in the still imperfect glassmaking process.*

Opposite: *By 1850 Pittsburgh had become a preeminent glassmaking center, with thirty-four factories, which often turned out heavy pieces like these: practical, durable, relatively inexpensive, and of great clarity. Not only middle-class households but also barrooms, hotels, and riverboats favored such glass. From left: an eight-ribbed clear pitcher with a silver spout, a bar bottle with a stopper, a cobalt blue decanter with a pewter jigger lid, and a cruet and stopper.*

The stoneware jar at far left, with an incised sailing ship and the inscription "25,000 MAJORITY GNL JACKSON," commemorates the election of 1824, which had embittering political results. Andrew Jackson had a plurality but could not carry the electoral college, and thanks to the maneuvering of Henry Clay, the victor was John Quincy Adams. At center is a log cabin in stoneware dated 1841: a souvenir of the inauguration of William Henry Harrison, who campaigned as the log-cabin and hard-cider candidate, though in fact he was an aristocratic Virginian. The stoneware jug at near left bears the date 1865. Decorated in cobalt blue with an American flag, a cannon, and what may possibly be Appomattox Court House, it is a memento of the surrender, on April 9, of General Robert E. Lee and the Army of Northern Virginia to Ulysses S. Grant.

One of the great rarities of the Museum of American History is this "Bible quilt," stitched in the early 1880s by Harriet Powers, born a slave in Georgia in 1837. According to the folk-art scholar Gladys-Marie Fry, the intricate appliqué reflects traditional needlework techniques from Dahomey in West Africa. But the design is Harriet Powers's unique creation. From top left: Adam and Eve with animals and the serpent; Adam, Eve, and Cain; Satan. From left center: Cain kills Abel; Cain in the land of Nod surrounded by bears, leopards, elk, a calico lion, and what Harriet Powers called a "kangaroo hog"; Jacob's ladder; Christ's baptism. From left bottom: the Crucifixion; Judas and the thirty pieces of silver; the Last Supper; and the Holy Family.

The wife of an independent but struggling farmer, Mrs. Powers took her quilt to the Cotton Fair in Athens, Georgia, in 1886. There she met Jennie Smith, a woman of the locality who evidently valued fine work. She offered to buy the quilt, but Mrs. Powers could not part with it. In 1890 she relented, but by then Miss Smith had no money. The next year, however, Miss Smith conscientiously recorded the transaction between herself and Mrs. Powers:

> She offered it for ten dollars, but I only had five to give. After going out consulting with her husband, she returned and said, "Owin ter de hardness of de times, my ole man he lows I'd better teck it." And not being a new woman, she obeyed.

The price may seem low for something now grown priceless. But Miss Smith preserved the quilt and—since Harriet Powers could not read or write—set down all that the creator had to tell her about her creation. Between the two of them Harriet Powers's name and her "darling offspring" were saved.

Above: *This banjo of about 1890 has an ebony fingerboard inlaid with stars and moons of mother-of-pearl; the tuning pegs are ivory. Banjos are of African origin: their prototypes were carried to the United States by slaves.*

Opposite: *The keyed bugle, which lacks valves, generally went out of use after 1835. But this ten-keyed B-flat handmade bugle was made by Samuel Graves of Winchester, New Hampshire, in the early 1840s.*

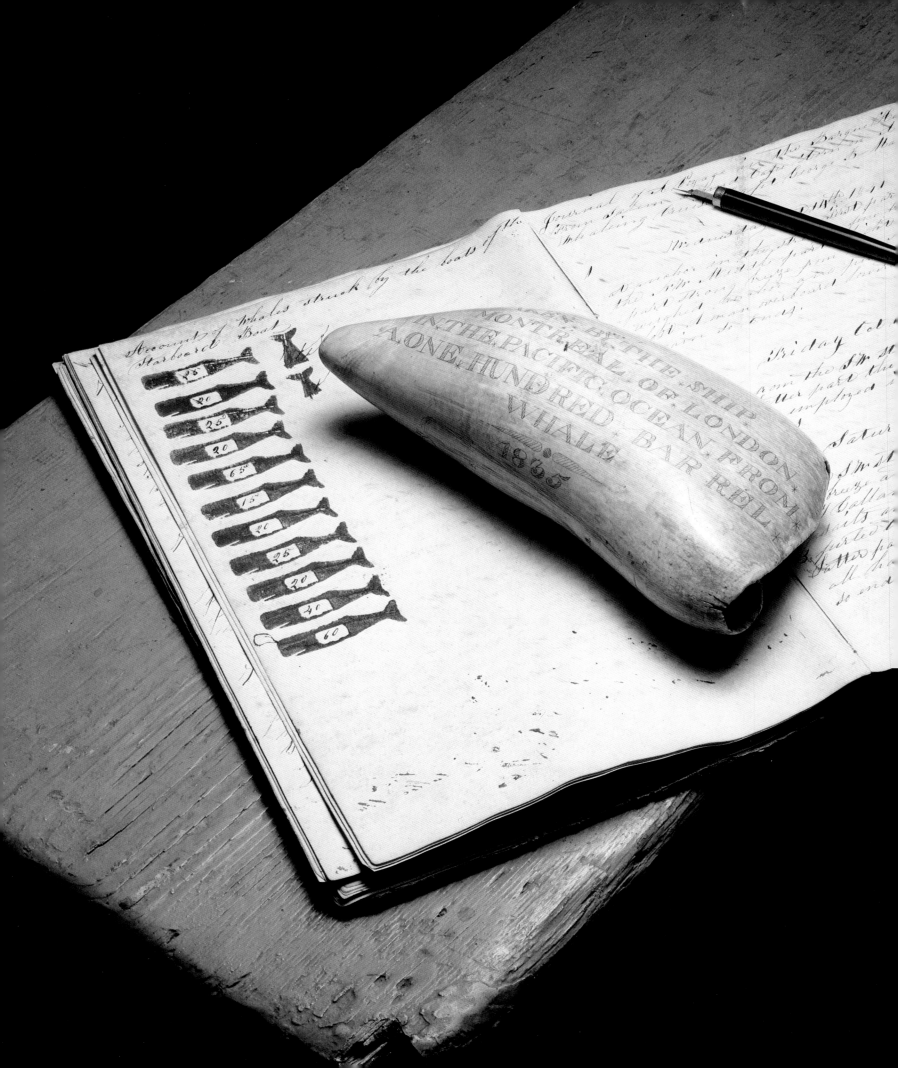

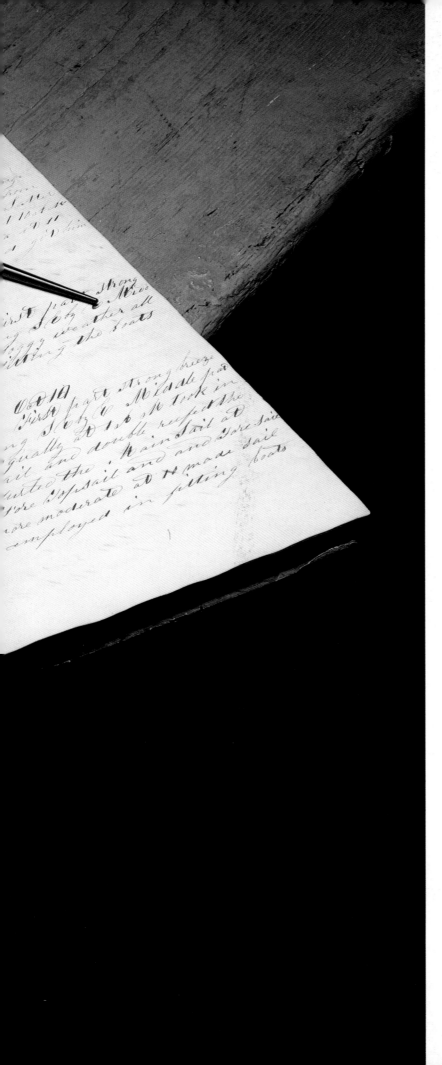

The open logbook displays a common bookkeeping device of whaleship captains—the whale stamp. This page records the almost incredible catch of eleven whales in a single day; the square in the center of the stamp was where the captain set down the number of barrels of oil extracted from each whale. The disembodied tails are ones that got away. Lying on the logbook, alongside the pen, is an example of a famous marine folk art—the carved whale's tooth, or scrimshaw. Where the name comes from is still debated—perhaps from "scrimp," since the carving space is cramped. (In Moby Dick, *Herman Melville refers to the carver as a "skimshander.") The carving of whale tooth and bone was a common pastime among whalemen. This tooth, dated 1835, was carved, it says, "aboard the ship Montreal of London in the Pacific Ocean from a one hundred barrel whale."*

And when this whale we did harpoon,
He gave one slap with his tail.
He upset the boat, we lost five of our crew,
Neither did we catch that whale, brave
*   boys.*
And for Greenland bore away, brave boys,
And for Greenland bore away.

—"The Greenland Whale Fishery,"
Anglo-American ballad

The link between the dainty-looking set of white glass lamps, at right, *and the sailors' gear,* opposite, *is as direct as can be. The lamps, manufactured in New England about 1830, burned whale oil, which was a superior illuminant in its time and was for many years the chief product of the American whaling industry. (Some whale oil went for other purposes—lubricating early steam locomotives, for example.) The wooden line tub with a harpoon and lance atop a coil of rope would have been standard equipment in any whaleboat ready for the chase; it sat in the bottom of the open boat. Only about thirty feet long, the chase boats were lowered from the main ship. A harpooned whale could easily capsize them. To the left of the harpoon can be seen a mast wrapped in a sail—carried horizontally to be mounted in case of need.*

*E*ven before it had a constitution, the United States had a postal service. It is one of our most ubiquitous, enduring, and useful institutions. Of all the post offices in our history, the combined post office and general store was among the most widespread and beloved. Scattered across the land, these stores served as community meeting places and ad hoc news bureaus, as well as hubs of civilization and museums of delights for millions of farm families and villagers. The post office and general store at left, now installed in the National Museum of American History, was built originally in Headsville, West Virginia, about 1861, just as the Civil War began. (West Virginia came into being that year when fifty western Virginia counties refused to secede.) The post office operated until about 1909, the general store until 1932. All the shelving, flooring, furnishings, and windows are in their original condition. At center is a pot-bellied iron stove. Among the items once for sale and still on view are highbutton shoes, suspenders, union suits, tins of cloves, poultry lice killers, and cow tonics. There are, as well, bean pots, dippers, glasses, and lantern globes, laxatives, tobacco, sewing caddies, and a hand-operated Singer sewing machine, not to mention tinware and silk ribbons. The costumed pair at the counter are bona-fide postal employees.

Hardtack, Salt Horse, and Coffee

*Just before the battle the General hears a
   row,*
*He says, "The Yanks are coming, I hear
   their rifles now,"*
*He turns around in wonder, and what do
   you think he sees?*
The Georgia militia eating goober peas!

Peas, peas, peas, peas, eating goober peas.
Goodness, how delicious, eating goober peas!

Goober peas are peanuts, of course, and
the Confederate Army (not only the
Georgia element) was usually ready to eat
peanuts or whatever else they could get. In
theory their Quartermaster Corps supplied them
with a plentiful daily ration of bacon, fresh
meat, biscuit, flour, sugar, meal, molasses, and
other necessities and luxuries. The South had
gone into war as an agricultural power, rich in
livestock, corn, rice, cotton, sugar, and acreage
under cultivation. And yet, even in the Army of
Northern Virginia, which ought to have been the
easiest to supply, rations were "alternately super-
abundant and altogether wanting," according to
an account by Private Carleton McCarthy of
the Richmond Howitzers. And things got worse,
not better.

> During the later years and months of the war,
> [Private McCarthy continues] so uncertain was the
> issue as to time, quantity, and composition, that the
> men became in large measure independent . . .
> and by some mysterious means, known only to
> purely patriotic soldiers, learned to fight without
> pay and to find subsistence in the field, the stream,
> or the forest, and a shelter on the bleak
> mountainside.

Not every soldier took quite so constructive
an attitude. One embittered Southerner, named

Randolph Shotwell, characterized life in the
C.S.A. as filled with "starvation, rags, dirt, and
vermin," and claimed that the "Quarter Master's
Department . . . really did a great deal more
to break down the army than to keep it up."
When General Lee crossed the Potomac (in
1863, before Gettysburg), said Shotwell, ten
thousand of his men were without shoes, hats,
or blankets. Under any sort of pressure, the
Quartermaster Corps occasionally ceased
functioning at all. At the Confederate fort of
Port Hudson, Louisiana, in the summer of 1863,
besieged rebels ate mules and horses and then
rats, which one officer calmly described as a
luxury—"superior, in the opinion of those who
eat them, to spring chicken."

One reason, in the spring of 1865, that Lee
surrendered when and where he did was that his
men had had almost nothing to eat for a week.
(One of Grant's first acts was to send 25,000
rations to the vanquished army.) The outcome
of the war might have been no different if the
U.S. Army had gone hungry while the C.S.A.
dined well. The Continental Army had starved
and won—an army does not always march on
its stomach. Hunger was merely a symptom of a
score of other problems that the Confederacy
could not solve. It is particularly ironic that the
upper-class South, which was fighting for the
right to remain a slave-based, agrarian society
with its roots in the land and not the factory,
could not provision its army nor even keep the
home front in victuals.

On the Union side no soldier (except those
in Confederate prisons) went hungry for long or
was obliged to fricassee a rat, but neither did he
live in any nutritional paradise. The standard
ration, as later described by John D. Billings, a
Massachusetts artilleryman in the Army of the
Potomac, was as follows:

Neither the Confederate nor the Union Army issued mess kits. A poor man might make do with a wooden plate and a coffee tin; this rather fancy set belonged to a Confederate officer. Clockwise, from left: a cloth-covered metal canteen; a lidded stew pot; a small mug; a mess kit with knife, fork, and spoon; the kit lid with a piece of hardtack; and two cloth bags for coffee and sugar.

. . . twelve ounces of pork or bacon, or one pound four ounces of salt or fresh beef; one pound six ounces of soft bread or flour, or one pound of hard bread, or one pound four ounces of corn meal. With every hundred such rations there should have been distributed one peck of beans or pease; ten pounds of rice or hominy; ten pounds of green coffee, or eight pounds of roasted and ground, or one pound eight ounces of tea; fifteen pounds of sugar, one pound four ounces of candles; four pounds of soap, two quarts of salt; four quarts of vinegar; four ounces of pepper; a half bushel potatoes when practicable, and one quart of molasses. Desiccated potatoes or desiccated compressed vegetables might be substituted for the beans, pease, rice, hominy, or fresh potatoes. Vegetables, the dried fruits, pickles, and pickled cabbage were occasionally issued to prevent scurvy, but in small quantities.

Not a very exciting diet (and in most units the men had to do their own cooking), but nourishing if issued in the quantities described and if the food was fresh. Often of course it was not. Marching rations were greatly reduced—salt pork, a little fresh meat if available, sugar, coffee, salt, and hardtack. What was hardtack? Billings himself, whose memoirs are entitled *Hardtack and Coffee,* explains. "It was a plain flour-and-water biscuit. Two which I have in my possession as mementos [he was writing more than twenty years after the war] measure three and one-eighth by two and seven-eighths inches and are nearly half an inch thick." These unappetizing slabs—standard issue on the Union and the Confederate sides—were granite-like in consistency and became the subject of a hundred jokes.

In his classic work, *The Life of Billy Yank,* Bell Irvin Wiley has gathered an impressive amount of hardtack lore from unpublished letters and manuscripts. Predictably, the biscuits were called "teeth dullers," "sheet-iron crackers," and "Lincoln pies." Soldiers claimed to have pulverized hardtack with their musket butts in order to make it edible. They crushed it into hot soup, soaked it thoroughly in water and then fried it in bacon grease, pounded it in canvas bags and then mixed it with stewed apples. They added it to boiling coffee and then skimmed off the scalded worms and weevils that floated upward. A few men even learned to like

Opposite: *The Bowie knife, known with grim affection as the "Arkansas toothpick," was the invention of James Bowie, the famous colonel of the Texas Army who died at the Alamo in 1836. This knife probably belonged to some Confederate infantryman. It was found several years ago on the Civil War battlefield at Perryville, Kentucky.*

Perhaps the most famous ships of the Civil War were a pair of ironclads, the Monitor (of which this is a model) and the Merrimac, a steam frigate rebuilt as an ironclad by the Confederates and renamed Virginia. Austerely simple in design, the Monitor is little more than an iron raft with a gun turret on deck. The brainchild of the brilliant Swedish immigrant, John Ericsson, she was launched on January 30, 1862, in Long Island, scarcely one hundred days after her keel was laid. She set out immediately for Hampton Roads, Virginia, where the Merrimac had just put to sea. On March 9, 1862, the battle was joined and the Monitor emerged the victor. Shortly afterward she sank in a storm, drowning sixteen hands. Nevertheless she changed the course of naval history: she is the progenitor of the modern battleship and the harbinger of the all-steel navy.

the biscuits. "I eat them in place of bread altogether now," one Pennsylvania soldier wrote home.

The meat given to the marching soldier was almost invariably salt pork or sometimes salt beef—"salt horse," it was called. Of this Billings observed, "it was the vilest ration distributed to the soldiers." It was yellowish green and so saturated with saltpeter that the taste of it could not be boiled out. In Billings's company the men used to make a little fun for themselves by staging a funeral over the salt beef, "making the appointments as complete as possible, with bearers, a bier improvised of boards or a hardtack box, on which was the beef . . . and then, attended by solemn music and a mournful procession, it would be carried to the company sink and dumped, after a solemn mummery of words had been spoken, and volley fired over its unhallowed grave." Salt pork was not so bad—sometimes the men even ate it raw in a hardtack sandwich.

Fresh beef was almost as hazardous as the salted kind, but for other reasons. It had to be eaten immediately or else it would spoil. Having come "quivering from the butcher's knife" (Billings' phrase), it was often tough, but the real risk was maggots. Bell Irvin Wiley quotes an Ohio man: "We drew meat last night that was so damd full of skippers that it could move alone." And having learned skepticism in a hard school, the soldiers were quick to suspect that what was offered to them as beef was actually some animal discarded by a cavalry unit.

Coffee was another thing. It was the favorite item in the ration, and the chief complaint was not to have enough of it. Billings describes the almost ritualistic way the coffee rations were served out. The sergeant, he says, would spread a rubber blanket on the ground, "and upon it . . . put as many piles of the coffee as there were men to receive the rations." The sugar would be mounded up on another blanket. Only the rawest greenhorn would attempt to keep the sugar and coffee separate. "Your plain, straightforward old veteran, who had shed all his poetry and romance, if he had ever possessed any," would simply scoop up sugar, grounds

and all into a cloth bag, which Billings says usually looked about as clean as the shirt of a coal-heaver.

Coffee was brewed in the time-honored fashion: water in a tin can was brought to a boil and the coffee and sugar added and boiled to taste. The finished product, according to one connoisseur in Sherman's army, had to be "strong enough to float an iron wedge." Its virtues were purely psychological. "It gave strength to the weary and heavy laden, and courage to the despondent and sick at heart." There was coffee every morning and at every halt. If the only available water was muddy, then muddy water was used.

Though no one would have perished on Union rations, the soldiers often grew disgusted and turned to sutlers—peddlers who went from camp to camp (taking care to arrive on payday) selling staples and some luxuries. Often what they had to offer—precooked meat pies, for example—left the consumer in worse shape than the army rations had done. In their detailed study of Civil War sutlers, Francis Lord and Thomas Yoseloff report that food poisoning from sutlers' wares was common. One Virginia merchant, who at least was honest about his materials, sold cat- and dog-meat pies. One of his soldier-customers remarked that it wouldn't do to eat pieces from different pies at the same meal lest "the ingredients, on coming together in one stomach, might remember and revive their ancient feuds." Moved to abandon both army rations and sutlers, soldiers occasionally foraged for food—with or without the permission of their commanding officers. They also begged and bought home-cooked meals in the houses of their enemies. In the South emancipated slaves sometimes set up impromptu kitchens to feed the bluecoats, and some even managed to make a business out of it.

Among the sutlers' wares, however, was one curious new type of foodstuff that over the years was destined to put an end to the dietary woes of the American soldier in the field—or at least to alter those woes. For it was during the Civil War—and partly because of the needs of the army—that food preservation got underway as an industry. In 1856, before the war broke out,

an inventor named Gail Borden had found a way to condense and can milk, and shortly afterward he invented a similar process for cider and fruit juice. Canned fish and a few vegetables (imported from France, where the food canning business was also getting underway) were among the sutlers' goods, along with Borden's milk. There were also some packaged cereals—"Hecker's Farina" was one brand. The processed-meats industry was as yet unknown. Philip Armour and Gustavus Swift got their start from profits made during and just after the war—Armour by some extremely sagacious dealings in pork futures. The K-ration and the C-ration, for better or worse, were not far off.

They too would find their John Billingses. Apart from the Continental and Confederate armies, the American soldier has been better fed than any soldier in history. He has also griped the loudest, as befits the station of a free man who, for the most part, would rather not be in the army, no matter what the quality of the cuisine.

The sixshooter at the top (its trigger folds out of sight) is the model that Colt first patented. Below it is a Remington revolver of the 1860s, manufactured in quantity for the Union Army. After the Colt it was the most widely used handgun of the period.

Overleaf: The Colt-Paterson revolver, patented in 1836 by Samuel Colt, had a rifled barrel, six chambers, and a revolving cylinder—it was the deadliest weapon yet seen on the American frontier. "Your sixshooter," two Texas rangers wrote to Colt in 1850, "is the arm which had rendered the name of Texas Ranger a check and terror to bands of our frontier Indians." The cased set of colt revolvers, made in the early 1860s, was a present to Major General Philip Henry Sheridan from the officers of the Third Division, 20th Army Corps.

Opposite: *This patent model—a curiosity in the history of arms—combines a thirty-six-inch cavalry sabre with a .40 caliber revolver. The patent was issued in 1866, but the sword-pistol, so far as anybody knows, was never a commercial success.*

Above: *The model of the machine gun for which Richard Gatling received a patent in 1862. An immediate success, it was the first practical machine gun. A crank on the right side of the breech-housing turns the barrels, each of which has its own bolt and firing pin.*

Opposite: *The ponderous-looking weapon at top is a "pepperbox" pistol with multiple barrels that fired shots successively with each trigger pull. This one, of a type widely successful in this country, was manufactured prior to 1865 by Ethan Allen of Grafton, Massachusetts. Deadly in aspect, the harmonica pistol of 1873 is breech loading with a six-rifled barrel. It was popular in France but never caught on in America.*

Overleaf: *These miniature weapons, all of them in working order, are from a set of sixty-nine that exemplify the history of firearms. At far left, in a case, is a pair of Belgian percussion pistols with folding triggers; at top, a U.S. pistol carbine of 1855 and below it an even smaller miniature carbine. The long gun at the table edge is a Winchester musket. The handguns at center are (counterclockwise from left) a U.S. Navy percussion pistol of 1842, two American flintlock pistols, a German wheelock ball-butt pistol of the sixteenth century, an English flintlock pocket pistol, and a Colt revolver of 1860.*

Above: *During Gold Rush days, when the vigilantes caught up with the criminal element, the weapons both sides brandished were likely to be Derringer percussion pistols like these. Henry Derringer manufactured such arms at Philadelphia in the early nineteenth century. Universally popular, "Derringer" became a generic term for all small handguns and in fact was the gun used by John Wilkes Booth to kill Abraham Lincoln.*

A Nation to Show

*I*t was a near thing. There might have been no
Centennial Exhibition in 1876 at all. Congress
not only declined to provide funds but even passed
a bill relieving the United States of liability for
"any expenses attending such an exhibition."
Congress, or part of it, doubted that the nation
had anything worth showing. Moreover, times
were hard—1873 had seen a stock market crash.
Would people be able to afford to come?
Nevertheless, thanks to a few believers, chief
among them a newspaperman named Joseph R.
Hawley, the exhibition opened in Philadelphia
on May 10, 1876, two months short of the
nation's one hundredth birthday. It was one of the
grand public events of our history.

There were millions of things to see—lathes,
drills, locomotives, livestock, plows, paintings,
statuary (including the arm and torch of a
"Statue of Independence," later the Statue of
Liberty). There were lamps, beds, hatracks,
gadgets, and a talking box from Alexander
Graham Bell. In sum it was overwhelming
testimony to what the new nation had
accomplished, and what it intended to become, a
nation of FORTY MILLIONS OF FREEMEN RULING
FROM OCEAN TO OCEAN, as one poster read.
Joseph Hawley remarked that while we might
not have any Raphaels, "we had a nation to
show." And an announcement to make, to
ourselves and the world, that a new industrial
giant had arrived.

Almost ten million visitors passed through the
gates (admission, 50¢) before the Centennial
closed in the fall. Most of the exhibitions were
sent home, but a freight train loaded with
donations was soon packed up and on its way to
Washington—and the Smithsonian had no place
to put any of it. Congress soon after established
the U.S. National Museum and built a house for
it—the Arts and Industries Building (its facade is
opposite), completed in 1881. Today, of course,
it is no longer the main part of the Museum,
but it does house one of the most ambitious
ventures in Smithsonian history: the replication,
on a reduced scale, of the 1876 Centennial. The
new exhibition opened in 1976; a reminder of
the optimism and pride, the expanding faith in
machines, and the belief in progress that
characterized America as it embarked on
its second century.

Above: *This Continental Army uniform is a
replica of one displayed by the War Department
in 1876.*

Opposite: *The Arts and Industries Building,
completed in 1881, is now the permanent home of
one of the Smithsonian's most impressive
displays—the re-creation, so far as possible, of
the Philadelphia Centennial of 1876.*

Opposite: *The Rotunda of the Arts and Industries Building has been decorated and restored to capture the flavor of that grandest of all world's fairs—the Philadelphia Centennial.*

Right: *The fifteen-inch Rodman seacoast gun at top and the array of post–Civil War machine guns (bottom) were part of the impressive array of ordnance sent to Philadelphia by the War Department. At center is a hyper-radiant lighthouse lens.*

Above: *An age that prided itself on progress and hoped to live in peace did not, nevertheless, overlook the production of firearms. This is a re-creation of the Colt Company display in 1876.*

Opposite: *Matthias Baldwin built his first locomotive in 1831, and by 1861 his Locomotive Works in Philadelphia had turned out 1,000 train engines and had become the major American manufacturer. In 1876 the Baldwin Company made this locomotive for the Santa Cruz Railroad of California. It eventually was shipped to Guatemala where it stayed in service until the 1950s.*

Opposite: *Since the mid-nineteenth century the American market has been an important one for French fashions. Charles F. Worth, for example, the premier designer of the 1880s, advertised his dresses through American department stores. This extravagant Worth evening gown had a second bodice—for daytime wear—of the same pale green silk brocaded with velvet.*

"But there, we must believe in good luck!" She took up the half-empty glass and held it against the light.

   Niel liked to see the firelight sparkle on her earrings, long pendants of garnets and seed-pearls in the shape of fleurs-de-lys. She was the only woman he knew who wore earrings; they hung naturally against her thin triangular cheeks. Captain Forrester, although he had given her handsomer ones, liked to see her wear these, because they had been his mother's. It gratified him to have his wife wear jewels; it meant something to him.

            —Willa Cather, A Lost Lady

Above: *The delicate parure (matched set) of seed pearl jewelry is still in its original box. Made between 1820 and 1850, it consists of a necklace, earrings, two bracelets, and two brooches.*

"Shall I Never See Thee More Alas"

They had pictures hung on the walls—mainly Washingtons and Lafayettes, and battles. . . . One was a woman in a slim black dress, belted small under the armpits, with bulges like a cabbage in the middle of the sleeves, and a large black scoop-shovel bonnet with a black veil, and white slim ankles crossed about with black tape, and very wee black slippers, like a chisel, and she was leaning pensive on a tombstone on her right elbow, under a weeping willow . . . and underneath the picture it said "Shall I Never See Thee More Alas." . . . There was one where a young lady was at a window looking up at the moon, and tears running down her cheeks; and she had an open letter in one hand with black sealing-wax showing on one edge of it . . . and underneath the picture it said "And Art Thou Gone Yes Thou Art Gone Alas." These was all nice pictures, I reckon, but I didn't somehow seem to take to them, because if ever I was down a little they always give me the fantods.

—*Mark Twain*, Huckleberry Finn

Huckleberry Finn may not have liked having "the fantods," but in his day morbidity was an essential part of gentility. Not without reason, for death was a constant in life. Women died in childbirth, children in infancy, young men in their prime. Even as late as 1900 the average life expectancy of a white man was only forty-eight and of a black man thirty-two. To be in a state of bereavement was commonplace, and grief required its formalized display. The memorial jewelry in this collection, opposite, *is all made from or made to contain human hair. The large brooches at bottom each house a curl; the other pieces—rings, earring, watch fob, and bracelets—are all woven from hair. (Mail order houses were at pains to guarantee that the locks submitted would be the locks returned—no substitutions.) Not all such jewelry, of course, commemorated the deceased or absent.*

Mourning clothes were also a necessity. The crepe hat, above, *made in the 1890s, has the traditional heavy black veil and tarlatan border. But the veil is attached in such a way that the wearer's face could not be covered— a breach of the strict traditions of an earlier generation.*

Opposite: *The card case was once essential equipment for gentlemen and ladies. This gold and green enamel one and the watch case (with Patek Philippe movement) were made by Tiffany and Company about 1855.*

Right top: *This Florentine intarsia parure—bracelet, brooch, and earrings—has hard stones cemented into the base stone to form a picture.*

Right: *Made between 1860 and 1880 and intended for evening wear, this tiara-like hair comb is of tortoise shell trimmed with gold.*

Right: *"JB Callen on the 17th anniversary of his Birth with Love from his Father 'old Grizzly' Junction City Kansas, Sept. 22, 1886" is the inscription on this watch fob. It is set with Colorado or Arizona gold nuggets, as is the watch—a lady's.*

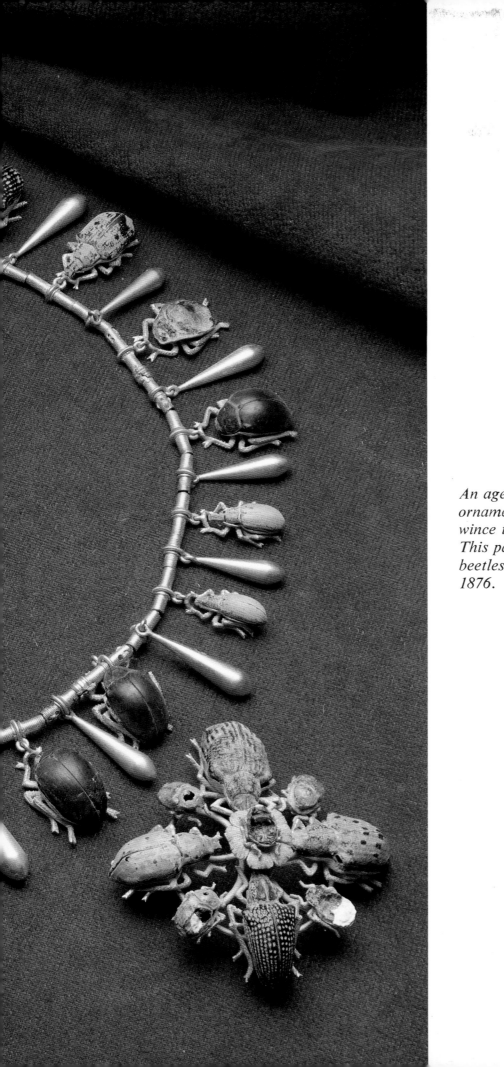

An age that fancied stuffed birds as
ornaments for ladies' hats certainly did not
wince to see preserved insects used in a necklace.
This parure featuring the backs of Brazilian
beetles was made by a Philadelphia jeweler in
1876.

INSTRUCTION BOOK

DRAFTING and CUTTING

Dresses, Basques, Sacques, Coats, &c.

Garment Drafting Machine

AS INVENTED AND PATENTED BY

A. McDOWELL

The McDowell Garment Drafting Machine Company,

West 14th Street, New York, U.S.A.

Seventy-third Edition.

sweatshop walls. And not too surprisingly, according to a report made in 1884 by the Massachusetts Bureau of Statistics of Labor, "The running of heavy sewing machines by foot power soon breaks down a girl's health." Not to mention poor light and bad air.

Not just women but men and thousands of children toiled over sewing machines. In 1907, according to an article by the poet Edwin Markham, 60,000 children were shut up in sweatshops or sent out as messengers on the lower East Side of Manhattan. "Nearly any hour on the East Side of New York City you can see them—pallid boy or spindly girl—their faces dulled, their backs bent under a heavy load of garments piled on head and shoulders, the muscles of the whole frame in a long strain. The boy always has bowlegs and walks with feet wide apart and wobbling."

Another journalist of the day spoke of the fate of the young immigrant—"a bronzed, wirey young peasant, coming here to the land of freedom and hope from the oppression of Russia, sat down at a sewing machine in a hot, dusty, fetid tenement-shop in East Broadway or Clinton Street; and sometimes he lasted five years, sometimes seven, rarely ten." What it all led to, aside from a flood of cheap and excellently crafted clothing for the nation, was one of the most important events in the history of organized labor. In 1900 with 2,000 members and $30 in funds, the International Ladies' Garment Workers Union was formed.

In these and other ways, the clothing industry has been a democratizer on multiple levels. It has made the United States the best-clothed nation in the world. It has discouraged class distinctions in clothes (if not entirely eliminated them). *Suiting Everyone,* a Smithsonian book by Claudia Kidwell and Margaret C. Christman, recalls a memorable event of the recent past. In 1959 when Soviet chief Nikita Khrushchev paid a visit to Nelson Rockefeller, then governor of New York, he was astonished to see that this multimillionaire, like most other men, dressed in an ordinary shirt and suit: "not just a capitalist but the biggest capitalist in the world" as Khrushchev wonderingly observed.

From the point of view of those who make the clothing, the industry has also been a democratizer—one of those chinkholes through which immigrants have traditionally been able to squeeze into the economic system of America. Once through the chinkhole, however, the newcomer might be enriched or devoured. Might one day own the factory or die of overwork in it or merely (and what a "merely") earn a decent living and survive.

Opposite: *This hand loom, brought from the French textile center of Lyons, is equipped with a Jacquard attachment of the 1840s. Introduced in 1804 by Joseph Marie Jacquard, the device consists of punched cards that select appropriate warp yarns to be raised or lowered for each successive shed in the pattern. Fancy and intricate patterns are thus produced automatically (the principle is similar to that of the player piano).*

224

Above: *The demand for machine-made shoes and boots accelerated during the Civil War, and this machine (here is the 1860 patent model) came along at the right time. It cut boot and shoe soles automatically and featured a novel combination of toggle levers operated by a connecting rod powered by a crank.*

Opposite: *This 1870 hat-shaping patent model gave hat brims the proper snap by means of a steam-filled ring that lowered to soften the brim and a plate that came up from below to curl it.*

Overleaf: *(Clockwise from upper left): Embroidered baby booties, about 1900; two-toned brown leather shoes for a girl, about 1865; leather riding boots, half-lined with pink and white, about 1860; an Iowa boy's leather high-tops with fabric insets, about 1902; leather-and-wooden clogs with brass nails— working-class shoes in the nineteenth century; leather shoes with pointed toes, Vermont, 1802; and a girl's red leather slippers that were worn in both the late eighteenth and mid-nineteenth centuries.*

Right: *If ready-made clothing is by origin an American phenomenon, so is the idea of work clothes: not that the worker should look worse than other people, but that evenings and Sundays he can put on his good clothes and look like everybody else. A selection of men's work clothes is in this shop window: from left, a checked cotton shirt of about 1883; brown duck pants by Levi Strauss and Co., also made in the late nineteenth century; a blue chambray shirt of about 1915; and fishermen's cotton pants of the early 1880s.*

Opposite: *An idea with a splendid future was the "wash" dress. The black-and-white dress at far left, made about 1899, was advertised as such. The two silk shirtwaists at center, made in the early 1900s, represent an enduring American fashion—blouses and skirts, which make one's wardrobe seem bigger than it is. The sheer white linen "lingerie" dress (about 1910) is meant for summer Sunday best.*

Right: *By 1800 almost every kind of ready-made clothing was available for men. From left, the dress coat of navy blue wool with a silk velvet collar was worn about 1845 by a Philadelphia lawyer; the black satin vest, of about the same date, has a buckle at the back to ensure a closer fit; pantaloons of brown wide-wale corduroy (about 1820) have instep straps to keep the trouser legs taut; and the white cotton dress shirt of 1820–40 was worn, it is said, by a Vermonter at his wedding.*

Below: *Some but by no means all of these artifacts have been banished from the dressing table. The thirteen-inch fruitwood curl stick (for doing long ringlets) and the crimping iron with wooden handles (it made parallel waves) have departed. But scissors-style curling irons, like the one in the foreground, are still in use, although they no longer have to be heated in a flame. Hair dye—in the bottle—is more widely used than ever, and so, probably, are hairpieces, like the two frizzled "postiches." Even beauty patches like those in the paper envelopes still occasionally appear.*

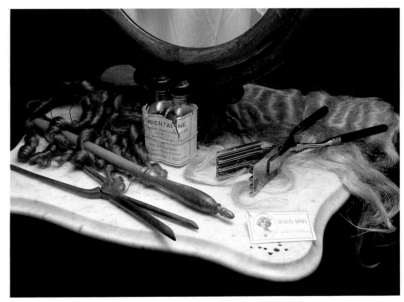

Left: *Looking rather like a surgeon's kit, this brassbound rosewood grooming case was selected in Paris by one W.R. Kibbey in 1849 while he was doing the Grand Tour—an essential part of the gentlemanly education. His case contains three bottles, four jars, three boxes, a letter opener, an ink well and pen, an "Inimitable" razor strap, brushes for shaving, for fingernails, for hair, and for clothes, and a box of matches. It all folds up to a scant $9\frac{1}{2}$ by $13\frac{1}{2}$ by $5\frac{1}{2}$ inches—carry-on luggage even for the Calais packet.*

Water pipes are one of many pieces of basic technology that make urban life possible—and in the last century the pipes were often made of logs, not metal. These augers, of graduated sizes, were used to bore the hole through each section of log pipe. The two specialized rotary planes in the foreground shaped the male and female ends of the pipes so that they could be fitted together.

← Farm Machinery
  Maritime Enterprise

↑ Vehicles
  Railroads

Machinery & Tools
Electricity→
Bridges & Tunnels

AGRIC

Above: *Classically simple in concept, this handsomely crafted shaving horse was used by a cooper to hold barrel staves while he shaved them with a drawknife. Sitting astride the horse, the cooper pushed the treadle with his feet, as he pulled back with the knife, forcing the "dumbhead" at top to grip the end of the stave more tightly the harder he shaved.*

Opposite: *This water-powered sawmill of the late eighteenth or early nineteenth century stood originally in eastern Pennsylvania. Its vertical "sash" saw, so called because it is carried in a reciprocating frame or sash, could make up to 130 strokes per minute. The log on the carriage was fed into the saw at about a quarter inch per stroke.*

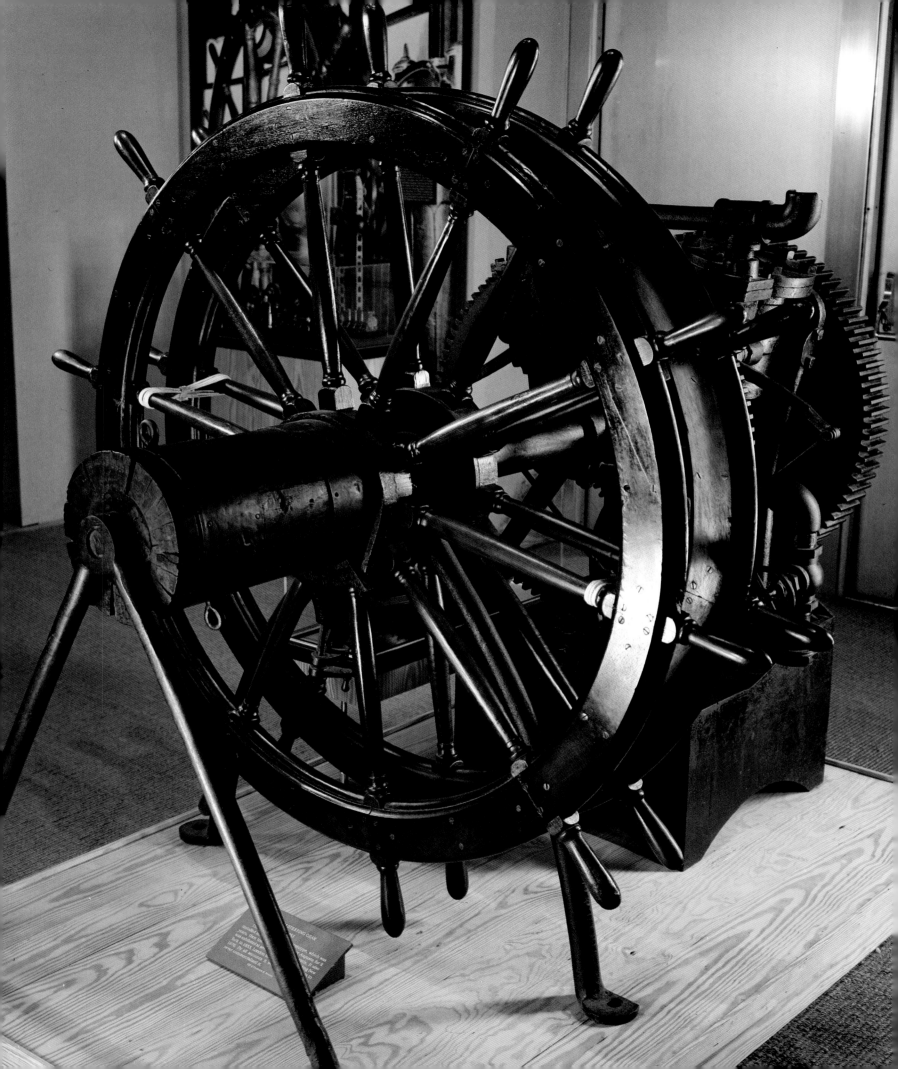

Overleaf: *Built by the Harlan and Hollingsworth Company of Wilmington, Delaware, this ivory and green steam engine—of commanding elegance—powered the Southern Railway's machine shop at Charleston, South Carolina, from 1852 to 1927. The walking beam, which rocks or "walks" as the engine runs, transmits the power from the piston at one end to the crankshaft at the other.*

Opposite: *Invented in 1853 by Frederick E. Sickels of Providence, this is a steam-powered steering gear for a ship. It worked well enough to be installed in at least one coastal steamer, the* Augusta, *in the mid-1850s, and to be shown at several world's fairs, including the Centennial at Philadelphia in 1876. But it taxed the capabilities of steam engines of that day and hence was never widely produced.*

Overleaf, right: *In 1829 Matthias Baldwin, a manufacturer of textile printing machinery who later became famous for his steam locomotives, designed and built this six-horsepower steam engine to power his works. It is of extraordinary technical sophistication and visual elegance for an American engine of that time—possibly a reflection of Baldwin's apprenticeship to a watchmaker early in his career. The engine saw service for almost half a century in the boiler shop of the Baldwin locomotive works in Philadelphia.*

*W*hether a printing press is powered by human muscle or by electricity or steam, the process is the same: an inked surface must be pressed against a clean one. The simplest kind of press is the flatbed-platen press, of which these two are examples. The forme, or surface to be printed from, is laid in the bed of each press and then inked; next the platen is lowered—usually, in such early presses, by means of wooden screws. The screw press, opposite, which is no different in principle from the famous one devised by Johann Gutenberg in 1450, was made about 1820 by Adam Ramage, a Scotsman who emigrated about 1795 and became a pre-eminent manufacturer of printing presses in America. The hand press, right, patented by S.P. Ruggles in 1859, is a clam shell platen press: the platen is hinged to the bed. Presses like this were used for small jobs like printing tickets.

Above: *This job print shop, set up as it might have looked about 1860, had no Linotypes or power machinery. Typically the job printer was a small craftsman who made his living printing broadsides, invitations, announcements, and billheads. He set type by hand and needed only a platen job press.*

Opposite: *The greatest advance in typesetting since Gutenberg's moveable type was the Linotype, which made typesetting as easy as typewriting. This Mergenthaler Blower Linotype, first used in 1886, is still in working order. "Hot type," as cast by Linotypes, has now been rendered almost obsolete by phototypesetting processes.*

The hand casting of type, for so many centuries the basis of the printer's craft, was laborious and fairly dangerous. Opposite, *in a demonstration conducted weekly by the Museum, molten typemetal (12 percent tin, 64 percent lead, and 24 percent antimony) is stirred with a ladle; in the foreground are other kinds of ladles and a type mold. Above left, the molten metal is poured into the type mold; the letters on the paper below have already been cast and now will need trimming. Above right, trimmed letters are set in place, ready for shipping to the print shop. During the 1840s machines began to take over all this work.*

Overleaf: *From the 1860s well into our century, most small towns had a newspaper office more or less like this. A steam-powered press is behind the editor's desk, type frames against the wall, and on the desk itself a press for printing handbills. Besides its other functions, the editor's office was often the telegraph office as well, since most of the news (if any) arrived by wire.*

This six-passenger Concord coach, made in the Lewis Downing coach shops at Concord, New Hampshire, in 1848, hauled travelers back and forth between railway depot and hotel. Suspended on leather thoroughbraces rather than steel springs, the coach could carry a hefty amount of baggage on the rear rack, the roof, and beneath the driver's seat. Coaches of this kind were shipped as far away as South Africa and Australia and saw service well into the automobile era.

The peddler in America is a species almost extinct, but a hundred years ago a peddler's wagon was a welcome sight to farm families with little opportunity to go to town and shop. This handsome wagon made the rounds in New England in the post–Civil War years, offering a variety of manufactured goods: brooms, tinware, lengths of fabric, pins and needles, rub-boards and soap, teakettles, tobacco, and medicines—the conveniences and necessities of life.

This pint-sized delivery wagon, pony-drawn, was a veterinary ambulance (for carting sick and injured dogs) in Washington, D.C., at the turn of the century. At some earlier date, it had been the delivery cart for the Connecticut Pie Company, one of the capital city's bakeries. The wagon has been restored half-and-half to show its history.

Preceding pages: *From 1898 when it was built in St. Louis until 1912 or so, this streetcar, "number 303," ran on Seventh Street in Washington, D.C. The city had a strict ban against overhead wiring in the central sections and hence was one of the few cities that developed an underground conduit system. The "303" has a "plow" on its underside that connects with the contact rail in the conduit between the running rails.*

Today cable railways survive in no American city except San Francisco, but at one time they seemed the hope of the future so far as urban transit was concerned. In the 1890s nearly every big city had at least one cable railway. This single-truck open cable car, built in 1888, was used on the Yesler Way Line in Seattle, Washington, until about 1910.

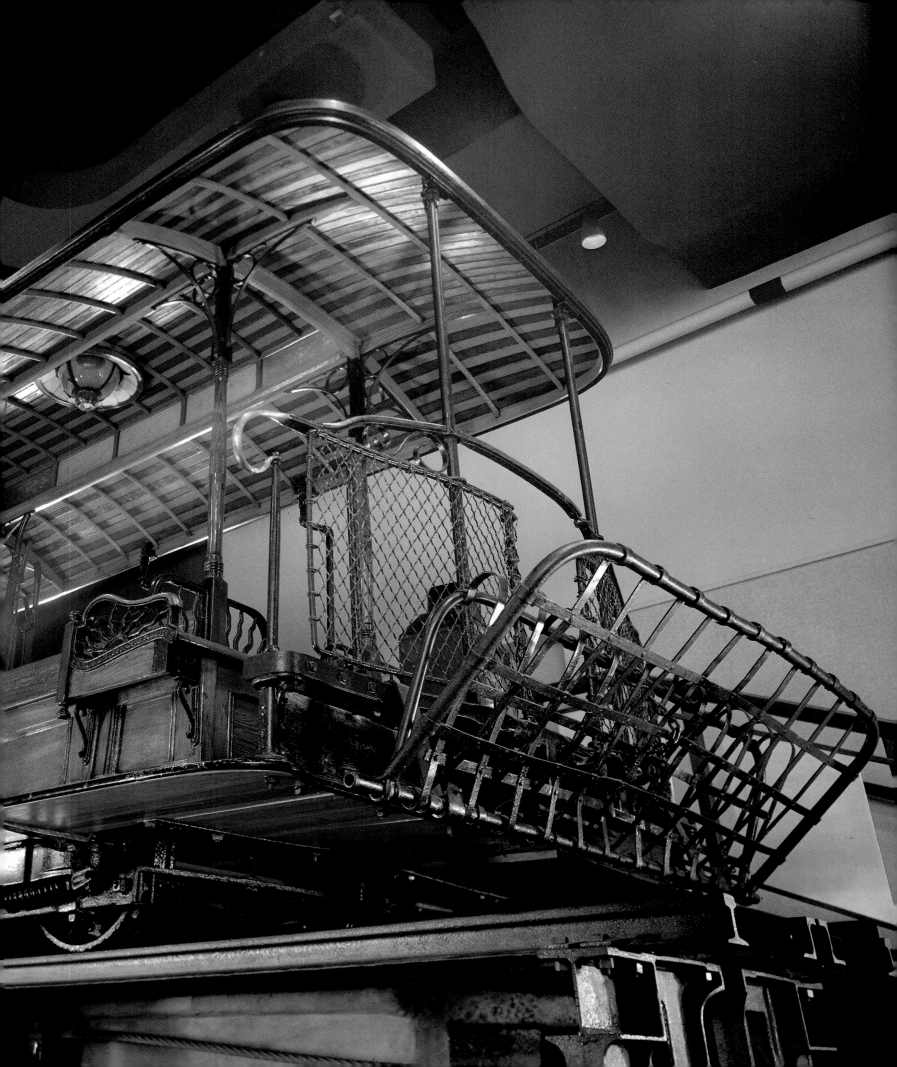

Above: *Americans sometimes fall in love with speed for its own sake, and this steam-powered, charcoal-burning velocipede testifies to what lengths we sometimes go in order to go faster. The tank between the iron-banded, wooden-spoked wheels is a vertical fire-tube boiler with its chimney angled back. The cylinders and rods on either side of it drive the rear axle. Under the saddle is a water tank—not to cool off the rider but to supply the boiler. Built by Sylvester H. Roper, this is one of the oldest self-propelled road vehicles in the Museum.*

Opposite: *This clean-lined wagon (a patent model) is one of the earliest automobiles with an internal combustion engine. It has all the basics—a clutch, foot brakes, muffler, front-wheel drive, and a power shaft that turns faster than its propelling wheels. George B. Selden claimed to have designed the car in 1879 and got his patent in 1895. It led to a famous legal fight. Alone among automobile manufacturers, Henry Ford refused to pay Selden a royalty. Selden sued and won, but was overturned in the Court of Appeals.*

Opposite: *This heavy and elaborate key was probably for the vault in the Department of the Treasury when the U.S. capital was at Philadelphia.*

Right: *From about 1819 until the late 1840s, this bill hopper and another like it stood in front of the Senate Chamber. New bills were put into the bottom tier and rose upward, if and when they passed through committee. Logically enough, the tiers grow smaller as they rise. The Sheraton style hopper is made of mahogany and white pine.*

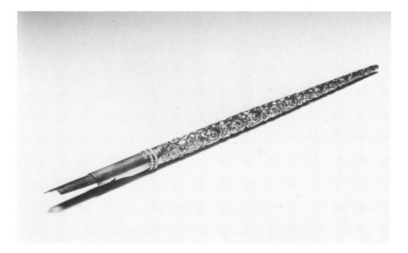

These two small objects—a diplomats' pen and a delicate silver pipe—connect with momentous themes in American history. The silver-handled, steel-tipped pen, at left, belonged to John Hay, Secretary of State to both William McKinley and Theodore Roosevelt; he used it to sign several important treaties. One was the Treaty of Paris of 1899; at the conclusion of what Hay had called "a splendid little war," Spain relinquished all claim to Cuba, ceded Puerto Rico and Guam, and sold the Philippine Islands to the United States. Four years later, in 1903, Hay took up his silver pen again and signed the paper by which the Panama Canal Zone was leased to this country. The peace pipe, opposite, with an urn-shaped bowl and twenty-one-inch stem, was given to the Delaware Indians in 1814 by General William Henry Harrison, in recognition of their pledge to fight on the American side against the British.

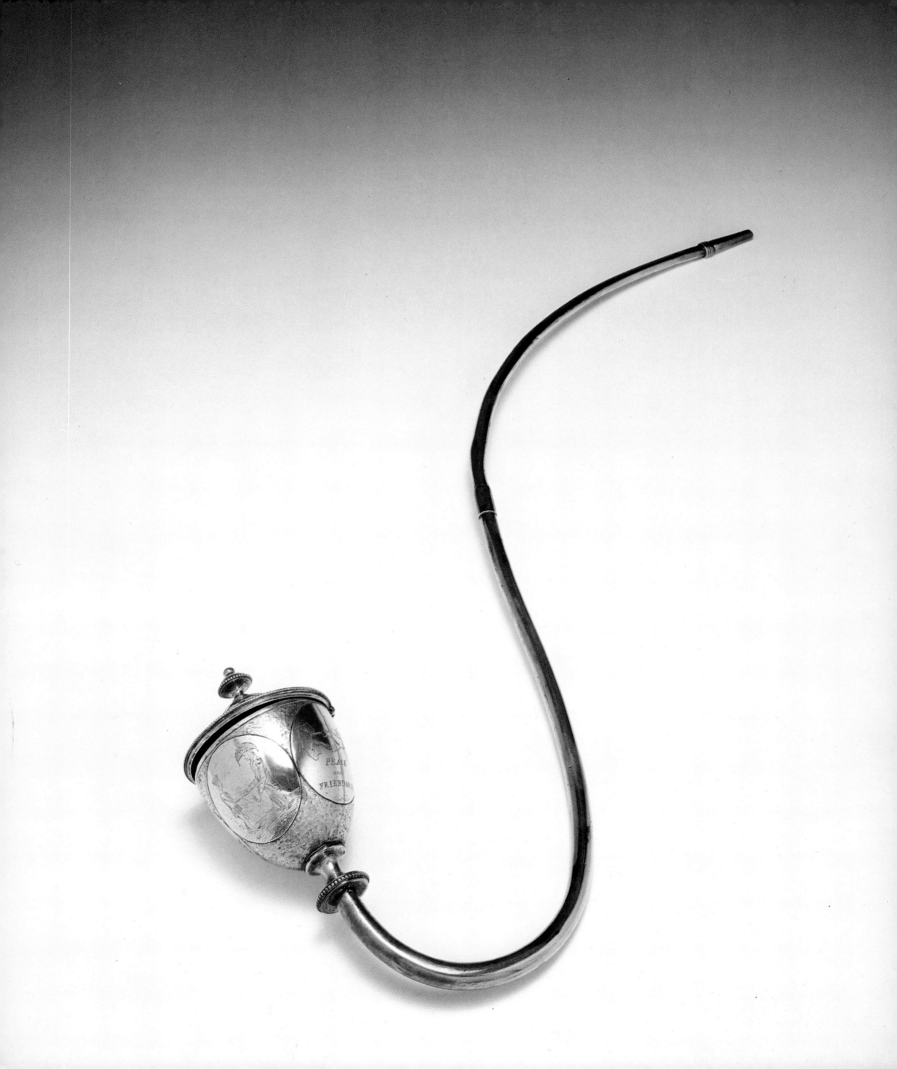

Opposite: *Louisa Adams, wife of John Quincy Adams, was born in England—the only First Lady not native born. (The manikin is not her likeness, nor are any other manikins in the First Ladies Hall meant as portraits.) The Empire style dress is of white net over satin trimmed with silver braid; her linen handkerchief measures a yard square. The harp and music stand were hers—the harp is sixty-three inches tall, with a gold column decorated with rams' heads and Egyptian motifs.*

Above: *John Quincy Adams, in a rare daguerreotype made in his old age, some time after 1842. Adams was the sixth President and served only one term but perhaps his most distinguished service was afterward, during the 1830s and 1840s, when he was Representative from Massachusetts. Among other things, he was the most effective Congressional advocate for establishing the Smithsonian Institution.*

This doll named "Sally" has a bisque head, china eyes, and a cloth body. It belonged to Mary Louisa Adams, the adored granddaughter of John Quincy Adams, Jr. Her parents, Mary Hellen and John Adams, were married in the White House early in 1827. While the bisque head might have been added by a later generation, the cloth body is the one that was loved and played with by the baby born in the White House. While she was still a small child, her father died—an event that increased the grandfather's devotion. He even found time to write poetry for her. In 1839, upon the occasion of presenting her with a Bible, he wrote the following lines for his young granddaughter:

> Walk by that light! fix firm thy steadfast eye
> On yon celestial boundless realm on high,
> And thither let thy faithful footsteps stand.
> So shall thy maker and creation's Lord
> Thy pure and fervent constancy reward
> And thine shall be the joys that never end.

Above: *This detail of a U.S. Henry Repeating Rifle shows its gold-plated receiver, inscribed "LINCOLN/President/U.S.A." It is one of several elaborately finished weapons made by the Winchester Arms Company for presentation to important officials, presumably to promote government contracts.*

Nature they say, doth dote,
And cannot make a man
Save on some worn-out plan,
Repeating us by rote:
For him her Old-World moulds aside she
   threw,
And choosing sweet clay from the breast
Of the unexhausted West,
With stuff untainted shaped a hero new,
Wise, steadfast in the strength of God, and
   true.

—*James Russell Lowell, "Ode"*

Opposite: *This plaster life mask of Abraham Lincoln was made in the White House in the spring of 1865, about two months before the President was assassinated.*

271

This bronze of Lincoln, from a group called "The Council of War," is the work of John Rogers, an immensely popular sculptor of the latter half of the nineteenth century. From his large studio in New York City, he marketed thousands of small, sentimental sculptures, mostly in plaster.

This chair, which seems to lack the proportions to accommodate the Lincolnesque frame, was nevertheless Abraham Lincoln's cabinet chair; and when he sat for his portrait as the "Great Emancipator," this was the chair in which he chose to be portrayed.

Opposite: *On September 22, 1864, the city of San Francisco (where gold had been discovered in 1848) sent President Lincoln this gold nugget from Sutter's Mill, along with the heavy gold snuff box topped with the applied gold initials, "A. L."*

*M*ary Todd Lincoln's resplendent silver tea
service gleams on a marble table top in this
setting similar to a White House parlor of the mid-
nineteenth century. Here too are five First Ladies'
gowns. The manikins represent (from left):
Martha Patterson Johnson in an evening cloak
with a tasseled hood (she was hostess for her
father, Andrew Johnson from 1865 to 1869 in
place of her invalid mother); Mary Todd Lincoln
in royal purple velvet with white piping; Jane
Appleton Pierce, wife of Franklin Pierce (she
served from 1853 to 1857; Mrs. Pierce was in
mourning during the administration, and social
life was very low key); Abigail Powers Fillmore,
First Lady from 1850 to 1853; and Harriet
Lane, who served during the administration
of her bachelor uncle, James Buchanan, 1857–61
(she wears her wedding dress of white moiré
taffeta and a lace veil).

*T*his ornate gilt box—emblematic of the epoch Mark Twain called the Gilded Age—was presented by the City of London to Ulysses S. Grant in June, 1877. Given as a token of a "Unanimous Resolution conferring upon General Grant the Freedom of the City," the box features a view of the U.S. Capitol, Grant's monogram, and the arms of the Lord Mayor. Grant made his visit to London on the first leg of a two-year world tour. Having served two terms in the White House, from 1868 to 1876, he ended his administration in scandal and political bankruptcy. Republican Rutherford B. Hayes, chosen after a highly controversial electoral decision, took office in 1877. Grant was persuaded to run for a third term in 1880, but failed even to win the nomination. Out of money and seriously ill, he spent his last years writing his military memoirs and died in 1885.

Above: *One of the many exploits that endeared Theodore Roosevelt to his public was that in spite of his aristocratic background he had gone as a young man to Dakota Territory and turned himself into a cowboy-rancher. These are his leather chaps that he wore as he rode the range. The harsh winter of 1886–87 killed all his livestock, and he came back east to make his re-entry into public life.*

Opposite: *Roosevelt, an impassioned conservationist, was also an impassioned hunter (his mansion at Oyster Bay, Long Island, still bristles with taxidermy). But on one famous hunting trip in 1902, he made news by refusing to shoot a bear cub—and thus the "teddy bear" was born. The cartoon that inspired the toy was drawn by Clifford Berryman for* The Washington Star.

AS IT SHOULD BE

TARIFF

TARIFF HEDGE

Berryman

The Sweetest Dream that Labor Knows

Robert Frost, who drew his poetic inspiration from the spare, small farms of New England, wrote in his poem "Mowing" that he heard his long scythe whisper to the ground,

"as it laid the swale in rows,

"The fact is the sweetest dream that labor knows. . . ."

Far away on the Great Plains, the horrendous engines of the late nineteenth century did not whisper. Juggernauts on the land, they rattled, shrieked, clanked, and huffed. They also achieved, as Frost's silent and ancient scythe could never have done, the sweetest of all human dreams: plenty to eat, in a nation that may have known drought and bad times but has had no first-hand experience with famine; a nation where the selling, not the buying, of surplus wheat has been a perennial problem.

Steam power, for many years the chief means of carrying farm produce to the cities, was just as vital to the farmer in another way. It conquered the land for him. The engine, opposite, manufactured in 1869 by the J.I. Case Company, is an eight-horsepower jenny for driving threshers and sawmills by belt. It was moveable: a team of horses hauled it around. The stack folded down so that the operator could drive the horses and use the rear wheel brakes.

Above: *This detail from the front of the engine is the trademark of the Case Company—an American eagle with folded wings and arrows in its talons, the symbol of preparedness.*

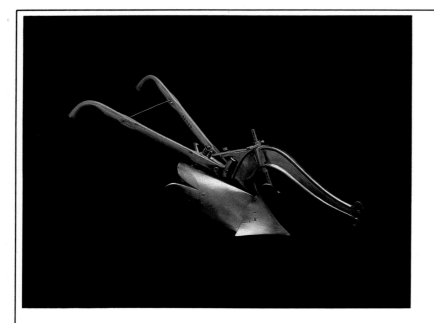

Left: *This model of a side-hill plow, patented in 1878, features a moldboard that operates on the right or left side and a handle that shifts in such a way that the plowman can walk in the furrow as he works the hillside.*

Left: *A model of a mechanical flail, which proved unsuccessful.*

Opposite: *Windmills, like steam engines, were critical tools for making the Great Plains habitable and productive. This model, for which a patent was granted in 1879, has a governing vane that will turn the blades out of the wind when a certain speed is reached.*

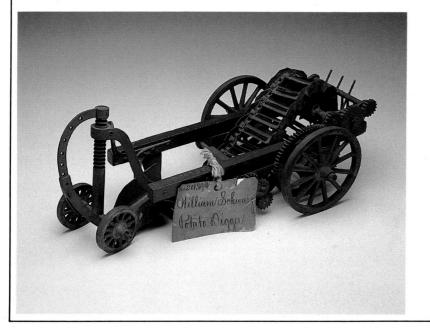

Left: *William Schwarz, a German immigrant, patented this potato digger on April 2, 1878.*

Above: *This experimental gas turbine tractor (a veritable racing car of its kind) was made by International Harvester of Chicago in 1965. A model of efficiency compared with the Huber, opposite, its ninety-pound motor produces eighty-five horsepower, and thus causes the sleek mechanism to rear back. For commercial purposes a less powerful engine would need to be installed.*

Opposite: *At the turn of the century the Huber Manufacturing Company of Marion, Ohio, was the largest and most famous maker of tractors and threshers in the world. This behemoth, a steam tractor built in 1924, is sixteen feet long and ten feet high. Its running speed was only two miles per hour although it burned a whopping 150 pounds of coal per hour.*

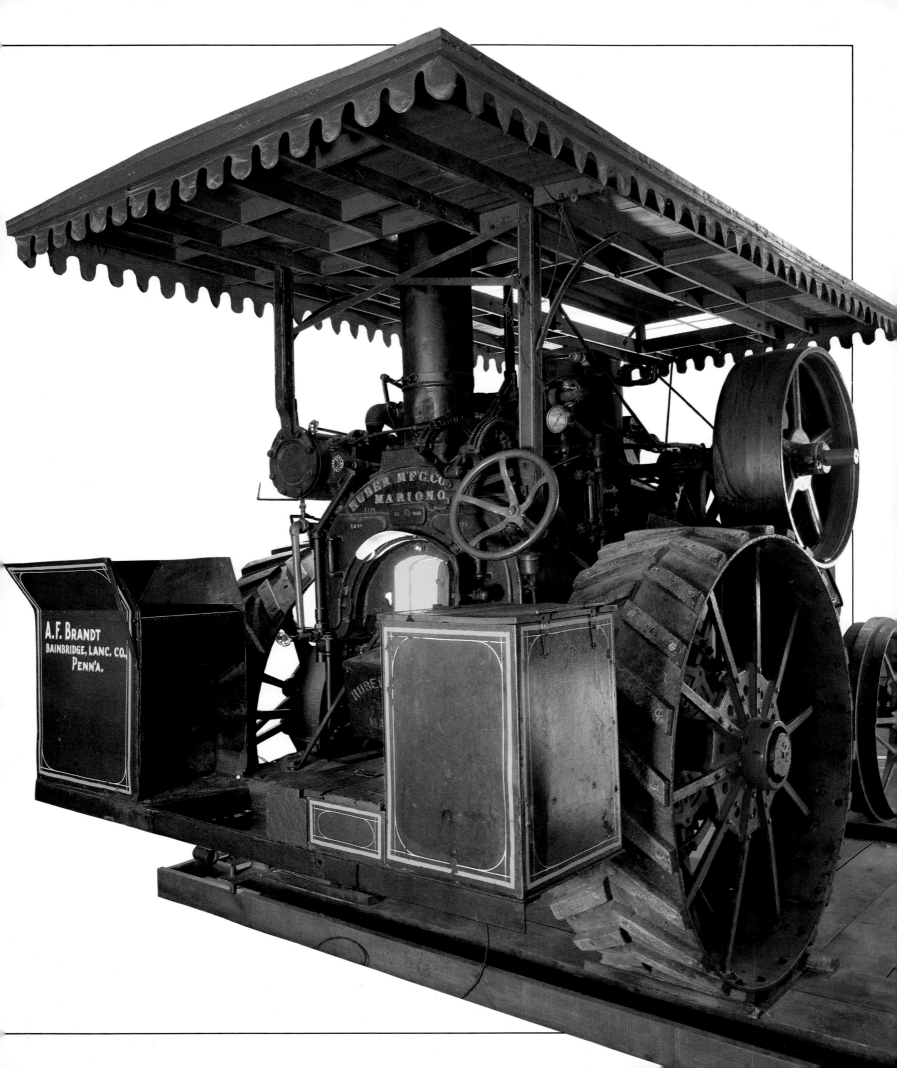

Above: *"Old Red" is a cotton picker, which in its working days, from 1943 to 1959, brought in more than 8,000 bales. The trend that Eli Whitney's cotton gin inevitably enforced— sweated labor on the land—was reversed by such machines as this. As cotton farming underwent mechanization, it also moved westward; the sharecropping system declined and then vanished as millions of Americans moved off the land forever.*

Left: *In tractors, steam soon gave way to gasoline. This kerosene-burning model, manufactured in 1918 by the Waterloo Gasoline Engine Company and used on a North Dakota farm, is basically a steam tractor that happens to have another kind of engine: two cylinders, twenty-five horsepower. The tractor was designed for the heaviest kinds of farm work.*

The Man Who
Made a Business of Invention

If Benjamin Franklin was the quintessential American of the eighteenth century, Thomas Alva Edison might well claim the title for the nineteenth. The two had more than fame in common. Both rose from modest beginnings (Franklin's more so). Neither had much formal education, nor any advantages at first—except ingenuity and ambition. Both were first-rate inventors—pragmatic, quick, eager to find mechanical solutions to every problem. Both spent years in the study of electricity. Both wrought enormous social change—Franklin through his political more than his scientific work. Not too surprisingly, the lives of both have been turned into allegories. The legends of Franklin's kite and of the irate railway conductor boxing Edison's ears echo down the corridors of American schoolhouses. From their adventures we learn what America is.

Nevertheless, they were very different men: from 1776 to 1876 is a long way. Seated at the same dinner table, they might have thoroughly disliked each other. Franklin was a generalist, a humanist, a worldly philosopher at ease with even the Queen of France. Like his great contemporaries Washington and Jefferson, he was rooted in the Enlightenment. Edison, the Mid-westerner, was all practicality—not a humanist or a philosopher or a mathematician. He once remarked that Isaac Newton's *Principia Mathematica,* which he had read as a youth, had turned him permanently against mathematics. He worked mainly by trial and error, not theory. His eye was ever on the marketplace. In what has become a deflating cliché, he once defined genius as two percent inspiration and ninety-eight percent perspiration. Genius though he was, he might not be able today to get a top post at General Electric or Westinghouse. His lack of education would

disqualify him, and his personality quirks would decidedly not endear him to the corporation psychologist. For in spite of his genial smile and good looks—and immense popularity— Thomas Alva Edison was hardly a normal, well-adjusted man.

He was born in 1847 in Milan, Ohio. (James K. Polk was in the White House then, and Edison lived to shake the hand of President Herbert Hoover.) His childhood, by present standards, was calamitous. At age five, he witnessed the drowning of a boyhood chum and ran home without telling anyone. He never forgot the incident, and some biographers have gone so far as to attribute his compulsive working habits in later life to the guilt he felt. At age six, in an experimental frame of mind, Thomas set fire to his parents' barn. His punishment was a ferocious thrashing from his father in the village square.

Some time afterward the family moved to Port Huron, Michigan, where Edison's next misfortune overtook him—a bad bout of scarlet fever that kept him out of school until he was eight. Instead of trying to help the boy catch up, his teacher pronounced him "addled," whereupon his indignant mother removed him from school and educated him herself. Her love must have brought him through these childhood tragedies; certainly it was she who encouraged his scientific bent. Despite the public flogging, he never stopped experimenting, playing jokes, and trying to repeat Franklin's electrical experiments in the cellar of the Edison house. Mrs. Edison did not baby her son—she once thrashed him herself after he had almost poisoned a playmate in the interests of science. "My mother was the making of me," he remarked years later.

The tutoring ended early. Like most boys

Page 288: *Many inventors before Edison had tried to make an incandescent lamp but had never found the right material for a filament. This bulb, a reproduction of Edison's first successful model, dated October 21, 1879, uses a high-resistance filament, in this case carbonized cotton sewing thread.*

Above: *Patented in 1873, this printing telegraph was one of many such devices perfected by Thomas Edison. By supplying needs for the largest electrical industry of the time—telegraphy—Edison quickly developed a reputation as a brilliant and practical inventor. He also generated funds to equip his laboratories for further inventions.*

in those days, Edison went to work at age twelve. His job was selling newspapers and candy on the Grand Trunk Railway, which made a daily run between Port Huron and Detroit. He liked the job—he was a hustler and a profit-taker. He also set up an experimental laboratory in the baggage car and almost set fire to the train. One persistent fable is that the conductor boxed the boy's ears for this and deafened him. But according to Edison's own account, the deafness that now began to torment him had a different cause. Lingering too long on the platform with his newspapers, he said, he had had to grab the rear step of a departing train and the trainman hauled him aboard by the ears. "I felt something snap inside my head," he later wrote. The real culprit may actually have been the scarlet fever. In any case, the man who invented the phonograph could scarcely hear what it played.

His railroad days reinforced the enduring passion of his life—electricity. The railroad system was already served by the telegraph, which was thus far about the only practical use for electricity. On an April afternoon in 1862, as he picked up his consignment of newspapers at the *Detroit Free Press,* Edison noticed that the front page carried a story about the battle of Shiloh in Tennessee—60,000 dead, presumably, including the Confederate general, Albert Sidney Johnston. Edison bribed the telegraph operator in Detroit to wire the news on down the line where it would be posted with the train schedules. Then he persuaded the editor to let him have 1,000 copies of the paper on credit and that evening—thanks to the advance publicity—sold the papers at inflated prices. He considered becoming a mechanic; then he bought a printing press with the Shiloh proceeds and thought of going into journalism. But he ultimately decided that telegraphy was the career for him. In 1863, at the age of sixteen, he became a full-fledged operator.

For the next five years he tramped all over the Mid-west and South as a telegraph man, a member of the brotherhood of telegraph men, a society of bachelors and drifters, almost like hoboes. He was a crack operator and had no trouble finding work, except that he was always tinkering with the equipment. He set up laboratories in the shabby furnished rooms he inhabited and tried obsessively to invent a multiplex transmission system, so that more than one message could travel simultaneously over the same wire. Arrogant, careless, and anti-social, he was fired from several jobs. His indifference to certain standards almost cancelled his skill. At the Western Union office in Louisville, the youthful inventor spilled sulphuric acid on the floor. It dripped through the ceiling and ate up the manager's carpet and desk. Another time, neglecting his duty at the key, he almost caused a train wreck. He was also a practical joker. His speciality, of course, was electric shocks.

He arrived in New York in 1869, twenty-two years old and broke. In a few years he was destined to transform the city's entire appearance and economy, but he spent his first night with only a dollar to his name, sleeping in a cellar on Broad Street in the city's financial district. Trading in gold was a big thing in that year, as it is now, and Edison made friends with a man who worked at the Gold Indicator Company, a firm that reported gold prices via a primitive telegraph. A few days later, in the midst of hysterically heavy trading, the telegraph broke down and Edison quickly repaired it. The result was a job at a substantial salary, and an invitation to experiment. At last Edison was in the right place. His inventiveness began to flow—an improved stock ticker, a stock printer, a gold price printer, a printing telegraph. By the end of one year he was the holder of seven patents.

The Gold Indicator Company was soon acquired by Western Union, and Edison along with it. He was the youngest of a number of inventors that the company nurtured and exploited. Shrewd as he was, Edison was none too smart about his own fortune. He did complain that his partners made all the money while he did all the inventing. At length he invented a stock ticker so ingenious that Western Union felt it had to settle up accounts. They bought Edison out for $40,000—a sum that astounded him. He was almost too nervous to negotiate the check at the bank.

He used the money, eventually, to set up his

laboratory in Menlo Park, New Jersey, and soon afterward chose a pretty sixteen-year-old named Mary Stilwell as his bride. Right after the wedding, Edison went to his lab and worked until midnight (he later claimed it was only until dinnertime), leaving his bride to weep alone. He habitually spent most of his time at work, nights and days. Eighteen hours at a stretch was a normal workday for him, and he had the peculiar ability to go sleepless for two or three days. When his daughter and son were born he nicknamed them "Dot" and "Dash." Except for brief periods of frenzied attention on Sundays, he ignored them as he ignored their mother. She worshipped him, nevertheless, from the distance at which he kept her.

Edison invented or perfected so many things that now make life pleasant and convenient that it is hard to say where his real fame rests. By the time he began work on the incandescent light bulb in 1878 he was already a celebrity and the holder of many patents. Edison's eye was always on the market. He knew there was money to be made out of cheap, safe, controllable electric light. And more than money, he wanted the glory of it. "I don't care so much about making my fortune," he told a newspaper reporter on one occasion, "as I do for getting ahead of the other fellows." Gas light was smelly, potentially dangerous, hot in the summer, and dim. Electrical arc lights, already in use on some thoroughfares, in industrial and public buildings, and in lighthouses, were blinding in their glare and utterly unsuited for lighting a home. A functional light bulb—with some incandescing substance that would not burn out within a few minutes—was yet to be invented. But the bulb was only part of the problem. There were no power plants, no transmission stations, no delivery systems. There was as yet no way of metering electricity—hence no way of selling it.

There was an unspoken intellectual problem as well. As Elting E. Morison of the Massachusetts Institute of Technology observes in *From Know-How to Nowhere*, ". . . electricity reversed the classical learning process. Men had put up buildings for a long time before they began to construct a theory of arches. They had

Opposite, above: *In 1877, interested in making what he called a "talking telegraph," Edison designed a hand-cranked recording machine. (The one shown here is a commercial model produced for Edison.) It has a blunt needle attached to a diaphragm. The vibrations of the spoken word activate the diaphragm, and the needle makes a series of varying indentations in a sheet of tin foil covering the rotating cylinder. The first thing it recorded was Edison's shouted recital of "Mary had a little lamb." When he heard the play-back, he was astounded. "I was always afraid of things that worked the first time."*

Opposite, below: *Emile Berliner is by no means a household word, but in most American households he ought to be. The disk phonograph record is his invention. This machine with its turntable and speaker, which Berliner demonstrated in Philadelphia, on May 16, 1888, has a zinc disk etched with acid. Celluloid copies could easily be stamped from it. He called the whole system—machine, process, and record—the "gramophone." By the end of the century he had made many improvements, but competitors had begun to appear. Berliner disappeared in a fog of patent fights, and Columbia and Victor took the field. The gramophone became, in everyday usage, the victrola.*

The earliest attempt to record sound was made by Leon Scott in Paris in 1857 with this phonoautograph. Using a brush and a vibrating membrane, the machine "recorded" sound waves on lampblacked paper. The next problem, which Scott did not solve, was to turn the tracing into sound once more.

run heat engines for a long time before they began to develop the field of thermodynamics. The customary way was to start with the thing and work out the thought. With electricity the problem was to translate the thinking into mechanisms that did work." Moreover, electricity was mysterious—completely unlike steam, water, wind or any other energy form then in use. As Morison writes, "Compared to these it was more subtle, more intricate, and followed far more sophisticated paths of logic." So far its only apparent advantage was in telegraphy, where it could carry a message faster than a steam engine could move.

Edison was not the first who had tried to conquer this mountain of difficulties, nor the first to imagine the advantages of electric lights. He felt sure that incandescence was the answer, that is, to turn electric current into usable light, it had to be run through a filament. This filament worked best in a vacuum—and someone had already invented a pump for creating a near vacuum inside a glass bulb. The problem was finding a filament that would give off enough light and last more than a few minutes.

From the fall of 1878 to the end of 1879, Edison experimented. He found that carbonized cotton thread and even carbonized cardboard worked better than anything—so well, in fact, that he was able to stage one of the great publicity stunts of the century. Having devised a circuit that produced an even-flowing current, he lit electric lamps outdoors at Menlo Park just after Christmas in 1879 and invited the public. Just how many lamps glowed in the holiday twilight is moot: some say there were 500. Probably there were no more than about forty at first, but Edison promised 800 as soon as his newest generator was in working order. Whatever the number, it was a grand American celebration. By New Year's Eve the Pennsylvania Railroad had to schedule special trains to carry the throngs to and from New York—3,000 people on that day alone. A rival inventor stalked the grounds and, in apparently drunken despair, attempted sabotage. Like the villain in a melodrama, he was led offstage by the righteous.

Edison went on experimenting with his

filament. He claimed to have tried 6,000 different materials before deciding that carbonized bamboo was the best solution. (The tungsten filament we use today was perfected later by William Coolidge and Irving Langmuir at General Electric.) More important than the filament or the bulb or the socket was Edison's profoundest conception: he invented the power and light company. He devised a way to manufacture electricity by means of a steam-powered dynamo and to deliver it—by means of underground wires—to different neighborhoods and separate houses. He understood that investors had to be brought in. By the end of 1880 he had formed the Edison Electric Company—the embryo of the giant known to New Yorkers today as Consolidated Edison. Soon afterward he installed the world's first central power station at No. 255–257 Pearl Street in lower Manhattan—"the biggest and most responsible thing I had ever undertaken." He had already got permission from the municipality to lay electrical conduits under the streets of the city: his political wizardry also deserves its due.

J.P. Morgan had been an early investor in Edison's company, and so his Wall Street offices were among the first to get service from the Pearl Street Station. On September 4, 1882, every wire was in place and the lamps screwed into their sockets. Edison bought a new coat and derby for the occasion, and a white cravat. At three in the afternoon, someone at Pearl Street threw a switch and somewhat to everyone's astonishment, the lights went on in the offices of J.P. Morgan. "The light was soft, mellow, and grateful to the eyes," reported the *New York Times* wonderingly the next day. Edison always called it the greatest adventure of his life. Electric power was still in a primitive state. Metering and billing were two problems remaining to be solved, as well as attracting big capital. But if we have Edison to thank for the steady glow we read by, we should not omit to thank him, too, for the inexorable meter in the cellar and our electric bill.

Edison's work was not unique. Brilliant inventors had preceded him and now succeeded him, refining his work and developing such critical systems as high-voltage transmission and alternating current. But, as Edison's biographer Matthew Josephson observes, that hardly matters. "Leadership in inaugurating the Electrical Age was almost universally attributed to Mr. Edison. What James Watt had been to the Age of Steam, Edison was to the new era of technology. . . . Edison symbolized electricity—thoughts and words soaring across great distances; energy freed from the engine and belt by smokeless motors; cities wreathed in light." He was a folk hero, a giant, the living embodiment of American striving and success. As Josephson puts it, "Almost every other American dreamed of making that 'better mousetrap'; yet Edison's devices were no mere mousetraps, but creations that served both to transform society and to lighten men's burdens." And to everybody's intense satisfaction, he had got rich and famous by doing what he did. If Edison had not existed, William Dean Howells or Mark Twain would have been compelled to invent him.

Edison never looked upon his work as complete—never stopped inventing. When he died, aged eighty-four, he was working out a system to extract latex from goldenrod. It was one of his less promising notions, but Edison managed to squeeze enough rubber out of the weeds to make four tires for a Model A. His death, on October 18, 1931, caused as much international and national concern as the demise of any president or monarch. As a final tribute, someone proposed that all the electricity in the United States should be turned off for two minutes. "But no sooner was the thought uttered than it was realized that such action was unthinkable," writes Matthew Josephson. A national blackout would, by 1931, have been like a national heart attack. His countrymen could no longer live without Edison's gifts—not even for an interval of two minutes.

Making money out of his idea never seemed to concern him particularly.

—Thomas Watson, speaking of Alexander Graham Bell

*I*f Edison sometimes behaved unlovably and Isaac Singer led a scandalous private life, Alexander Graham Bell was one American inventor who apparently never committed an ungentlemanly act. A Scot by birth, he migrated to the United States by way of Canada. He was not, at first, ambitious to invent the telephone and surely did not yearn to lay the foundations for that giant among American corporations, AT&T. He began his career as a teacher of the deaf, and to the end of his life aided the cause of the deaf and gave large amounts of money to it. (His mother had been deaf, and so was his wife.) But he also had the mind of an inventive genius. Hoping to devise an instrument to teach articulation to the deaf, he became interested in telegraphy. Then he realized that, "If I could make a current of electricity vary in intensity, precisely as the air varies in density during the production of sound, I should be able to transmit speech telegraphically." That was in 1874. In March, 1876, he and his colleague Thomas J. Watson built their first telephone, and Bell uttered his famous words into the transmitter: "Mr. Watson, come here, I want to see you."

Opposite: *This carved ivory telephone, which was used both as receiver and transmitter, is a duplicate of one designed by Bell for Queen Victoria and installed in 1878 in her summer house on the Isle of Wight.*

Above: *Nikola Tesla, who migrated to the United States from Croatia in 1884, made fundamental contributions to alternating-current technology, including the design of the induction motor, which was patented in 1888. It is the first practical motor using alternating current rather than direct. At the time, Westinghouse and Edison were engaged in a noisy public debate on the relative advantages of AC versus DC, with Edison dogmatically devoted to the latter. Tesla's inventions were key elements in the AC victory.*

Overleaf: *In June, 1876, when his device was only three months old, Bell demonstrated it publicly at the great Centennial Exhibition in Philadelphia. For about two weeks, these two instruments were on view. "My God, it talks," exclaimed the Emperor Dom Pedro of Brazil. It was a great crowd-pleaser, but no one quite grasped, apparently, that a communications revolution had been born.*

*B*lack-and-white photography had hardly got underway before experimenters began looking for a way to capture the color image. In 1861, scarcely two decades after the daguerreotype was invented, an English scientist, James Clerk Maxwell, made the first color photograph. He combined three separate color positives, which he projected simultaneously onto a screen each through a color filter—blue, green, and red corresponding to the color filters used for exposing the negative. The 1890 tri-color camera at left produced a color picture using the same principle—by means of three exposures made simultaneously with three colored filters. Modern color films depend upon multi-layered, photo-sensitive emulsions, each of which responds to one color, on a single film or paper.

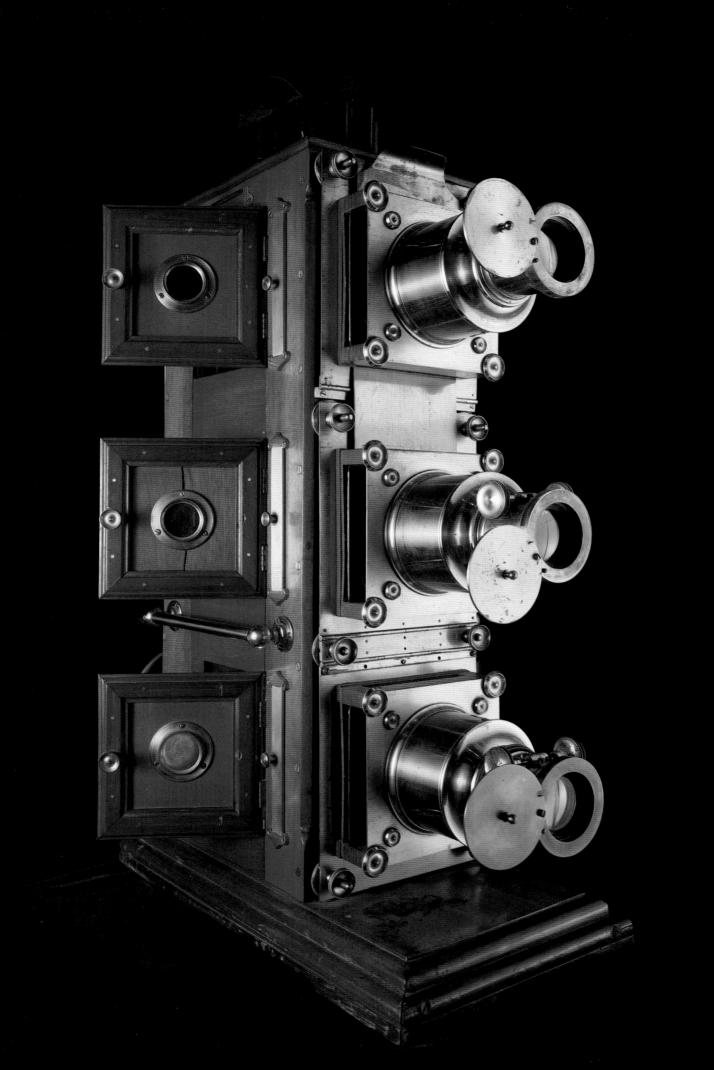

Opposite: *This stereopticon (magic lantern) of 1890—with the look of advanced industrial technology about it—is capable of projecting three images at once. A tool of lecturers, the stereopticon could produce "dissolves," that is, it could blend one image into the next if the light in one lantern was dimmed while in another it was increased.*

Above: *By combining two photographic images taken from slightly different viewpoints, the stereoscope produces the illusion of depth. This table-top instrument was made about 1860. Instantly popular, the stereoscope became one of the earliest commercially produced forms of home entertainment, something for the family to enjoy when charades had begun to pall.*

Right: *This daguerreotype camera, made in 1839, was used by Samuel F.B. Morse. The daguerreotype shows L.J.M. Daguerre, inventor of the daguerreotype process.*

Opposite: *This compact photographic kit, manufactured in London about 1869, had all the equipment and chemicals necessary for making photographic negatives. To make the negative the photographer had to coat a glass plate with collodion, a viscous liquid, and then (to make it light-sensitive) dip it into a solution of silver nitrate.*

Right: *Tintypes were photographs taken on sheets of black-varnished iron coated with a light-sensitized collodion. They were cheap, mailable, and very popular. This tintype camera of 1870 has four lenses, which produced four images of each pose.*

Among its other consequences, photography altered the forms by which our history is transmitted. The miniature portrait on ivory, above, left, *made in 1843 by J.W. Dodge, is Henry Clay—one of the "war hawks" of a young republic eager to drive the British out of this hemisphere permanently. Later on, Clay was a skilled conciliator between Northern and Southern interests.* Above, right, *a daguerreotype of Cyrus Field, who in 1858 made his first attempt to lay the Atlantic Cable. With or without cameras, the likenesses of such men as Field and Clay would no doubt have been preserved for posterity, but probably not that of Keokuk,* opposite, *a chief of the Sac tribe who aided the Americans in the Black Hawk War of 1832. His daguerreotype was made in 1847 by Thomas Easterly.*

S ome inventions—the digital computer, for example—arrive before most people know they need them, while others, like the typewriter, arise almost by public demand. All over Europe and the United States, hundreds of inventors struggled throughout the nineteenth century to perfect a writing machine. The winners, in the end, were Christopher Sholes, a Milwaukee newspaperman, and his backer, James Densmore. In 1867 Sholes and two lesser collaborators, Carlos Glidden and Samuel Soule, applied for a patent on the machine at far right, and the next year filed an application on the machine in the foreground, which looks like a toy piano. (Since it is a patent model, the inventors included only a few keys.) On both machines, the paper lay flat on the tops, and the keys struck it from underneath. Densmore pronounced the machine worthless. One variant after another was tried but none of the early machines allowed the user to see what he was writing. In 1873, the inventors approached the Remington Arms Company, which, in a post–Civil War business slump, was diversifying. Glidden and Soule bowed out; Sholes sold his rights for $12,000, and Remington itself helped design the more familiar looking machine with the QWERTYUIOP keyboard at near right. Christened Type Writer, it went onto the market in 1874 and was not a great success. But by the end of the century, Remington typewriters were in offices all around the world.

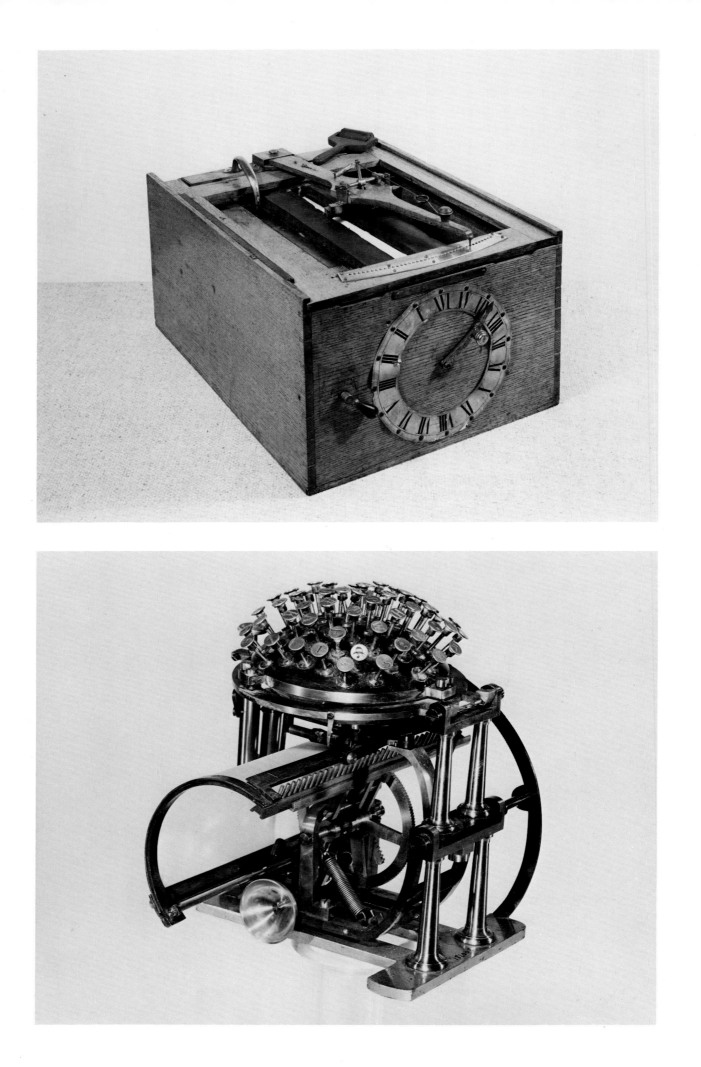

Opposite, above: *This is a reconstruction of the "Typographer," the first American writing machine. The original, built by William Burt in 1829, was destroyed in a fire.*

Right: *E. Remington & Sons, the arms manufacturers, added sewing machines to their line after the Civil War, and then typewriters. The first typewriter cost $125.*

Opposite, below: *The "writing ball," a Danish invention of 1865, was the first writing machine to become a commercial success. Pastor J.R. Malling Hansen designed it.*

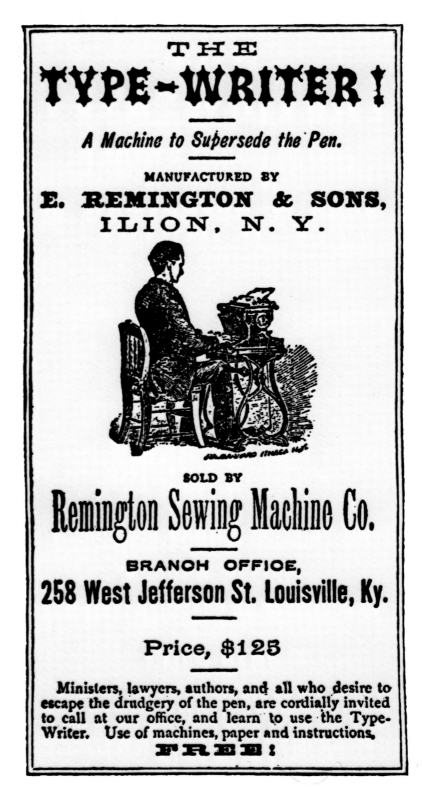

THE
TYPE-WRITER!

A Machine to Supersede the Pen.

MANUFACTURED BY

E. REMINGTON & SONS,
ILION, N. Y.

SOLD BY

Remington Sewing Machine Co.

BRANCH OFFICE,

258 West Jefferson St. Louisville, Ky.

Price, $125

Ministers, lawyers, authors, and all who desire to escape the drudgery of the pen, are cordially invited to call at our office, and learn to use the Type-Writer. Use of machines, paper and instructions, **FREE!**

*T*his pocket-sized medicine kit—it contains 196 vials of different medicated pellets, and tiny papers to wrap them in—belonged to one of the innovative spirits of nineteenth-century medicine, Dr. Samuel Hahnemann. Born in Germany in 1755, Hahnemann died rich and famous in Paris in 1843, renowned as the founder of homeopathy, a popular medical approach during the nineteenth century now generally discredited. One of Hahnemann's ideas was that doctors ought to mix their own prescriptions instead of relying on apothecaries and that the curative power of a drug could be determined by trying it out on healthy persons. Observing that quinine could either cure fever or cause it, he evolved his homeopathic theory—"A disease can only be destroyed and cured by a remedy which has a tendency to produce a similar disease." Hence for scarlet fever, which produces sore throat, he used belladonna, which makes the throat dry. To relieve poison ivy, a highly diluted dose of the poison from the plant would be given. (As with much medical practice of the time, the patient got well in spite of the treatment.) Hahnemann was opposed to such favored remedies of the day as bleeding and violent emetics, and he also thought medicines should be given in small doses (the smaller the dose, the stronger the medicine). For these reasons, if no others, his patients loved him, and homeopathy was widely acclaimed in both Europe and the United States.

*T*hough the American drugstore eventually developed into a unique combination of apothecary, notion counter, luncheonette, book shop, ice cream parlor, and perfume purveyor (functions which were most often kept under separate roofs by European shopkeepers), the American pharmacist is nevertheless rooted in an ancient tradition. Throughout the centuries professional druggists have divided their shops into two rooms (as even the most modern pharmacy does today): one where the pharmacist meets the public and another where he compounds his formulas away from public view. At right is a detail of a public room in a typical European pharmacy of the eighteenth century. The shelves, carved cherub, drawers, and furnishings come from a shop in Freiburg im Breisgau, Germany. The jars, variously made of glass, ceramic, wood, and metal, were made and used from about 1500 through 1800 in England, France, Holland, Germany, and Italy.

Above: *These hand-blown glass apothecary jars with tin lids were used in the nineteenth-century pharmacy to hold raw drugs and herbs.*

Opposite: *Reassembled in the Museum with antiques from Germany, this seventeenth-century apothecary's compounding room is the immediate ancestor of the American drugstore on the following page. Here on the pharmacist's table is his herbal, or recipe book, and behind it a pair of glass containers, a writing stand, and various spoons, bowls, and measures.*

Above: *This medicine chest belonged to Dr. Edward R. Squibb (founder of E.R. Squibb and Sons pharmaceutical manufacturers), who was a U.S. Navy surgeon from 1847 to 1857. The bottles are numbered and there is an explanatory key—so that the captain or an ordinary seaman could use the kit in case the doctor was not aboard or had been killed or wounded in battle.*

Opposite: *This drugstore compounding room of about 1890 would have been behind the stained glass partition of the pharmacy on pages 8–9. On the shelves are liquids and powders in jars; in the foreground are a mortar and pestle and pill-making equipment. Pre-manufactured pills were already common.*

Right: *In 1886 an Atlanta, Georgia, druggist named John Pemberton invented Coca-Cola syrup as a headache remedy. He also thought up the mellifluous name. Someone else added carbonated water, thus stumbling upon a product even more lucrative than a headache cure. This Coca-Cola syrup jar was made about 1890.*

Dentistry, along with other branches of medicine, progressed in the late nineteenth century from a form of torment practiced by amateurs, into one of the healing sciences. This dental office, quite recognizable as such, was used by Dr. Greene Vardiman Black—an inventor, researcher, and Professor of Dentistry at Northwestern University until his death in 1915. In 1871, Dr. Black invented the foot-operated dental drill; he also improved methods of cavity preparation and filling. The anesthesia apparatus, which contained pure nitrous oxide, was an 1884 invention of Amos Long.

The speciality of orthodontics did not develop by hazard. It had its founding father, Edward H. Angle, who graduated in 1878 from the Pennsylvania College of Dental Surgery and later practiced in California. His first patent (for a device that corrected imperfect "bite") was issued in 1889, and he went on to perfect most of the instruments now used for the regulation and retention of teeth. Apart from its cosmetic aims, orthodontics is a form of preventive dentistry—saving teeth that would otherwise decay or be useless. It was an inevitable development as dentistry changed in the nineteenth century from a trade into an important branch of the medical sciences.

Above: This laboratory and study, re-erected at the Museum, belonged to Dr. Edward H. Angle, whose portrait hangs on the wall at left.

Opposite: Detail of the worktable above, with models of gums and teeth and assorted dental instruments.

The most historic engine in the entire Smithsonian is the John Bull, *built in England by Robert Stephenson and shipped, in late August, 1831, first to Philadelphia and then to Bordentown, N.J., for service on the Camden and Amboy Railroad. (The Americans added the cab, pilot truck, bell, whistle, and headlight.) The engine pulled construction trains, then passenger cars. By 1866 the engine was retired, probably the first locomotive in the United States to be set aside as an historical relic. In 1893, it traveled from New York to Chicago for the great Columbian Exposition.* John Bull *is still in operating order.*

The General and the Locomotive

"I can scarcely think of him without weeping."

The first regular steam-powered rail service in the United States began not in some Great Lakes boomtown but in the genteel southern city of Charleston. In December, 1830, the South Carolina Railroad, with an American-made locomotive called *The Best Friend of Charleston,* inaugurated freight and passenger service on its first six miles of track. The kick-off celebrations were vigorous—an artillery salute, a brass band, and much feasting and oratory. Six months later the locomotive exploded, but this did not deter anybody. By 1840 the United States had 5,000 miles of track. Pennsylvania had the most (947) and New York was second (773). In spite of their ambitious beginning, the southern states were lagging: all together they had only about 1,200 miles of track.

So rapidly did the technology of steam advance and so vital a role did the railroads play in the developing economy that by the beginning of the Civil War (less than thirty-one years after *The Best Friend* made its first run), railroads took on a crucial military role. The Civil War, to a great extent, was fought on the railroads—the first such war in history. In 1861, although the Confederacy and the Union were about equal in area, the North had more than two miles of rail for every mile in the South— 20,000 against 9,000. Over these superior miles of rail the Union would move troops, guns, ammunition, and food. Early in 1862, Abraham Lincoln, who understood that railroads were crucial, picked two capable, tough-minded men to make the railroads serve the army. Their names, Captain Herman Haupt and Daniel Craig McCallum, have hardly gone down on the roster of American heroes, but one way and another they managed to keep the supply trains running and the bridges rebuilt. As much as Ulysses Grant, these two railroad generals won the war.

The Confederates meanwhile, desperate for new rails and with no domestic source for them, tore up whole lines in border states like Texas and Florida and moved the tracks to where they might do some good. But the attempt was hopeless. They also tried hard to destroy and disable the border railroads. The Baltimore & Ohio, the Louisville & Nashville were ripped up, rebuilt, and destroyed again. Stonewall Jackson made it his particular business to attack Union rail lines. Systematically he confiscated rolling stock and tore up bridges. In one of the many futile and tragic acts of the war, Confederate General John Bell Hood blew up the railroad yards of Atlanta before abandoning the city to Sherman. He then went out into the countryside, ripping up tracks. Sherman retaliated by having his own rail lines built as he marched through Georgia, and then, when he moved out, destroying them to keep the Southerners from using them.

In the years leading up to Appomattox, not surprisingly, enough railroad lore accumulated to fill several volumes. The war began and ended on trains. In October, 1859, advancing toward Harpers Ferry, John Brown and his raiders stopped a Baltimore & Ohio express eastbound from Virginia, and in the skirmish shot and killed the train's porter—a free black. And in the spring of 1865, a season of unparalleled national tragedy, a long and darkly shrouded train carried Lincoln's body back to Springfield, Illinois.

Not all that happened on and around the rails was of such high solemnity. One of the classic epics of absurdity occurred in April, 1863, when some Yankee spies in plain clothes

Below: *Thomas Davenport, a blacksmith of Brandon, Vermont, was the first inventor to build an electric motor capable of useful work. This one, built in 1838, was intended to drive a small electric train of several carriages (seventy or so pounds) at a speed of three miles per hour on a circular track four feet in diameter. The train was exhibited in London soon after it was built.*

Right: *Built about 1836, this is the oldest surviving eight-wheel passenger car, one of fifteen such cars built for the Camden and Amboy Railroad in New Jersey. With its low ceiling, narrow little seats only a foot deep, poor ventilation, and dim illumination, it testifies to the fortitude and pluck of early railroad passengers. About 1870, the Pennsylvania Railroad acquired the Camden and Amboy and sold the car off: a farmer bought it and converted it into a chicken roost. By 1892, however, the Railroad decided to retrieve and refurbish it in order to display it at the Columbian Exposition in Chicago. It found its way, eventually, to the National Museum.*

Prairie

Walbland

Ein Beginn auf der Prairie.

Ein Beginn im Walde.

Auf der Prairie nach 6 Jahren.

A. T. & S. F. R. R.

Cottonwood Trees on Polk St. Topeka. 26FT HIGH, FOUR YEARS OLD FROM CUTTINGS.

Im Walde nach 10 Jahren.

Opposite: *Railroad hand cars started out as simple four-wheel push cars in the mines of Europe. As steam locomotives and railroading developed, maintenance cars had to keep pace, too—for necessary work on signals, fences, water tanks, and bridges, and for railroad track gangs. Steam-powered hand cars appeared in the 1840s but motorized hand cars did not come into their own until the twentieth century. This iron-and-wood track car, built for the Atchison, Topeka, and Santa Fe in 1928, has a one-cylinder, eight-horsepower engine and weighs about 900 pounds.*

Above: *Santa Fe Railway land poster in German, 1876.*

Overleaf: *The* Pioneer, *a small six-wheeler built in 1851, was used on the Cumberland Valley Railroad in Maryland and Pennsylvania for almost thirty years.*

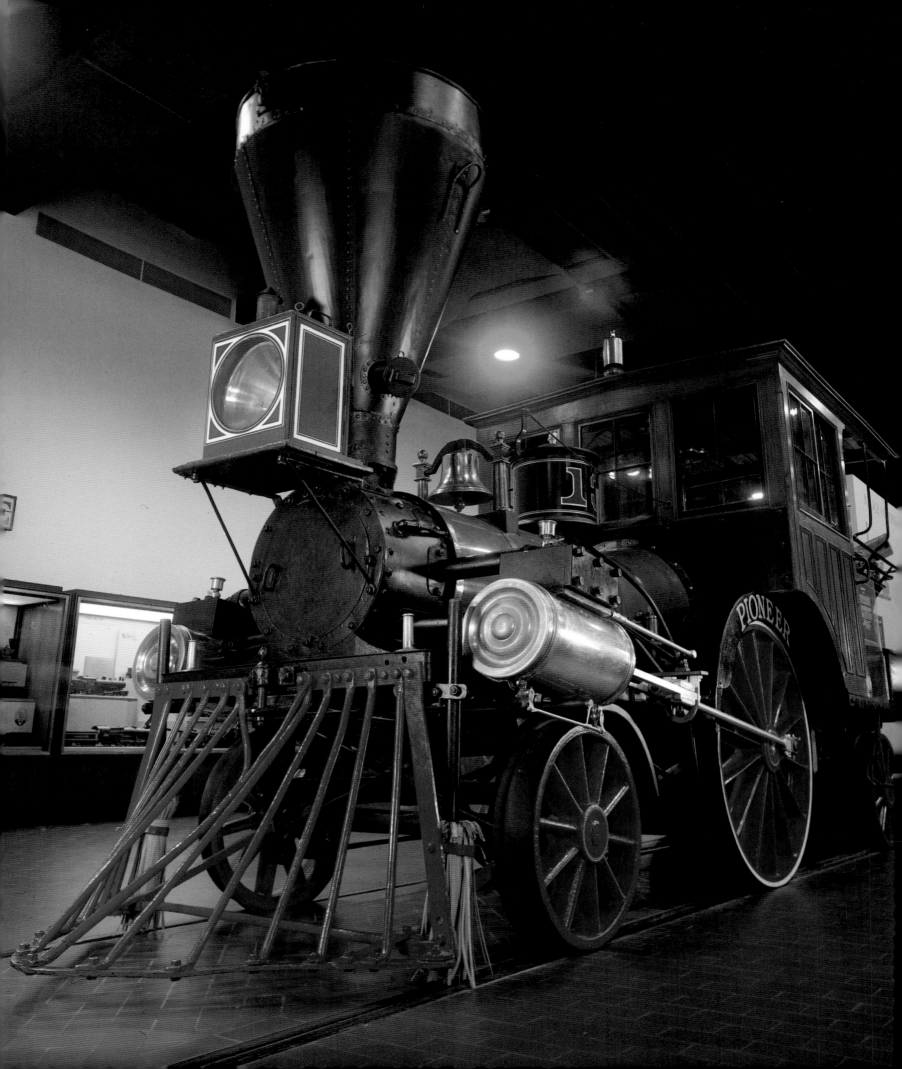

stole a Western & Atlantic locomotive from the station at Big Shanty, Georgia, and set off in it. Their leader was James Andrews, their master plan to blow up bridges all the way to Chattanooga. They steamed on up the line—a single track—pulling off on sidings to dodge oncoming freight trains. Before they could do much damage, they noticed that a pack of rebels were in furious pursuit in another locomotive, boiling along in reverse. There was no question, then, of disembarking to set off explosives. Inevitably the stolen locomotive ran out of water. Though the escapade had not the slightest military result, the Southerners ill-naturedly strung up James Andrews and seven of his party.

Another event of mythic rather than tactical importance was the burning of the locomotive *Pioneer*—now a centerpiece of Railroad Hall at the Museum. As the label on the locomotive says, the deed was done by Jeb Stuart—General James Ewell Brown Stuart—the Confederate cavalry chief, whom his biographers like to characterize as "the last of the cavaliers." The *Pioneer,* vintage 1851, saw service on the Cumberland Valley Railroad, which ran from Chambersburg, Pennsylvania, to Powells Bend, Maryland. A lightweight six-wheeler, it was atypical even in its day. Unlike most other American locomotives, it had no separate tender (to hold the water and fuel) and only one set of driving wheels. It was meant only for light passenger traffic, but, despite these limitations, it was economical to operate. On the morning of October 11, 1862, Stuart set fire to the shops of the Cumberland Valley Railroad in Chambersburg, severely damaging much equipment, including the *Pioneer*. Both Stuart and the locomotive were, in their separate categories, mavericks, or even dinosaurs. In an era of fast-changing technologies, styles of soldiering, like the design of locomotives, were subject to revision. Both these remarkable oddities were doomed to be phased out.

Stuart could only have been a Southerner—it is hard to imagine a Union officer of any rank—let alone a general—getting away with such high-jinks. At West Point, from which he graduated in 1854, Stuart had earned the derisive, affectionate nickname "Beauty," which

he took in good humor. Like many other future Civil War officers, he served his apprenticeship in Texas as an Indian fighter, and his dandified habits did not flower until the outbreak of the Civil War, when as Brigadier General of the Virginia Cavalry he took to carrying a French saber and wearing a plumed hat, gorgeous high boots, a scarlet-lined cape, gauntlets, and a yellow silk sash. "We must substitute *esprit* for numbers," he once remarked.

This attitude, as well as his get-up, exactly suited the temper of his men. They were volunteer state militia mustered into the army in groups that styled themselves "Hussars," "Lancers," "Dragoons," and "Light Horse." They must have been an amazing sight—no wonder their whiskery, plain-faced commander took refuge in finery. In the early days, before the Confederate States of America adopted its historic gray, the men turned up in anything from zouave jackets to coonskins—the fancier the better. The horsetrappings of an average recruit were worth considerably more than his horse.

With or without his plumed hat, Beauty Stuart was anything but a fop. His silk-lined cloak may have made the mountain men grin, but he took the untrained, undisciplined, touchy young men who volunteered for service in his regiment and turned them into a fighting force. Most of them had been riding and shooting since childhood; now they had to learn to obey orders. Early on, Stuart won the respect and confidence of Robert E. Lee, who had been his commandant at West Point a few years earlier. But for all his skill, he remained a kind of stuntman—a specialist in the mad dash and the suicide mission—a dazzling military talent but not quite fit for the regular run.

Years after the war was over, William Tecumseh Sherman uttered his famous aphorism about the hellishness of combat—"There is many a boy . . . who looks on war as all glory, but. . . it is all hell." Yet Jeb Stuart surely did not think war was hell. He liked to fight. Late in 1862, he captured a station on the Orange & Alexandria Railroad, some fifteen miles from Washington, and sent off a wire to Quartermaster-General Meigs of the U.S. Army complaining about the inferior quality of the army mules he had just captured, "which interferred seriously with our moving the captured wagons." It became one of the great jokes of the war and grew into a tall tale. The Chambersburg raid was just as much fun—a comic entr'acte in a dance of death.

In October, 1862, Confederate hopes still ran high. Stuart and his men were comfortably encamped in Dandridge plantation in northern Virginia, when the order came from Lee to move northward behind enemy lines with a detachment of 1,200 to 1,500 cavalry. The objective was to proceed "to the rear of Chambersburg, and endeavor to destroy the railroad bridge. . . . Any other damage that you can inflict upon the enemy you will also execute. You are desired to gain all information of the position, force, and probable intention of the enemy which you can. . . . " Hostages were to be taken and to be courteously treated. In short, it was a combination of guerrilla warfare and intelligence work—dangerous but just what Stuart liked. Lee promised a diversionary action upstream from where Stuart and his men would have to ford the Potomac.

This plan failed: on October 10, the column was sighted as it splashed across the river. When word reached General McClellan, he was for some reason unable to decide what to do. Frantic telegraph messages flew between him and Washington while Stuart pushed quickly on through Maryland and into Pennsylvania. His scouts often got close enough to enemy encampments to be able to count the cannon. By noon he was at Mercersburg, more than halfway to the designated railroad bridge. According to John W. Thomason's biography of Stuart, the Mercersburgers had never seen Confederate cavalry before and refused to believe they had been invaded until several of the squadron stopped off to buy boots and paid in Confederate money. As Stuart's raiders went along, they cut telegraph wires and seized an occasional terrified traveler. (Needless to say, Stuart forbade his men to stop any ladies.) So well did they cover their tracks that McClellan soon had no idea where they were. At dusk in a downpour they reached Chambersburg and

Stuart decided to spend the night.

What happened that evening was set down by the local newspaper editor, Colonel A.K. McClure, on whom the rebel cavalry descended. The colonel had had the foresight to pour out all his liquor and empty two kegs of rye whiskey on the ground, but the invaders smoked his tobacco and drank up all his coffee and tea. Though they need not have done so, they paid for everything, and McClure wrote them down as "men of more than ordinary intelligence and culture," with a demeanor "in all respects eminently courteous." At 4 A.M. the bugle sounded and Stuart went out for the morning report. It was still raining hard, and he was worried about re-fording the swollen Potomac—if they were lucky enough to see it again. A demolition crew had gone out in the night to take down the railroad bridge, as Lee had commanded, but had been unable to budge it. Time was short. Stuart forbade any looting but as his column moved out at dawn, he ordered his rear guard to blow up the army depot and set fire to the railroad yards.

Then he rode eastward a few miles and turned southward into Maryland. Only one federal detachment managed to catch up with him, and he quickly repelled and outmaneuvered them. Miraculously, in the dawn of October 13, the whole column—bugles blaring—returned to camp at Dandridge plantation. They had failed to blow up the bridge but had gathered important intelligence. They also came with a herd of 1,200 captured horses, and some thirty hostages. The raid was an astonishing success, and most important, it had made McClellan look foolish in the eyes of his commander-in-chief.

The citizens of Chambersburg were quick to recoup. The *Pioneer,* outmoded and far too light to pull the heavy passenger trains now in wartime use, was nevertheless rescued from the wrecked machine shops and repaired, and put back into service. In 1871 it was overhauled once more and remained in regular use until 1890. Then it went into storage and in 1901, having taken on the patina of an antique, went on the exhibition circuit, ending up eventually at the Chicago World's Fair of 1933–34, then at the Franklin Institute in Philadelphia, and finally where it is now—one of the unique and beguiling relics in the Railroad Hall. Jeb Stuart, fire-eating Southerner that he was, would surely not have minded that he failed to destroy this Yankee appliance, which is now linked in history with his name.

He did not survive the war. After Chambersburg, he and his men fought gallantly at Fredericksburg and at Chancellorsville, the terrible battle where Stonewall Jackson was wounded to death, and at Gettysburg. On May 11, 1864, battling to hold back General Sheridan's advance down the Shenandoah Valley, Stuart sent a cheerful dispatch to headquarters:

> The enemy is marching on at Yellow Tavern, the head of the turnpike, six miles from Richmond. My men and horses are tired, hungry, and jaded, but all right.

That afternoon at Yellow Tavern, in the front of the line as always, harrying the regiments of Michigan with saber and pistol, Stuart was wounded in the abdomen by a bullet from a Colt revolver. As he was taken off the field in a horse-drawn ambulance under heavy fire, he saw that his leaderless men had begun to panic and turn tail. So he called out as loudly as he could—he was still wearing his yellow sash—"Go back! I had rather die than be whipped." His troopers rallied for him and beat back the bluecoats, at least for that day. The ambulance took Stuart to Richmond, and a mournful crowd gathered outside the house where he lay. Jefferson Davis came to the deathbed; gunfire rattled the windows while the two of them talked. The next day the bearded warrior died—he was just past his thirty-first birthday.

By 1864 Robert E. Lee was wearily practiced in battlefield eloquence on behalf of his fallen lieutenants. He never failed to produce some nobly phrased eulogy. But when they brought him the news about Jeb Stuart, all he could manage were eight words: "I can scarcely think of him without weeping."

The 1401, above *and in detail* overleaf, *is one of the most magnificent of American steam locomotives. It is a PS 4 Pacific—a twelve-wheel passenger engine capable of hauling fourteen steel passenger cars, or about 800 tons, at a speed of eighty miles per hour. This one was manufactured in 1926 for the Southern Railway and saw service mainly in the Carolinas. Wishing to distinguish his engines from run-of-the-mill black ones, the president of the Southern, Fairfax Harrison, selected the "livery"—bright green with gold trim. The 1401 was one of ten locomotives that pulled the funeral train of Franklin D. Roosevelt from Warm Springs, Georgia, to Washington, D.C., in April, 1945. In 1951, as the age of steam came to its close, the 1401, an aristocrat of railroading, was taken out of service.*

OUR TIMES

The self-service restaurant had its American beginnings in Philadelphia in 1902, when Joseph V.
Horn and Frank Hardart, Sr., installed the first
automat. They had bought the installation in Germany, where the idea originated. The decorative
framework from that first "waiterless" restaurant
is here combined with a later vending device. The
automat became immensely popular, particularly
in New York City. The food was cheap and good,
and patrons could sit talking for an hour over a
nickel cup of coffee. And the gadgetry—put the
money in the slot and turn the knob—appealed
to almost everybody. The automat was wonderfully modern, quintessentially urban, and available to all.

The New Kitchen

To call this pleasant, old-fashioned "Italian-American" room a modern kitchen would surely sound eccentric to most readers. It is more an exercise in nostalgia—grandmother's kitchen as we remember it. And it also stands as an emblem of the way immigrant groups embraced American living standards, for this was the kitchen of an immigrant Italian family, as small details (the clusters of onions and garlic, the oil cruet) show. And yet with all its virtues as a period piece, it bears ample evidence of rapidly encroaching technology. All the signs are there.

Unlike the large colonial kitchens pictured elsewhere in this book, the room is divided into logical work "areas"—places to cook, eat, store, and prepare. Instead of an open hearth, there is a gas range (not visible here). On the door is an ice company card, and somewhere in the room there is an icebox with a drip pan—not anything to delight a contemporary kitchen designer but an impressive advance for its day. The Hoosier cabinet against the wall is a rational if limited solution to the problem of storing kitchen staples close to the place where they will be measured and mixed. And finally, there is the most modern kitchen appliance of all—the telephone, which both simplifies work and keeps any at all from being done. Today its ubiquitous presence has turned many kitchens into part-time offices, where a desk, pencil pot, an in-basket, and a filing cabinet are decidedly not out of place.

The kitchens of the 1920s are a far cry from the futuristic workspaces of the 1980s, with continuous hard-surface counters, a battery of under-counter appliances, precisely organized storage cabinets and pantries, a microwave oven in the wall, and possibly even a computer. Nevertheless, the 1920s are closer to the space age than to the eighteenth century. Perhaps no technological advance has altered women's lives more fundamentally than the design of the modern kitchen. Until recently, preparing and preserving food was a year-round, full-time job for as many women as a given household could provide (not only because of primitive conditions at home but also in the field and the marketplace). Now on an average weekday in most households the kitchen stands empty and silent except for a few hours a day around mealtimes.

For thousands of years, the kitchen was the scene of endless and usually dangerous work. Its distinguishing feature was an open hearth. In modest homes with only one chimney and one hearth, the kitchen might be the only room. In larger houses the kitchen, because of its heat and strong smells, might be attached to the back of the main house in a kind of lean-to, or even set up away from the main house in an outbuilding. (The kitchen at Mount Vernon is a famous example of the latter arrangement.)

In any case, no one at this time gave much thought to improving kitchens. There were no clean, flat counters on either side of the sink, no running water, and except for the cellar or the well, no refrigeration. The number and kinds of cookpots and other utensils were limited. In summer the fire was murderously hot and hardly more bearable in winter. Keeping it stoked up to just the right temperature, raking the glowing coals under the three-legged skillets, making sure that quickbreads were not scorching in the Dutch ovens were tasks requiring agility and skill. Skirts, sleeves, and small children were in constant danger of catching fire. Scaldings were a regular occurrence. To cook breakfast and dinner for a crew of ten farmhands in even a well-equipped kitchen might take four women from dawn until mid-afternoon. To modern eyes the classic colonial kitchen is romantically beautiful, bringing a catch to our throats in a way that formica and stainless steel could never do. But to the women managing those kitchens the open fireplace must have sometimes seemed a fiery furnace, and the kitchen a prison.

One of the first to perceive that kitchen drudgery had a direct connection with economic and moral issues was the American reformer

Catherine Beecher. The daughter of a famous New England family, Miss Beecher devoted her life to the cause of female education. In 1869, she and her celebrated sister, Harriet Beecher Stowe, published *The American Woman's Home,* "a guide to the formation and maintenance of economical, healthful, beautiful, and Christian homes." Like *Uncle Tom's Cabin,* the mission of this book was to stir people up. The American housewife, it implied, was not much better off than Uncle Tom. The book maintains that "the honor and duties of the family state are not duly appreciated," and avers that "family labor is poorly done, poorly paid, and regarded as menial and disgraceful." The result was that the housewife and her family—hence American society—suffered.

One way to set matters right was to reform the kitchen—to make it clean, workable, and convenient: to save steps for the women working there. Miss Beecher and Mrs. Stowe knew very well that these women were hardly likely to be hired cooks and scullery maids. For even in 1869 Americans had a servant problem. Nobody wanted to be a servant. "Every human being stands (according to the Declaration of Independence) on the same level," the sisters wrote. "All are to be free to rise and fall as the waves of the sea. . . ." Stranger still, most Americans disliked having hired help around the house. "Every mistress of a family knows that her cares increase with every additional servant." There was not, nor would there ever be, a genuine servant class in the United States the way there was in Europe. American families had to learn to care for themselves.

This was no piece of feminist radicalism. Catherine Beecher, in particular, shrank from the notion of woman's suffrage (she was also opposed to abolition, ice cream, and cold drinks). Woman's place was in the home, she thought, but that was no reason for a kitchen to be medieval. "In most large houses," she wrote, "the table furniture, the cooking materials and utensils, the sink, and the eating room are at such distances apart, that half the time and strength is employed in walking back and forth to collect and return the articles used." One of her line drawings showed exactly what was needed—shelving on every wall, a sink with a dish drainer and a pump nearby, under-counter bins for flour, meal, and sugar, convenient storage under the sink for clean towels and soap. She got the idea for her kitchen from looking at a ship's galley. "The cook's galley in a steamship has every article and utensil used in cooking for two hundred persons, in a space not larger than this stove room, and so arranged that with one or two steps the cook can reach all he uses."

Her basic principle was efficiency, her goal to lighten the load of the cook and increase her comfort. Every implement is stored near where it will be used. To cut down on bad smells and keep the temperatures from reaching inhuman levels, the wood-burning cookstove was to be in its own small but adequately ventilated room, separated by sliding doors from the main kitchen. Although technology has long ago outstripped even Miss Beecher's imagination, she would recognize her logic in any modern kitchen today and could probably cook a meal in one.

According to Sigfried Giedion, the historian of technology, what Catherine Beecher did was to organize the work process itself. She had few tools at her disposal—not even running water or ice for the kitchen. True mechanization would be many years in following. But part of the process was conceptual, and that was her forte. As the Italian-American kitchen shows, it was hard to get away from the idea of furnishing the kitchen with a dozen separate pieces and instead to conceive it as an integral unit, with the sink and range as part of the counter surfaces and the storage areas built smoothly into the walls and under the counters. In the 1920s European architects—Mies van der Rohe, Walter Gropius, J.J.P. Oud, and Le Corbusier—took the lead in this movement for rationalizing home kitchen design. Probably few of them acknowledged an American woman as their predecessor.

Another enormous step—this one mechanical —was the elimination first of the hearth and then of the wood-burning or coal-burning stove. Fearing explosions, people were slow to accept gas heating appliances of any kind. Gas cookstoves had been patented in England as early as the 1850s, but only in the 1890s did the American public begin to lay aside its suspicions and to buy gas cooking ranges in quantity. By the 1930s, when gas cooking had at last been fully accepted, electricity began to be a rival. By the late 1930s mechanical refrigeration had become commonplace. A freezing machine had been displayed in London as early as 1862, and the first practical electric refrigerator was manufactured in the United States by Kelvinator in 1916. Soon afterward the Frigidaire and the Servel (gas-powered) came on the market; yet by the mid-1920s only about 20,000 households had refrigerators. By 1936 that number had increased to two million. In the years since, refrigerator "styling," if not technology, has evolved markedly in each decade. No appliance dates a kitchen so definitely as the refrigerator.

And there were other innovations besides the concepts and the gadgets. As Russell Lynes has shown in *The Domesticated Americans:*

> The most humane contribution that the nineteenth century made to the kitchen, and the most unsung, was window screening. Compared with its contribution to comfort, to sanitation, to the preservation of sanity and good temper, the gas range, the electric range, the refrigerator, and the freezer pale into nothing. Flies were a far worse trial to the housewife of the last century than the pump in the kitchen sink or the scuttle that needed filling with coal. The literature of the nineteenth century household is filled with them.

The modern kitchen was by no means an exclusively American invention. Many of the basic appliances came from England, France, or Germany. Nevertheless, the great momentum and motivation was always here. There were a hundred reasons for this: the scarcity of servants, a factor reckoned with by Catherine Beecher; the pressure on the servantless housewife to do many things besides kitchen work; the steady—if muted and even unvoiced—conviction of some women in each generation that the principles laid down in the Declaration of Independence applied to them, too; and finally the fact that "modernizing" very quickly turned into a self-perpetuating and lucrative industry in itself. The kitchen was not the only part of the home that underwent a revolution because of women's demands. But the revolution began at the hearth.

As if she knew that her notions might eventually let loose forces of which no right-thinking person could approve, Catherine Beecher appended an "appeal," authored by her and not her sister, to *The American Woman's Home.* In it she inveighed against improper ventilation, free love, the sewing machine, women working in factories, women going into politics, "the baneful influence of spiritualism," the suffrage movement, and other "malign influences" sapping the "foundations of the family state." Though historians of the women's movement usually mention her respectfully, she would have loathed being regarded as a "liberator" of women. But in spite of herself she was. Like many another reformer she mounted a frontal assault on one apparently mundane and clear-cut problem and ended up altering the basal metabolism of American life.

Opposite: *The upwardly mobile, second-generation immigrant family of the Wilsonian era could scarcely have a more telling monument than this 1915 dining room from the Bensonhurst section of Brooklyn, New York. In those days Brooklyn was largely suburban, a place where working-class and middle-class families moved in order to escape Manhattan's tenements. The oak furniture, vaguely "Tudor" in design, the china, glass, silver, and bric-a-brac are all mass-produced and were, in their day, inexpensive. All together, they reflect American taste of the time—and the fulfillment of a generation's dreams.*

To own a house was the goal of nearly every immigrant family, indeed of nearly every American. This living room with its lace curtains, antimacassar on the sofa back, hat rack, and comfortable rocker would have looked like home to almost anybody in about 1925. But the newspaper and the keepsakes on the table reflect the Italian origins of the family that lived here.

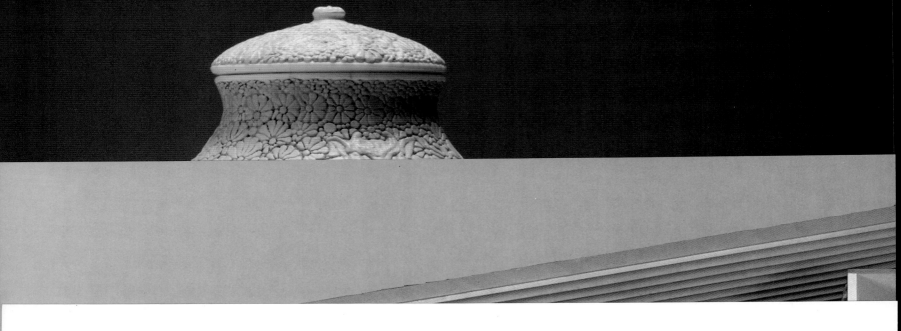

Preceding pages: *This doll house, created in the early 1900s by Faith Bradford, has the artistry of the best novels of that period: it is an intricate, self-contained world with a strong story line. Mr. and Mrs. Peter Doll—lively, cultivated, devoted—and their ten children live in the house with servants and a menagerie of pets. Their commodious rooms include a laundry, butler's pantry, kitchen, drawing room, library, study, parlor, and various bedrooms, guest rooms, and bathrooms. Miss Bradford acquired or made the furnishings to suit the family's needs (everything from Oriental rugs to spoonholders and goldfish bowls). There is even an attic (top left) with, as she wrote, "inherited treasures such as the hooded cradle. . . . Also there are some articles that are in need of mending, and they may get it, someday."*

Above: *Children's toys often reflect the technology of the grown-up world. The horse-drawn coal wagon at top was superseded by the motorized version below it. At center Happy Hooligan, an early comic-strip character, obviously in need of a better form of transportation, has been dumped out of his donkey-drawn cart. The miniature taxi is from an era when people wore hats: the high roof permitted them to do so. The tank truck on its side is copied from an oil truck.*

Above: *The "City Transfer Co." delivery truck or moving van, at top left, is made of cast iron and tin with a lithographed paper side panel. The horses are cast iron. The iron truck, top right, is also for heavy moving. The horse-drawn log carrier was once a familiar sight on country roads, as it carried its cargo out of the woods. A cast-iron racing car lies on its side, while a gentleman in a light gig spins away from the scene. The toys on both pages are early twentieth century.*

American Folk Art: The Pleasures of Excellence

F olk art, as collectibles, hardly existed here before the 1920s. Yet the creations of ordinary people (housewives stitching quilts, itinerant sign-painters, metalsmiths fashioning tools—to cite only three examples) have exhibited extraordinary richness and variety in America, often as a consequence of the traditional skills that immigrants brought with them from Europe and Africa. Perhaps nowhere is this artistry more plainly visible than in American woodcarving. From the time of Plymouth and Jamestown, newcomers to these shores were astonished by the limitless woods. Wood was everywhere, and mostly free. It provided the roof and walls and table and chair. It fueled the fireplace. It was the raw material for a thousand things: religious images, ships' figureheads, shop signs, decoys, furniture, household ornaments, and tools.

The examples of American folk art in this section are not of great antiquity—none much more than a century old. All were made with some apparently practical or commercial purpose in view, but one can sense in them a pride in technique and a pleasure in excellence that mark their creators as artists, untrained though some of them may have been.

Far left: *This hollow-form eagle weathervane was crafted from copper and zinc (beaten on an iron plate, which was itself cast from a wooden pattern) in the last quarter of the nineteenth century.* Center and near left: *Two fine nineteenth-century carved eagles.*

Among the most appealing and numerous of American folk sculptures are trade signs and shop figures. As cities grew and towns sprang up during the nineteenth century, the art naturally flourished. Above, left to right: Three such sculptures made in the 1880s: a mustachioed soldier (perhaps for a uniform shop or tailor) with a French dress hat, tight, striped trousers, short boots, and a hook nose; a fashionably dressed woman holding a fan (she surely belonged to a dressmaker or milliner); and a rare Santa Claus—a toy shop sign. He wears an ermine cloak and a backpack and originally— in his outstretched left hand—held a couple of switches.

Opposite: *The most famous of all American shop figures are tobacco-store Indians. They originated not here but in England during the reign of James I (who loathed tobacco in any form). The first English tobacco shops advertised their wares with carvings of Indians dressed in tobacco-leaf skirts, and the motif crossed the ocean. By the mid- nineteenth century, American cigar-store Indians were so widespread as to constitute an industry rather than a folk art. Both those here are hand- carved. The one at left, with curving feather head- dress, tunic, and curled collar, may come from central Pennsylvania. The noble native at right, holding a pipe and wearing a wampum necklace, is meant to be a distinguished chieftain. An eagle adorns his head; feathered ornaments carved of wood are on his arms and legs, more fantasy than historical fact.*

Opposite: *This splendid steed of painted wood, with floral carving along the neckline and a curly mane to serve as a handgrip for the rider, was carved between 1912 and 1916. By the late nineteenth century, the mechanical carousel, which was, at its best, an elaborate and fantastic work of whirling sculpture, was a common feature at country fairs, carnivals, and the seaside. A few of the craftsmen who made carousel figures were trained sculptors—and hence not "folk artists" in the strict sense—but others were simply talented woodcarvers.*

Right: *A trumpeting angel carved in the late nineteenth century served as a decoration on a carousel, or perhaps an amusement park proscenium.*

This orderly office, re-created as it was in the early years of this century, might have belonged to a marine underwriter; and though desks and ledgers may seem, at first glance, irrelevant to seafaring, marine underwriters have been a benevolent force in American shipping. Since before the American Revolution, they have exerted significant efforts to reduce perils to life and property. During the nineteenth century they helped prompt tighter safety regulations and often were involved personally as well as financially in rescue and salvage operations. Today, they continue their longstanding function of compensating for losses that sometimes occur in marine enterprise.

MARINE DISASTER BOOK 91

MARINE DISASTER BOOK 92

A ship's radio room of the early 1920s. This one is equipped with (from left) a medium-wave receiver, earphones, an Oliver typewriter, a Seth Thomas chronometer, and a 500-watt quench-gap spark transmitter. Messages were sent in Morse Code, using the key which can be seen behind the earphones.

A tattoo parlor used to be as inevitable a fixture of a port city as a tavern, for by the early twentieth-century tattoos—ships under full sail, serpents, the names of sweethearts—had come to be the favorite body ornament of the American seaman. Behind the manikin in this typically furnished parlor is a shelf with tattooing equipment and a selection of designs. The tattooer used an electric needle to puncture the skin and inject the colored inks. American and European sailors may have brought the practice back from Polynesia (the word itself is the Tahitian Tattau*) or from New Zealand or Japan. Over the centuries the Maoris and the Japanese had made tattooing virtually an art form. Americans have not been inclined to regard it as such although tattoos occasionally acquire a certain chic at society's upper levels. An indelible mark on one's skin has usually, however, been an emblem of the poor man—the sailor, the drifter, the working man, the miner. The tattoo kit in this parlor, in fact, comes from a mining camp in Arizona.*

Smithsonian Stamps: A National Treasure

Above: *This 24-cent airmail stamp—with its biplane upside down—is one of the great philatelic rarities of modern times. The first regularly scheduled airmail flight, on a "Jenny" biplane, no. 38262, took place on May 15, 1918, and of course the Post Office had to issue a new stamp. On the press run a sheet somehow got inverted, and on May 14, quite by mistake, a window clerk in Washington, D.C., sold the sheet of the stamps to William T. Robey, a stamp collector and obviously a man who could think on his feet: in spite of all entreaties, he refused to return the sheet. A week later he sold it for $15,000. These stamps still occasionally appear on the market in singles, pairs, and blocks.*

Left: *A pleasant relic from the days before zip codes, computers, and the 10¢ postcard, this post office from Dillsburg, Pennsylvania, as it looked about 1913, has prefabricated sorting racks and lobby sections.*

Essex, ss. **GEORGE** the Second, by the Grace of GOD, of *Great Britain,* *France* and *Ireland,* KING, Defender of the Faith, &c.

To the Sheriff of Our County of *Essex*   his Under-Sheriff or Deputy, Greeting:

WE Command you to Attach the Goods or Estate of *Jose Briant of Salisbury* in our said county of Essex Blacksmith

to the Value of *Six* Pounds, and for want thereof to take the Body of the said *Jose Briant,* (if *he* may be found in your Precinct) and *him* safely keep, so that you have *him* before Our Justices of Our Inferiour Court of Common Pleas next to be holden at *Salem* within and for Our said County of *Essex,* on the *Second* Tuesday of *July* next: Then and there in Our said Court to Answer unto

Stephen Coffin of the same Salisbury Inholder

In a plea of the case For that whereas the said Jose at Salisbury aforesaid on the ninth Day of January anno Domini 1755 by his promisary note of that Date for value received promised the said Stephen to pay him Two Pounds seven shillings and Ten pence lawfull money in one month from the Date of said note yet tho' a month is past the said Jose tho' often requested has not paid the same but denies to pay it

To the Damage of the said *Stephen Coffin as he says* the Sum of *Six* Pounds, which shall then and there be made to Appear, with other due Damages: And have you there this Writ, with your Doings therein. Witness *Thomas Berry* Esq; at Salem, the *First* Day of *May* in the *Twenty Eighth* Year of Our Reign. Annoque Domini, 1755.

Joseph Bowditch Cler

The Smithsonian's National Philatelic Collections have grown through gifts and acquisitions to some fourteen million stamps, covers, essays and proofs. The emphasis is on American postal memorabilia, but the collection also includes important foreign items such as the first adhesive stamp (an 1840 British issue with a portrait of Queen Victoria), a 1381 French letter on parchment, and microfilmed letters carried by pigeons during the 1870–71 siege of Paris in the Franco-Prussian War. Among the vast Americana in the collection are McKinley postcards issued after his assassination and hastily withdrawn because his widow objected to the portrait; a mailbox swept away in the Johnstown Flood; envelopes carried by plane, steamer, bicycle, and balloon; rare printing errors and important firsts in U.S. postal history.

Opposite: *Affixed to the upper left hand corner of this 1755 writ, ordering a sheriff to seize a blacksmith's property for nonpayment of a debt, is a three-pence embossed revenue stamp. The date of the writ, May 2, 1755, was the day on which these stamps were first used, making this the oldest "first day of issue" item in the Smithsonian's collection.*

Right: *The first adhesive stamp in the United States was issued in 1842 by a private company, City Despatch Post, with a portrait of Washington. The company offered its New York City customers the latest innovations in postal services; it was among the first to use street mailboxes and to deliver mail right to the doors of its customers' addressees.*

Opposite, far left: *The American postal system of the first half of the nineteenth century was a complex and recalcitrant creature. Some local postmasters issued their own stamps and envelopes—mailable only at the post office of issue. Once posted, they would go anywhere in the United States. The rate system was reformed in 1845 and two years later the first U.S. general postage stamps were issued for use all over the country—a five-cent stamp honoring Benjamin Franklin and a ten-cent one with a portrait of George Washington.*

Opposite: *Stamps with printing errors have long been a delight to collectors and an embarrassment to the Post Office. To publicize the 1901 Pan-American Exposition in Buffalo the Post Office issued five stamps with transportation themes—an undertaking that must have been jinxed. A small number of three denominations of the stamps, showing the Great Lakes steamer* City of Alpena *(top), a New York Central and Hudson River Railroad train (center), and one of the first electric automobiles (bottom), were printed with their vignettes upside down.*

Right: *In the 1850s the railroad was the fastest means of transporting mail, but postmasters were already looking to the sky in their quest for ever-speedier delivery. In 1859 the postmaster of Lafayette, Indiana, handed a packet of mail to balloonist John Wise, who had successfully flown the previous year from St. Louis to Henderson, New York. In the packet was this letter from Mary Wells, who expresses the tentative nature of the business: "Professor Wise . . . expects to land in Philadelphia or New York." This first officially sanctioned mailcarrying flight turned out to be a short one, as contrary winds dashed the pilot's and postmaster's hopes—the* Jupiter *had to land only thirty miles from its starting point.*

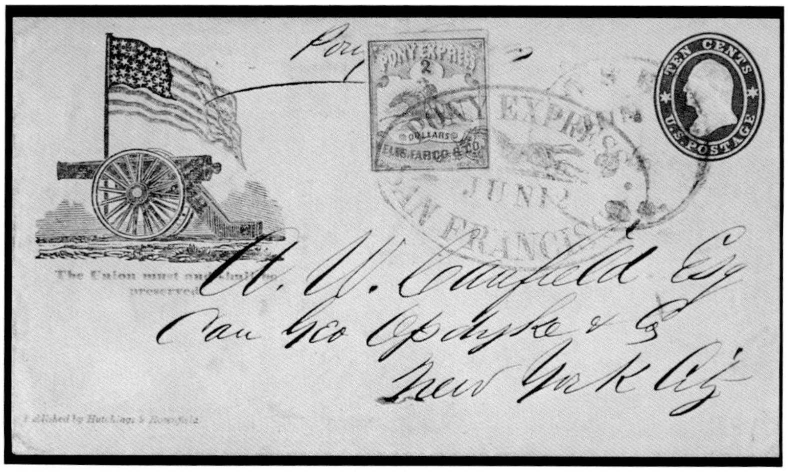
PONY EXPRESS
WELLS FARGO & CO
TEN CENTS
U.S. POSTAGE

PONY EXPRESS
DOLLARS
WELLS FARGO & CO
TEN CENTS
U.S. POSTAGE

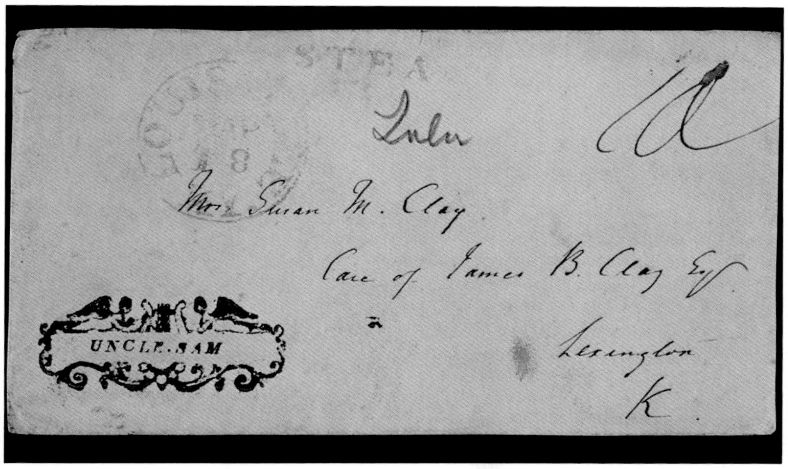
UNCLE SAM

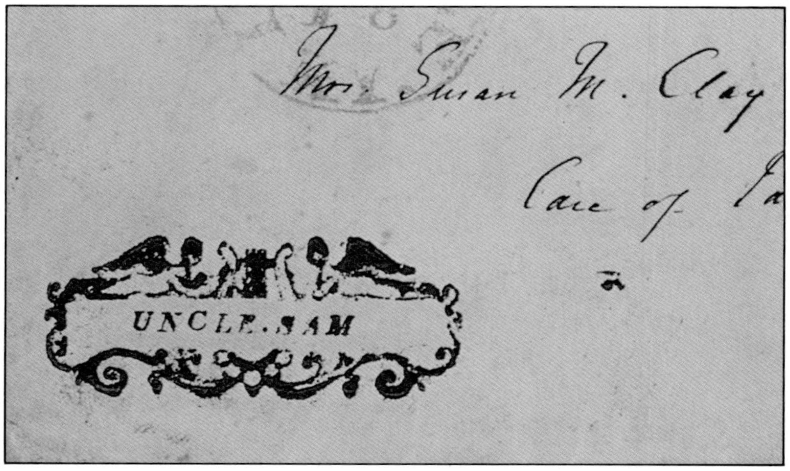
UNCLE SAM

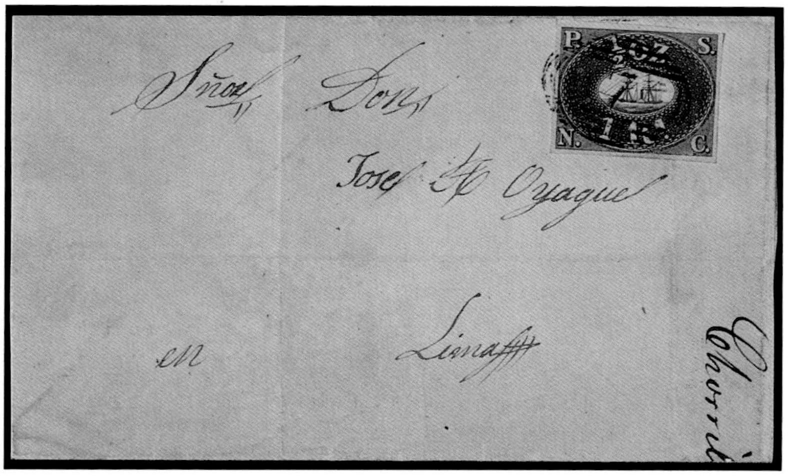
P. S.
N. C.

P. S.
N. C.

Opposite, top: *Wells Fargo & Company operated the famed Pony Express service for sixteen months in 1860 and 1861, when the new transcontinental telegraph put it out of business. The riders carried mail between San Francisco and St. Joseph, Missouri, where letters bound for points east were handed over to the U.S. Post Office. Hence this envelope, with a New York address, bears both a two-dollar Pony Express stamp and a ten-cent U.S. embossed stamp.*

Opposite, center: *Addressed by Henry Clay to a relative, this letter was carried by the steamboat* Uncle Sam *some time in the 1840s.*

Opposite, bottom: *One of the rarities in the Smithsonian's collection is this 1858 Peruvian letter, bearing the stamp of the Pacific Steam Navigation Company. That firm received a charter to carry British mail along the Pacific coast of South America and issued stamps that were later used by the Peruvian post office. This cancelled cover is one of only ten known.*

Right: *In 1863 the Louisiana Relief Committee sent twelve circulars to Douglas Hamilton in Mississippi and paid the postage with twelve two-cent Confederate stamps portraying Andrew Jackson. This cover bears the largest known block of these two-cent stamps.*

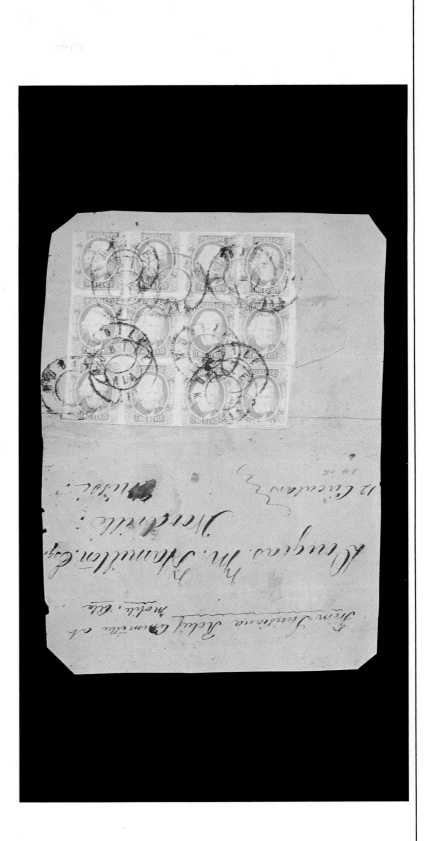

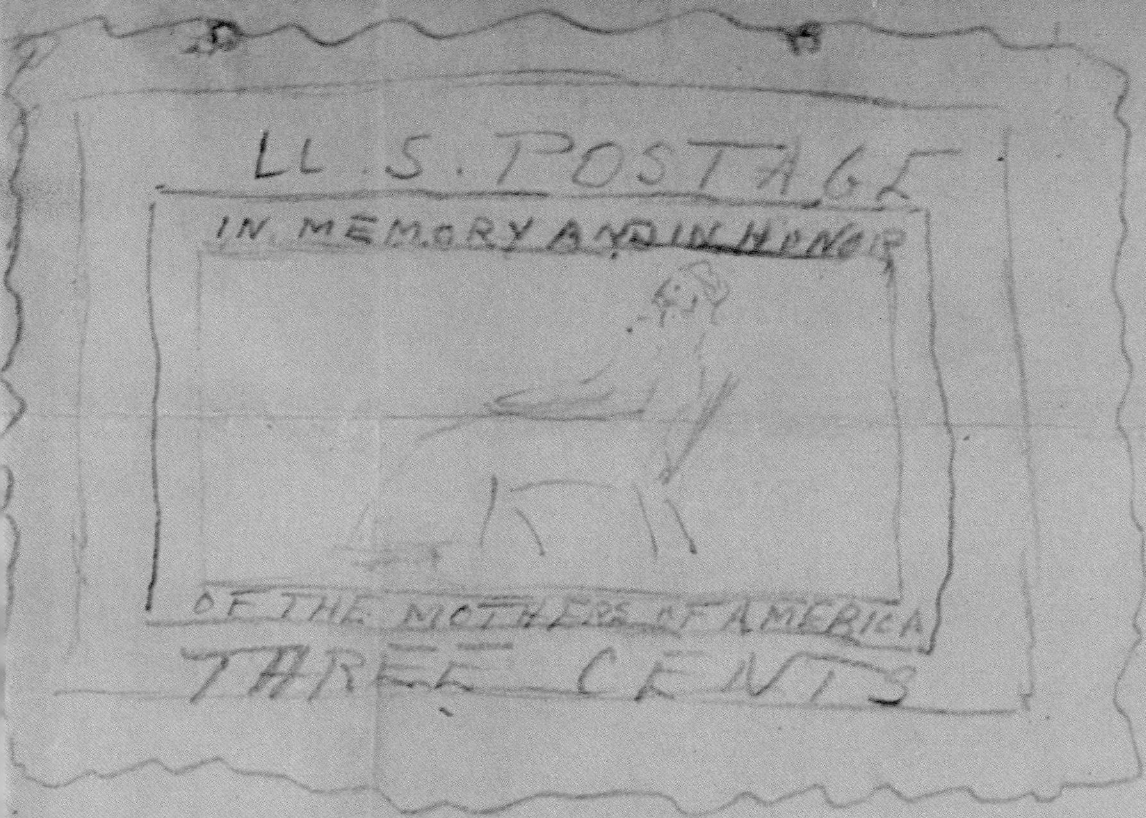

LL. S. POSTAGE

IN MEMORY AND IN HONOR

OF THE MOTHERS OF AMERICA

THREE CENTS

U.S. Postage
IN MEMORY
AND IN HONOR
OF THE MOTHERS
OF AMERICA
THREE
CENTS

For Jim Farley — "
The Original Design of the
Mothers Day Stamp
by Franklin D Roosevelt

2/16/34 FDR

Opposite: *Where motherhood and stamp collecting are concerned, the wheels of government move quickly. In January, 1934, President Franklin Roosevelt was visited by a Kansas City matron who urged that the Post Office issue a stamp honoring mothers. The President, who was reportedly devoted to his mother and well known as an avid philatelist, designed the stamp himself before a month had passed. He decided that a reproduction of "Whistler's Mother" would be an appropriate tribute. Roosevelt transmitted this original sketch to James Farley, his Postmaster General, in February, 1934.*

Right: *Airmail letters flown and autographed by the pioneer aviators Amelia Earhart (top) and Charles Lindbergh (bottom).*

Smithsonian Coins: The Wealth of Nations

The Smithsonian's National Numismatic Collection of coins, paper money, and medals covers virtually the entire history of currency from the first seventh-century B.C. coins of Asia Minor to today's copper-nickel-clad quarters. The collection holds countless foreign rarities of which fifteenth- and sixteenth-century Japanese coins once given to President Grant, and an 1882 Russian three-ruble gold coin, of which only six were struck, are just random examples. The checkered history of American paper money is told in the Revolutionary War era notes that inspired the phrase "not worth a Continental"; in nineteenth-century "broken bank" notes issued by banks that all too frequently went broke; and in emergency money, called scrip, issued by towns and private organizations during the Great Depression. The Smithsonian's holdings also reflect the nation's passion for coin collecting: there are six thousand gold coins collected by Josiah K. Lilly, the pharmaceuticals manufacturer, and donated to the Smithsonian by his executors in 1967. Among the most recent donations is the Chase Manhattan Bank assemblage of moneys of the world, one of the best-known collections in the U.S.

Opposite: *Sometimes called "America's most beautiful coin," this 1907 $20 gold coin is a trial piece designed by the eminent sculptor Augustus Saint-Gaudens at the request of President Theodore Roosevelt. The sculptor's sumptuous design, with a flying eagle on the reverse and a robust, striding Liberty (see page 386) on the obverse, was altered by mint officials because its high relief prevented stacking and required too many strikings. A low-relief version of the coin was issued, and the disappointed president kept this trial piece as a memento.*

Above: *Until 1882 private citizens could legally issue their own coins—a right that was exploited to the fullest in California during the Gold Rush when gold was abundant but U.S. coinage scarce. Fifteen private mints operated in California, including one run by John Little Moffat in San Francisco from 1849 to 1853. Moffat issued both coins and ingots, including this $20 coin and $9.43 ingot, which is the only surviving Moffat ingot of that amount.*

Opposite, top: *In response to a demand for large-denomination gold coins, U.S. mint engraver George T. Morgan produced this sketch for a $100 coin, and his colleague, William Barber, designed and struck trial pieces for a $50 coin. Neither coin was produced for circulation.*

Opposite, bottom: *In the 1830s Christian Gobrecht, an engraver at the Philadelphia mint, designed a seated Liberty silver dollar based on a painting by Thomas Sully. The stages of his design process are represented here by two drawings on paper, one on transparent mica, a brass die, a lead test stamping, and a finished dollar.*

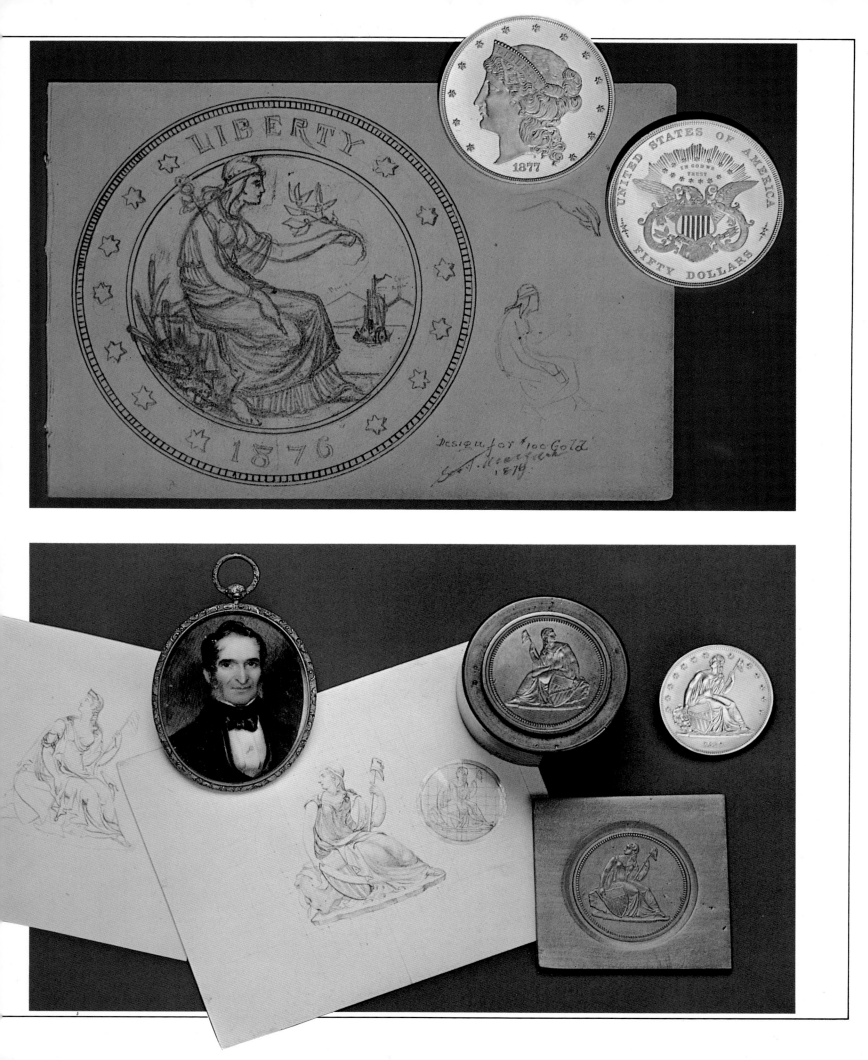

Left: *These two coins (shown in obverse and reverse) are dismes, precursors of the dime and pronounced the same way. The 1792 disme here was among the first patterns struck by the Philadelphia mint; only about a dozen survive today. The 1794 half disme shown here is unique.*

Opposite, top: *President Woodrow Wilson is portrayed on this 1934 $100,000 gold certificate—the largest denomination of U.S. paper money. Notes of this amount were used by Federal Reserve banks to make large-scale gold transactions.*

Opposite, bottom: *Aside from occasional brief issues of Treasury notes, the U.S. government did not issue paper money until 1861. In the first half of the nineteenth century, the issuing of paper money was left to private banks, creating a paradise for speculators and counterfeiters. When the expense of the Civil War began to drain the Treasury the government issued several kinds of notes, including this rare, interest-bearing 1864 Treasury note. Despite its age the note is still legal tender.*

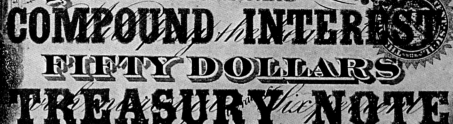

Opposite, top: *Among the foreign coins that circulated in the American colonies was this 1737 Spanish dollar (left), minted in Mexico. It is known as a "pillar dollar" after the Pillars of Hercules design on its reverse. On the right is Saint-Gaudens' 1907 $20 gold coin. This piece is an experimental striking.*

Opposite, bottom: *The figure of Liberty on this 1795 U.S. coin wears a Phrygian cap, a symbol of revolutionary causes. The history of the symbol goes back to Roman times, when ex-slaves wore this type of cap as a badge of their freedom.*

Right: *In 1787 New York jeweler Ephraim Brasher struck this gold doubloon and half doubloon—the first gold pieces struck in the United States. Probably proposals for New York State coinage, these pieces were never minted for circulation.*

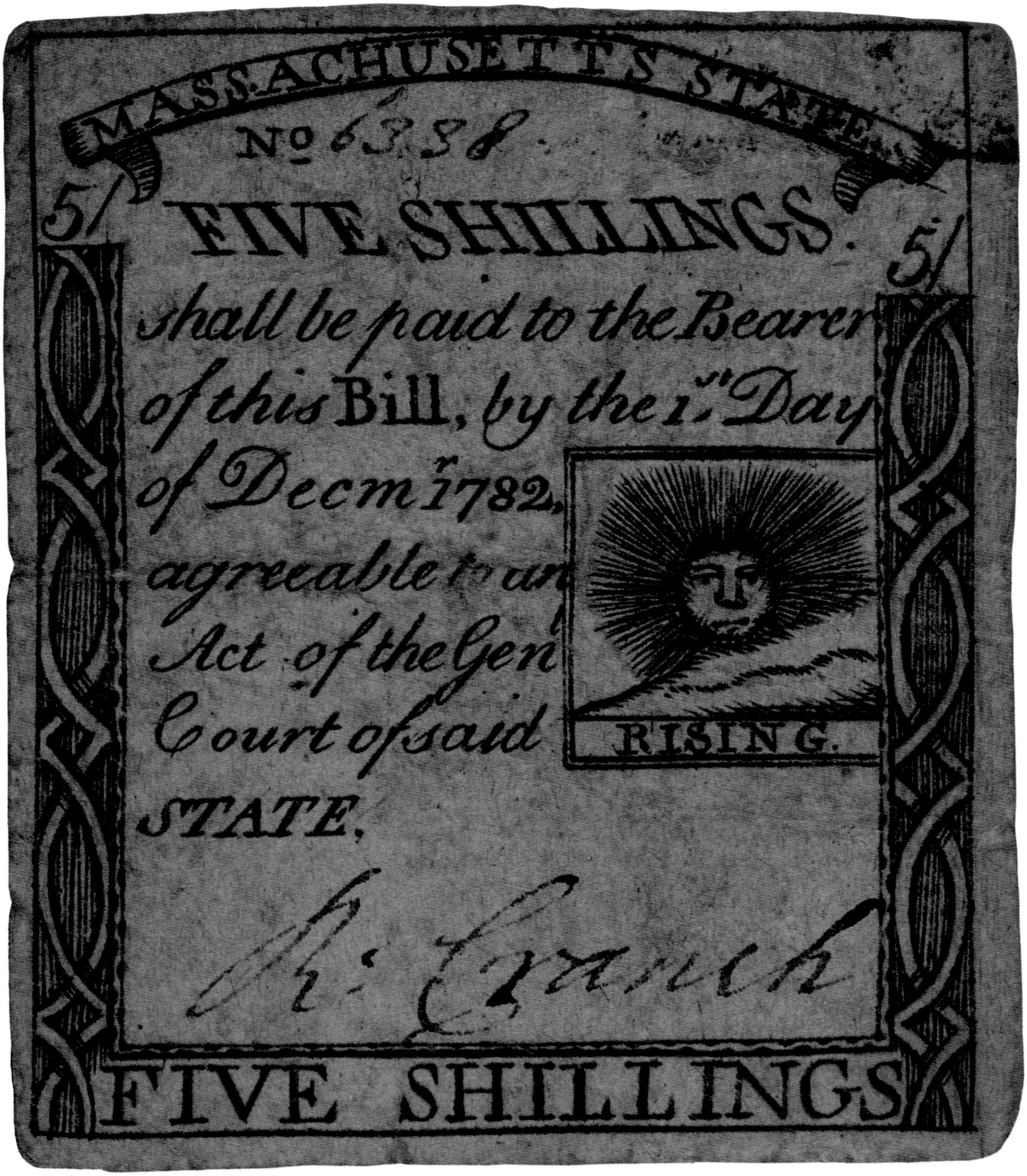

MASSACHUSETTS STATE

Nº 6338

FIVE SHILLINGS.

5/   5/

shall be paid to the Bearer
of this Bill, by the 1ˢᵗ Day
of Decmʳ 1782,
agreeable to an
Act of the Genˡ
Court of said
STATE,

RISING.

R. Cranch

FIVE SHILLINGS

Right: *Massachusetts became the first colony to issue paper money in 1690, when the colony had to raise funds to fight King William's War. This twenty-shilling note is part of that historic issue.*

Opposite: *This attractive 1782 Massachusetts note, with a rising sun vignette, was designed by Paul Revere.*

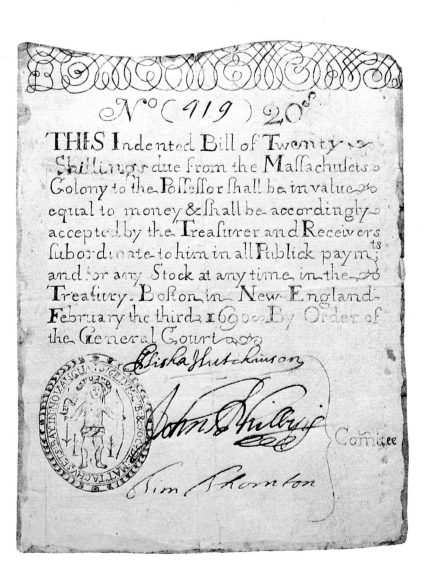

Measuring Time, Measuring Space

An industrializing nation cannot function without timepieces; a merchant marine needs chronometers and navigational aids. Inevitably, American inventors joined the historic quest for accurate, beautiful, and economical instruments to measure the turnings of the universe. Behind them, as they knew, lay a long tradition of craftsmanship— a tradition that the splendid collection of clockwork and navigational instruments at the Museum of American History amply reveals. One of the oldest calculating instruments is the astrolabe. A multipurpose instrument, it contains a two-dimensional map of the stars and can help the user tell where a given star can be found at a given date and time in the latitude for which the astrolabe is set. On the reverse side is a sighting bar and a scale to measure altitude: a simple way to determine the relationship of the heavens to the spot one stands on. The astrolabe was invented by the Arabs and was used to tell time, so that the faithful could be summoned to prayer.

Three Islamic astrolabes and, at right, a Persian Qibla indicator. The latter is a pocket instrument with a gazetteer of longitudes and latitudes from which the faithful could calculate the direction of Mecca, the direction they faced in prayer.

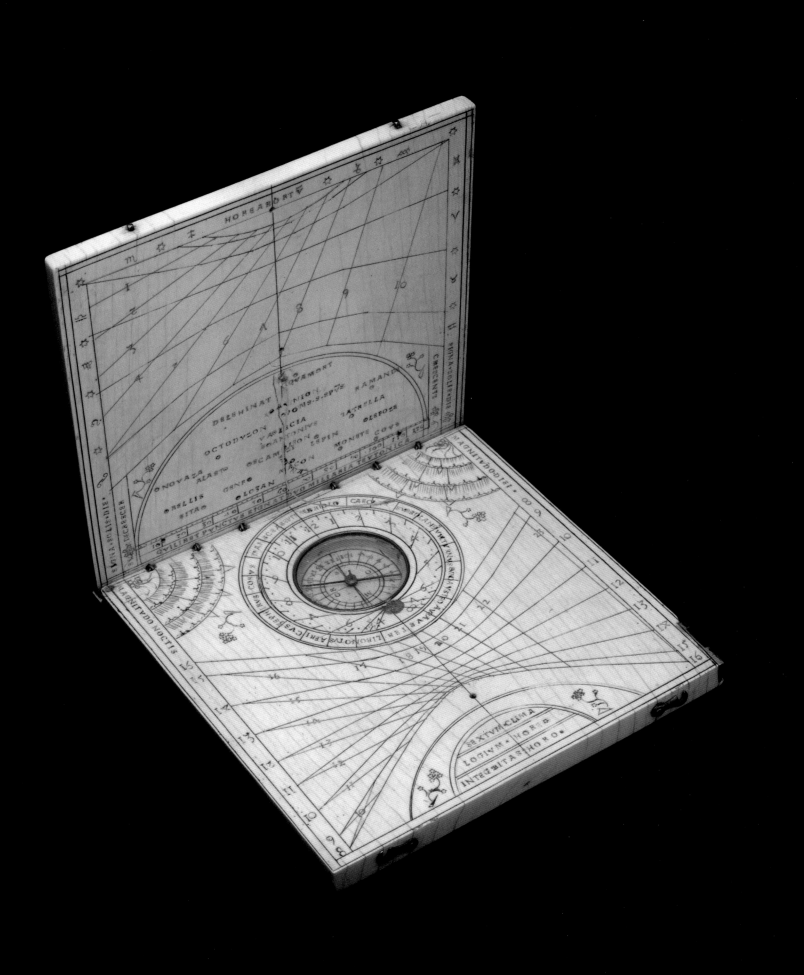

Above: *One of the most elegantly simple of all
calculators is the sector: two flat rules engraved
with a set of scales and hinged at one end. Used
with a pair of dividers, the sector can help solve
any problem concerning right angle triangles. Both
these sectors are brass, the larger one inscribed
"Thos. Harris & Son, British Museum, London,"
and was made in the early nineteenth century. The
smaller sector bears the signature of Nicholas Bion
of Paris, who probably made it in the early eighteenth century.*

Opposite: *One of the rarest of all sundials is this
ivory diptych or book-type dial with leaves hinged
to open at right angles. On the upper leaf is a
vertical dial; on the lower a compass is inset. The
instrument is dated 1518—the earliest ivory dial in
existence—and signed "L.S.," but the maker's
name and nationality are as yet unknown.*

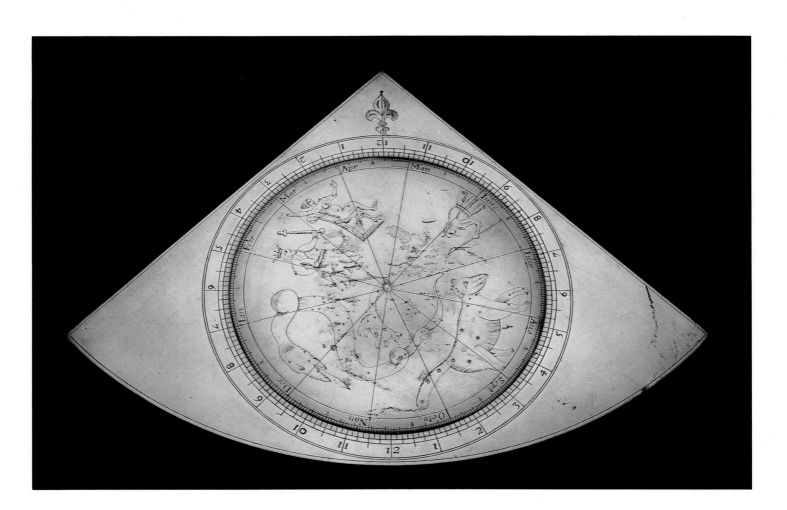

Above: *The quadrant, one of the early instruments for measuring altitude, is one-quarter of a circle. This brass one, made in 1657 and signed by Henry Sutton of London, is in fact a portable sundial. The user sighted along one radius and suspended a plumb line from the apex of the right angle. As he sighted upward, the plumb line would fall across the scale engraved on the reverse side and indicate the sun's altitude—and hence the time of day. The engravings on this side of the quadrant are the circumpolar constellations.*

Opposite: *A virtuoso example of the sundial-maker's art, this cube dial has a stylus placed on each side. It is signed "D. Beringer"—a dial maker of Nuremberg, Germany, who worked between 1728 and 1780.*

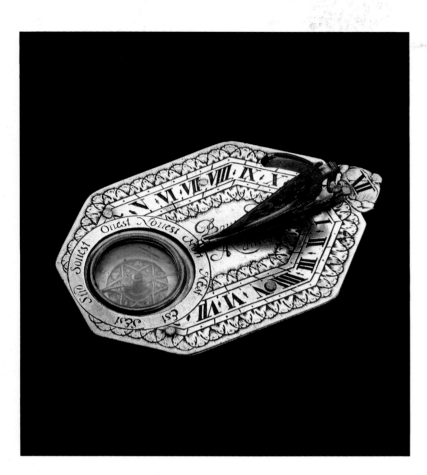

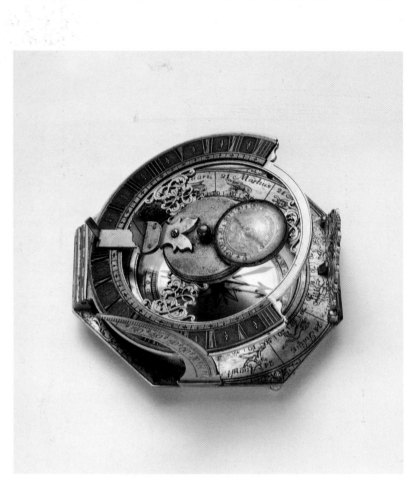

To travel without a timepiece is inconvenient, at best. This pocket-sized silver sundial was an eighteenth-century French aid to travelers. The dial is both portable and universal: the small octagonal plate is engraved with concentric hour scales for different latitudes and has a compass inset. The gnomon, or stylus, folds down for compactness and is adjustable according to latitude.

This instrument of 1557 which may have been the work of the famed Christoph Schissler of Augsburg, Germany, is really a multiplicity of instruments, in a single brass case. There is a map of central and western Europe and another of the world, a gazeteer, and a horizontal sundial with four scales for latitudes. "Compendia" of this kind and period are among the most beautiful instruments ever crafted; they usually served as expensive toys for princes and prelates.

Opposite: The passage of a few centuries can sometimes turn utilitarian objects into pure works of art, as these three exquisite pieces testify. At top left is a brass astrolabe made by Georg Hartmann of Nuremberg in the sixteenth century; at bottom left an English astrolabe, unsigned, of about 1325; and at center an astronomical compendium made of brass by Caspar Vopel of Cologne in 1541.

Above: *The art of making pocket watches did not originate in the United States, but the American contribution was to mechanize the process. Before that occurred, however, New England craftsmen worked in traditional ways. The watch at top left was made by Luther Goddard of Shrewsbury, Massachusetts, between 1807 and 1817. The Pitkin brothers of East Hartford, Connecticut, first applied factory methods; at upper right is one of their patent models. The watch at bottom, made in 1843, was an attempt to streamline without losing strength.*

Right: *This calm interior with its workbenches and tools replicates a nineteenth-century chronometer shop—that of William Cranch Bond of Boston, a celebrated maker of clocks and marine chronometers and, from 1839 to 1859, the first director of the Harvard College Observatory.*

Above: *One indispensable function of the National Museum of American History is to preserve the names of ingenious men and women that have been crowded out of the standard history books. One such is Henry Fitz of Newburyport, Massachusetts, the first successful commercial telescope maker in America—and hence a figure of importance in nineteenth-century astronomy. In his shop, above, as it looked in 1863, Fitz is at right; the female manikin represents an assistant.*

Left: *One of Henry Fitz's finest works was this thirteen-inch telescope made for the Vassar College Observatory, which opened in 1865. The instrument was used by Maria Mitchell, the director of the observatory and professor of astronomy at Vassar—one of the nation's first astronomers. In 1847, she discovered a comet, and was awarded a gold medal by the King of Denmark. She taught at Vassar from 1865 until 1889, the year of her death.*

Right: *Not quite so arduous as the building of the transcontinental railway nor so dangerous as Lindbergh's first trans-Atlantic flight, crossing the continent by automobile in 1903 was still nothing to be undertaken lightly. This Winton automobile was the first car to make the journey from San Francisco to New York City. The drivers were H. Nelson Jackson, who bought the car second-hand in San Francisco, and Sewell Crocker. They set out on May 23; on July 26, sixty-three days later, they reached New York. There were few roads and no gas stations or motels. The Winton wheels have wooden spokes, and the car body is wood. The two-cylinder, four-cycle engine is water cooled; each cylinder is fitted with a carburetor.*

Overleaf: *This low-slung wooden racing car, "Bullet No. 2," was built by Alexander Winton in 1903 for an Irish road race. Winton himself did the driving, but mechanical difficulties forced him out of the race. On January 8, 1904, at Daytona Beach, Florida, the celebrated racing driver, Barney Oldfield, drove this car at almost 84 miles an hour— a breakneck speed in those days. The Bullet has two four-cylinder in-line engines bolted together to form a straight eight.*

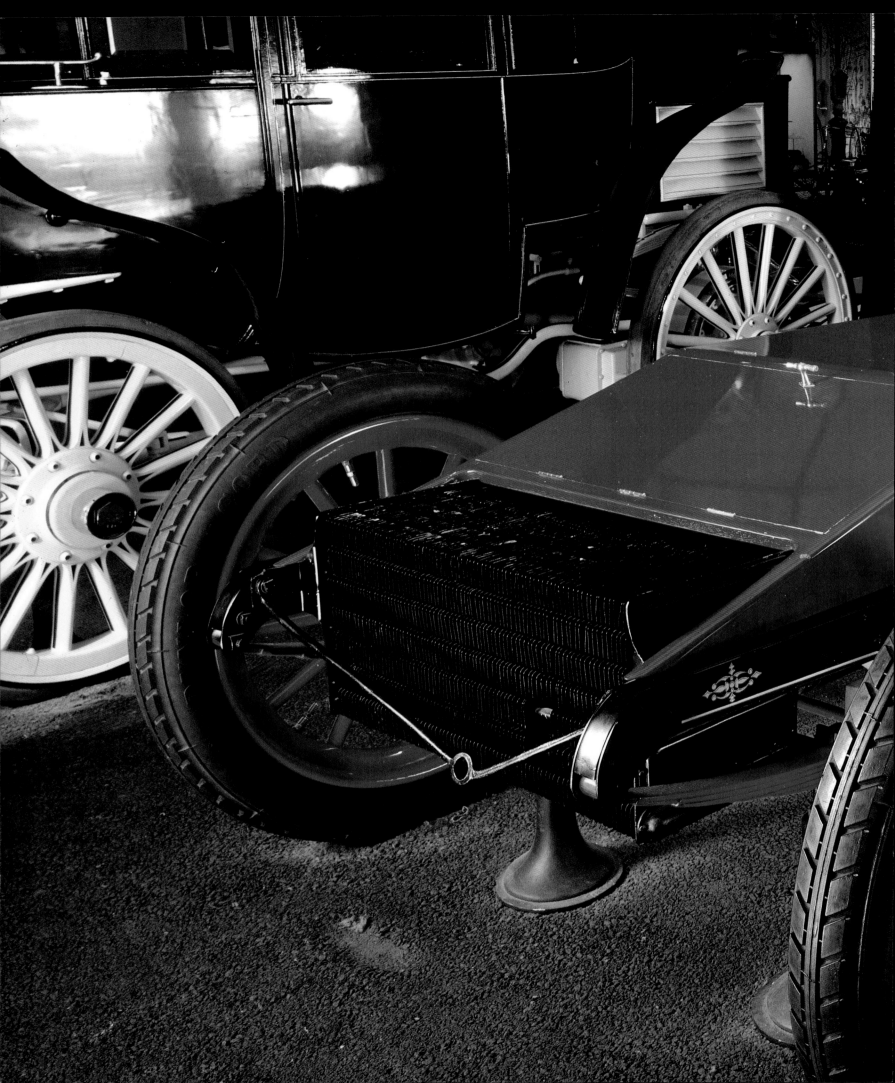

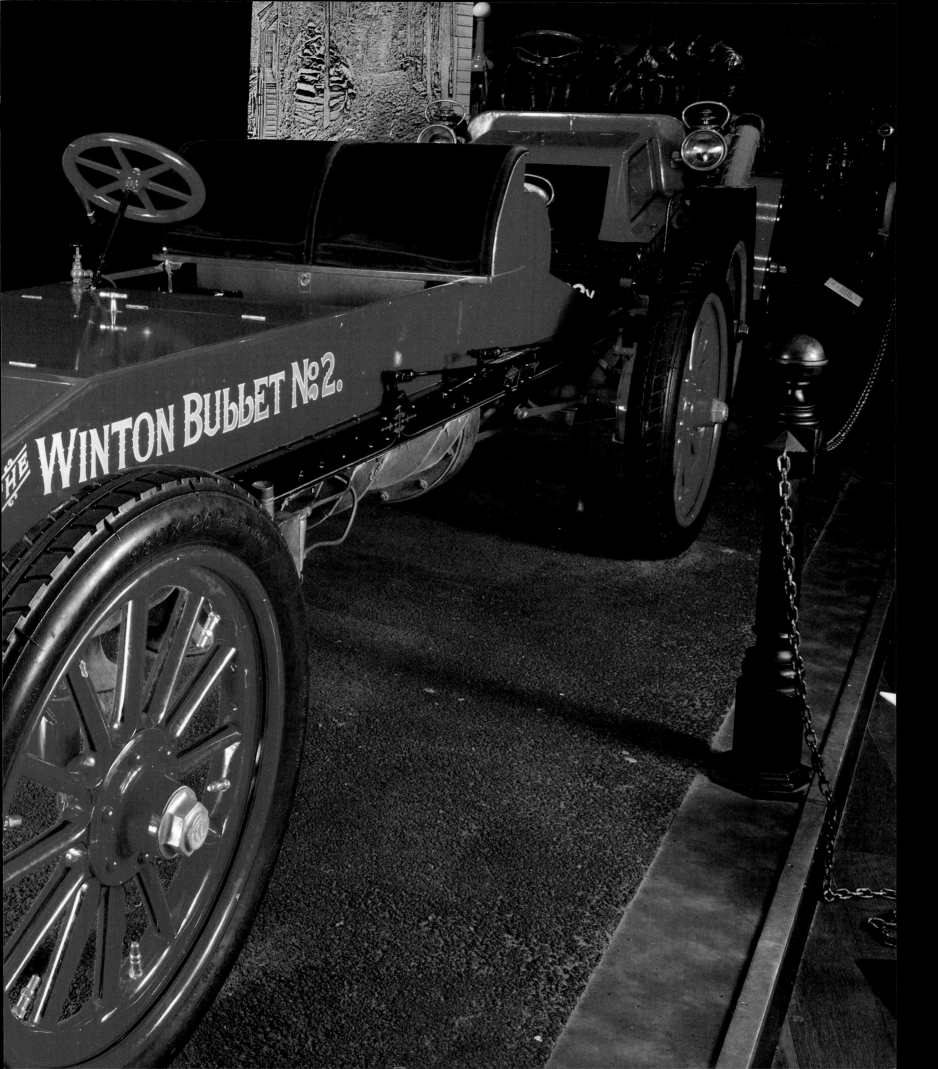

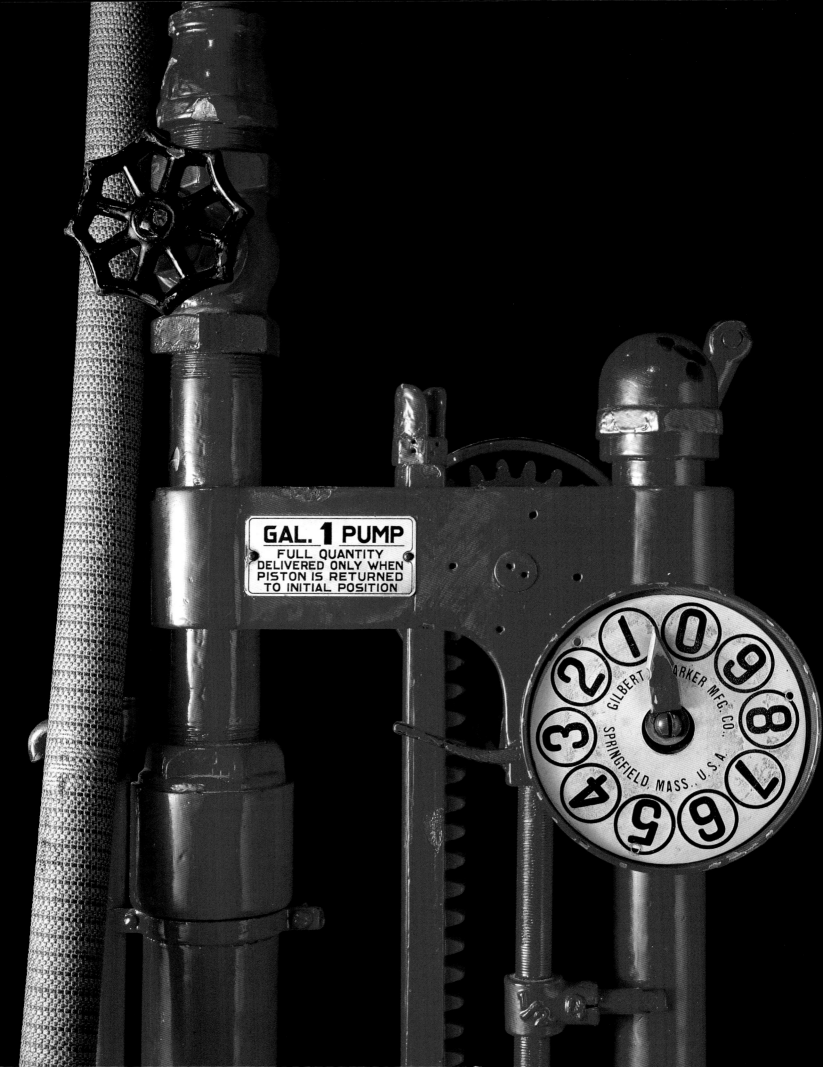

GAL. **1** PUMP
FULL QUANTITY
DELIVERED ONLY WHEN
PISTON IS RETURNED
TO INITIAL POSITION

GILBERT & BARKER MFG. CO.
SPRINGFIELD, MASS., U.S.A.

Opposite: *This 1920s gasoline pump was a step along the way toward efficient fuel deliveries— and, though no one knew it, toward the "energy crisis" of today. Before there were gas pumps, horse-drawn tank wagons delivered gas to the stations, and the customer took it away in cans. The pump was designed to eliminate the cans.*

Above: *New York City has hardly been known as a center for automotive manufacture, but it was the home of the Simplex Company, which made this car in 1912. One of the most powerful cars of the day, and among the most popular, the Simplex has a four-cylinder, four-cycle, T-head engine, right-hand drive, and bucket seats. The tire rims were demountable, and the car carried three spares. This model, which has acetylene headlights and kerosene side-lights and tail lights, stayed in operation until 1928.*

Above: *The open car soon proved to be the enemy of clean clothes and coiffures. This unbleached linen duster of about 1916 protected the dress underneath; the hat and blue silk veil kept the wearer's hair clean and unblown, and the goggles shielded her eyes from cinders, wind, and rain.*

Left: *On April 4, 1913, in Rochester, New York, some presumably satisfied customer bought this Model T for $600. The car first appeared in 1908; fifteen million of them were eventually on the road. It has a four-cylinder, four-cycle water-cooled L-head engine with a rated horsepower of 22.5. Its economic and cultural power was even more impressive: it changed everything from politics to courtship habits and quite literally remade the American landscape.*

This Sunoco blending pump of 1956 could deliver nine different grades of gasoline, each with the required number of octanes to suit various engines. It also incorporates the computer pump of the 1930s, which delivers fractions of gallons and calculates the price as the gas is pumped into the car.

The phrase "Mack truck" quickly came to denote something gigantic, as in "a hole so big you could drive a Mack truck through it." This Mack Bulldog, as the seven-ton Model AC was called, was made in 1930 with a four-cylinder, 40 horsepower engine. Mack Bulldogs first appeared in 1915 and were manufactured almost unchanged until 1937. This dumptruck belonged to Victor Ottilio, a New Jersey contractor who used it in two celebrated projects—the building of the George Washington Bridge and of the Lincoln Tunnel, both of which run between New York City and New Jersey.

He saw me looking with admiration at his car. "It's pretty, isn't it, old sport!" He jumped off to give me a better view. "Haven't you seen it before?"

I'd seen it. Everybody had seen it. It was a rich cream color, bright with nickel, swollen here and there in its monstrous length with triumphant hat-boxes and supper boxes and tool boxes, and terraced with a labyrinth of wind-shields that mirrored a dozen suns.

—F. Scott Fitzgerald,
The Great Gatsby, *1925*

*B*y 1925, when Gatsby *was published, the automobile had been assimilated into American letters. Gatsby's car may or may not have been a Packard; yet given the hero's penchant for owning all the right things, what else could he have driven? Perhaps the grandest name of American luxury cars, Packard was the Rolls-Royce of America. The first Packard was made in 1899, the last in 1956, two years after the company was acquired by Studebaker. Until 1923, the classic Packard had a 12-cylinder engine so powerful that it could accelerate smoothly from three mph in high gear. The car at left, a Model 902 made in 1932, is an eight. It is not restored but in its original condition—down to the tools in the toolbox.*

Overleaf: *The Packard 902, front view.*

Above and opposite: *An abbreviated history of pressing can be read in the three devices on these pages. The "tailor's goose,"* above right, *was for many years the only kind of iron there was in the clothing industry. It had to be heated on a stove, it weighed twenty pounds, and it could spoil the fabric. The gas iron,* above left, *of about 1910, was a welcome replacement. Gas was piped in through a rubber hose and kept the iron uniformly hot, though it was still awkward and weighty. The steam pressing machine,* opposite, *had one specific purpose—to press the collars of men's coats. The operator stood in front of it, put the collar in place, and lowered the pressing arm with a foot treadle. Made in 1924, the machine was not retired until 1969.*

Left: *With the look of some scientific monstrosity from Dr. Frankenstein's equipment cabinet, this is a permanent wave machine made by Nestle-Lemur of New York, N.Y., about 1928. Through a combination of heat and chemicals the machine—depending on which set of clamps was applied—could crimp the ends or the body of the hair. The process was tedious, costly, and likely to leave the patron with burnt locks. By the 1930s, however, every beauty parlor, even in the smallest hamlet, did permanent waves.*

Opposite: *With her hair cut short and properly waved by machine, the fashionable woman of the late 1920s might depart for the opera or dinner in a costume like this loose-fitting blue silk satin dress. The drapery is asymmetrical, and the dress fastens in front by means of snaps on the embroidered panel. The shoes are black silk satin with rhinestone straps.*

Jailed for Freedom

This curious object, displayed in the "We the People" section of the Museum, is circumspect and small: no sound effects, no moving gears. Those who are attracted by it might assume, at first glance, that it is an emblem from the Freedom Riders' epoch of the 1960s. But its date is 1917, and it commemorates one of the desperate and dramatic moments in the fight for woman suffrage. Like so many other small things in the Museum, it has a numinous quality, as though inhabited by a spirit —in this case, the spirit of the suffragist leader Alice Paul.

The pin belonged, in fact, to one of her lieutenants, Amelia Himes Walker, who on July 14, 1917, was arrested and jailed for picketing the White House in the suffrage cause. She was one of sixteen women arrested that day and sentenced to sixty days in the workhouse for "obstructing traffic." During the course of the year, 218 women were arrested and 97 jailed. Alice Paul was among them, for of course the leaders picketed along with the rank and file. Conditions in the District Jail and Occoquan Workhouse where the women were imprisoned were appalling—filthy, crowded, ill-equipped cells, unventilated in summer and cold in the winter. Nor were the women treated gently, once installed in these quarters.

The man responsible for the arrests, awkwardly enough for him, was President Woodrow Wilson. It was awkward because, though he had not shown himself a great friend of suffrage, he did not wish to be known as an enemy. Moreover, he was trying to wage a war in Europe and tended to regard any distraction as subversive. He had tried to ignore the pickets at the White House gates. But when they began to carry banners reading DEMOCRACY SHOULD BEGIN AT HOME, it was more than he

could endure. Alice Paul, the day she was arrested, carried one that said, THE TIME HAS COME TO CONQUER OR SUBMIT. FOR US THERE CAN BE BUT ONE CHOICE. WE HAVE MADE IT—the President's own words, apropos of the confrontation with Germany.

Alice Paul, a Quaker, invariably described by her contemporaries as "slight and frail," was by temperament and training a fighter. Born in 1885 in Moorestown, New Jersey, she had been educated at Swarthmore College and the University of Pennsylvania (she earned her Ph.D. in 1912). In England for part of her studies, she joined the militant wing of the suffrage movement there. The streets and jails of England were a rigorous training ground for a young American scholar. She returned to the United States in 1910 and by the end of 1912 (she was about to turn twenty-eight) was active in the suffrage movement. She had a very clear idea of what needed to be done. The so-called Susan B. Anthony Amendment, written to enfranchise women, had languished in a Congressional committee since 1896, and Alice Paul was determined to revive it. How would she do so? Her plan was simple, systematic, and legal. She would bring political pressure to bear on senators and representatives who had opposed suffrage or done nothing for it. And she would persuade the President to take a stand.

From the 1890s until about 1910, the American suffrage movement had fallen on bad times—its old leadership dying out, and many powerful interests allied against it. But it had already begun to wake up again when Alice Paul came back from England. For one thing, new leaders, in particular Carrie Chapman Catt in the ponderously named National American Woman Suffrage Association, were asserting themselves. Mrs. Catt was a practical, hardworking moderate

427

could be enslaved only if white women were also kept in subjection. The four founders of the Women's Rights movement—Elizabeth Cady Stanton, Lucretia Mott, Susan B. Anthony, and Lucy Stone—were all abolitionists first and, except for Susan Anthony, who remained single, they married prominent abolitionists. All but Mrs. Stanton also were Quakers—for the

criminals." In 1869 she and Susan B. Anthony formed the National Woman Suffrage Association, which campaigned for suffrage but also took a radical stance on many other issues, even going so far as to criticize the institution of marriage. Lucy Stone and Julia Ward Howe founded the American Woman Suffrage Association, which was more circumspect. Over

429

the next two decades, however, the differences faded, and in 1890 the two parties merged.

Though the 1890s were years of discouragement, some gains were nevertheless made. Wyoming came into the Union as a suffrage state in 1890. Colorado, Utah, and Idaho followed. By the time Alice Paul was organizing her Congressional Union in 1914, seven other states (Washington, California, Arizona, Kansas, Illinois, Nevada, and Montana) had granted full or partial suffrage to women, as had the Alaska Territory. More important, and thanks in part to the efforts of Susan B. Anthony and Elizabeth Cady Stanton, suffrage had lost its early "crackpot" image. By 1890 it was a serious movement, and those who fought suffrage had to fight it seriously—with money and political strategy. Catcalls and indignant Sunday sermons were no longer enough.

Alice Paul's particular political genius—or folly, according to Carrie Chapman Catt—was to realize that the President was the man to go after. Even at the conference tables at Versailles, Wilson was not to meet a more determined antagonist. (It was not a personal antagonism. "We respected him very much. I always thought he was a great President," Miss Paul remarked several years ago in an interview with Robert Gallagher of *American Heritage* magazine.)

On March 3, 1913, the day before Wilson was inaugurated, Miss Paul organized a suffrage parade—five thousand women marching up Pennsylvania Avenue. The crowds on the sidewalks were enormous and not always friendly; the District police were not prepared to handle such numbers. The day ended in a near riot, and the cavalry had to be called in. The police chief was later fired.

On March 17, Miss Paul led a small delegation to call on the new President. They asked him to ask Congress to debate the national amendment. Wilson replied—none too brilliantly—that the suffrage issue had never before been called to his attention and that he did not know where he stood. Helping him to find out became, for Alice Paul and her party, a full-time job. They sent one delegation after another, but he consistently refused to do

anything for the national amendment. In 1915 he did return to his native New Jersey to cast a yea vote in the suffrage referendum there. In spite of this well-publicized gesture—and heroic efforts on the part of the suffrage party—the referendum was defeated, as it was that same year in Massachusetts, New York, and Pennsylvania. Since no women were allowed to vote, the referendums in those states were unlikely to have any positive result. More than ever, Alice Paul was convinced that the national effort was the only hope.

Still the President did nothing, and in 1917 he refused even to receive any more suffrage delegations. So the Woman's Party began to picket outside the White House gates—every day, beginning in January, the "silent sentinels" stood with their banners. Today it is nothing unusual for men and women bearing placards to march up and down in front of the Executive Mansion. Unless their numbers are particularly large, they scarcely rate a line in the evening paper. But in 1917, picketing was a radical act, and women pickets were regarded as doubly outrageous. Still, everything went peacefully for a while. On March 4, there were a thousand pickets. In June the arrests began. At first the women would be rounded up and a few jailed and then, after two or three days, the President would pardon them. (Amelia Himes Walker was in such a group.) The traffic obstruction charge was a shaky pretext. The women were political prisoners, of course, and they knew it.

But the pickets did not go away, even after the arrests began, and the authorities began taking a hard line. On October 20, Alice Paul was arrested and sentenced to seven months in the District jail. In what proved to be a tactical error, her captors decided to make an example of the "ringleader." She and her companions were treated most roughly indeed. Held in solitary confinement and denied counsel, Miss Paul was several times forcibly fed. (Force feeding has little to do with nutrition; a tube is forced up the nose and down the throat of the victim and liquid poured through it into the stomach. It is a painful procedure and can cause illness or even death.) In a final attempt to discredit Paul, she was confined to the psychopathic ward. On November 14, thirty women in Occoquan Workhouse were beaten, threatened, and mistreated in what came to be known as the "night of terror." The subsequent storm of critical publicity was such that the Administration itself soon called for the release of all suffrage prisoners.

Even discounting the benefits of hindsight, it is amazing that so civilized a man as Wilson would ever have tolerated the arrests, let alone have allowed the women to be deprived of counsel, given maximum sentences for an offense they had not even committed, manhandled, and forcibly fed. It is impossible that he did not know exactly what was happening in the District jails, but perhaps he did not want to believe it. As Eleanor Flexner points out somewhat drily in *Century of Struggle,* her account of the women's rights movement in the United States, "It is difficult to locate the break in the chain of command which permitted them [jail conditions] to continue so long after the facts were known to Mr. Wilson."

It is certain that he hated the picketing and thought the women unseemly. On June 22, after the first arrests, he wrote to his daughter that the members of the Woman's Party "seem bent upon making their cause as obnoxious as possible." On October 31, having received a letter protesting the treatment of the prisoners in Occoquan, the President instructed his secretary to look into the matter, in the following curious terms: ". . . take this letter to Louis Brownlow and find out whether he really knows the conditions at Occoquan, letting him see how very important I deem it to see that there is certainly no sufficient foundation for such statements. . . ." And in November, receiving another letter on the subject of forced feeding, he told his secretary to reply that "no real harshness of method is being used, these ladies submitting to the artificial feeding without resistance."

It was hardly the President's most glorious episode, nor Carrie Chapman Catt's, either. For even in the dark days of November, 1917, she refused to come to Alice Paul's defense, and in fact carefully disassociated herself and her party from the militants.

In January, 1918, however, the District Court unceremoniously overturned all the sentences and invalidated all the arrests. On January 10, 1918, the President declared his support for the Susan B. Anthony Amendment and the next day the House of Representatives passed it. This was the beginning of another long battle to get it passed in the Senate (it failed the first time around and had to go back to the House again) and ratified by the states. But now the possibility was truly at hand. Whether these great events occurred because of Alice Paul or in spite of her is still debated by historians of the suffrage movement. But as Flexner says, "Too much emphasis has been put, subsequently, on the merits of the picketing—its aid or harm in winning votes for women—and too little on the fact that the pickets were actually among the earliest victims in this country of the abrogation of civil liberties in wartime."

When Alice Paul got out of jail, she went back to work. One thing she did was to have commemorative pins made for the women who went to prison for the cause. Perhaps Wilson, in the end, forgave the Woman's Party for making an aggressive nuisance of itself. In any case, Alice Paul eventually forgave him. Once converted, Wilson became a warm advocate of suffrage—and the Woman's Party never ceased picketing and demonstrating lest Wilson or anyone else forget that the suffragists meant business. Wilson played one role, Alice Paul another. On August 18, 1920, the goal was won at last when the legislature of Tennessee ratified the Nineteenth Amendment: "The right of citizens of the United States to vote shall not be denied or abridged by the United States or by any State on account of sex."

Left: *This finely crafted necklace and comb, produced by Marcus and Company of New York City, exhibits the Egyptian taste of the late nineteenth century. The scarabs, representing beetles sacred to the ancient Egyptians, are set into dulled gold.*

Opposite: *Though their husbands were not in each case universally admired, these dresses, belonging to three First Ladies, must surely have been. At left is Florence Kling Harding's white satin dress embroidered with rhinestones and baroque pearls and worn at the White House shortly after Warren Harding's inauguration in 1921. The slippers are also white satin with French heels and rhinestone buckles. At center, Grace Goodhue Coolidge's red chiffon velvet "flapper" dress, with a three-tiered skirt, a long train attached at the shoulders, and a rhinestone belt is one of the more outstanding designs in the First Ladies collection. At right, Lou Henry Hoover's dress of lustrous ice-green satin falling into bias folds and drapes is a typical early 1930s style, with draped cowl neckline and cap sleeves. The setting for this trio (the manikins are not portraits, but the coiffures are exact recreations) is the East Room as it looked during the first half of the twentieth century. The gold furniture from the room was transferred to the Smithsonian in 1937 by Eleanor Roosevelt.*

Above: *After his heart attack in 1955, President Dwight D. Eisenhower appeared for photographers in these maroon pajamas, embroidered with five gold stars on each collar to show his military rank and, on the breast pocket, "Much better thanks"—a message that the public was relieved to hear.*

Left: *Americans usually take keen interest in what their presidents do for relaxation, as these mementos testify. Clockwise, from the top: Woodrow Wilson's golf cap, Chester A. Arthur's fishing reel, Warren G. Harding's golf club and his monogrammed golf balls and playing cards, Grover Cleveland's fishing flies, and a life preserver from John F. Kennedy's Honey Fitz. They rest on Franklin D. Roosevelt's lap robe, complete with the presidential seal, which he used when riding in his automobile.*

Congress shall make no law . . . abridging . . . the right of the people peaceably to assemble, and to petition the government for a redress of grievances.

—First Amendment,
Constitution of the United States, 1791.

*I*n the exercise of this right—so forcefully set forth by the Constitution—Americans have, over more than two centuries, petitioned their government and have raised their voices against many kinds of injustices. No exhibition at the Museum more clearly reminds us of our courageous inheritance than this one. From left: "Target Freedom" (NAACP poster); "Brother Can You Spare a Dime" (mid 1970s Veterans' protest); "Funds for life not death" (anti-war protest); "I am a Man" (pro-Civil Rights); and "War is not healthy for children and other living things" (Women Strike for Peace).

Overleaf: *This American flag (details shown) is made of some 1600 national and local campaign buttons.*

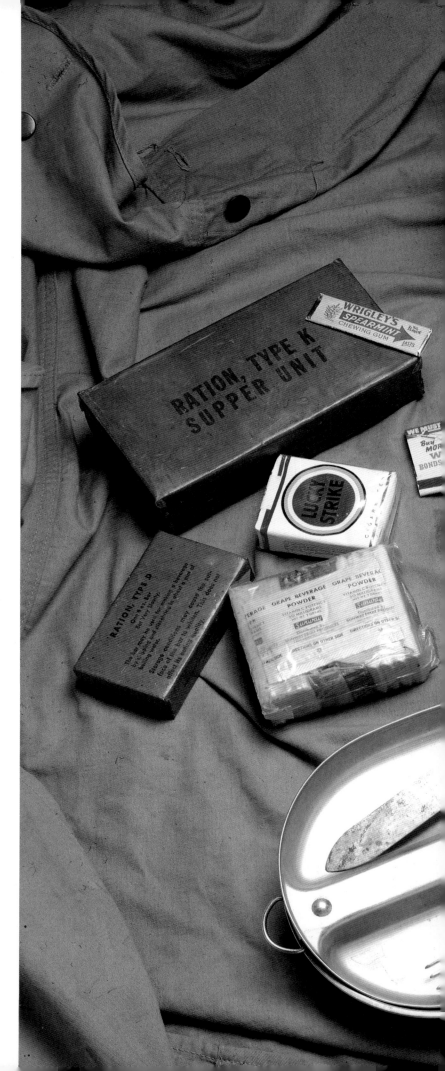

*C*omfort has never been the lot of the foot-soldier, but the design of his personal field equipment has come at least a modest distance since the hardtack slab and coffee can of Civil War times. Counterclockwise, from upper right: The M1 steel helmet adopted by the Army at the start of World War II; a bag of freeze-dried hash with a plastic spoon and two canned spreads (lightweight rations for long-range patrols); a mess kit with knife, fork, and spoon; C-rations (scattered) consisting of canned meats and such small amenities as cigarettes, matches, chewing gum, and toilet paper; the World War II K-ration, which had enough dehydrated edibles for three meals; and a canteen and cup with folding handle. Put into a canvas pouch, it hung from the rifle belt.

Above and right: *For the common soldier, the Army is a great leveller. For good and sufficient reason, it insists upon uniformity and conformity: things have to be done the Army way. This Army barracks from Fort Belvoir, Virginia, was built in the 1940s and used until almost the end of the war in Vietnam. The bunks are as alike as the window-panes; the helmets and shirts are stacked on their shelves with precision.*

Right: *A device fit for a secret agent is this shoe with a miniature camera in the heel (detail, above). It was made not for James Bond but for the* New York Daily News *in about 1940 in the hope that it could be used for taking photographs surreptitiously.*

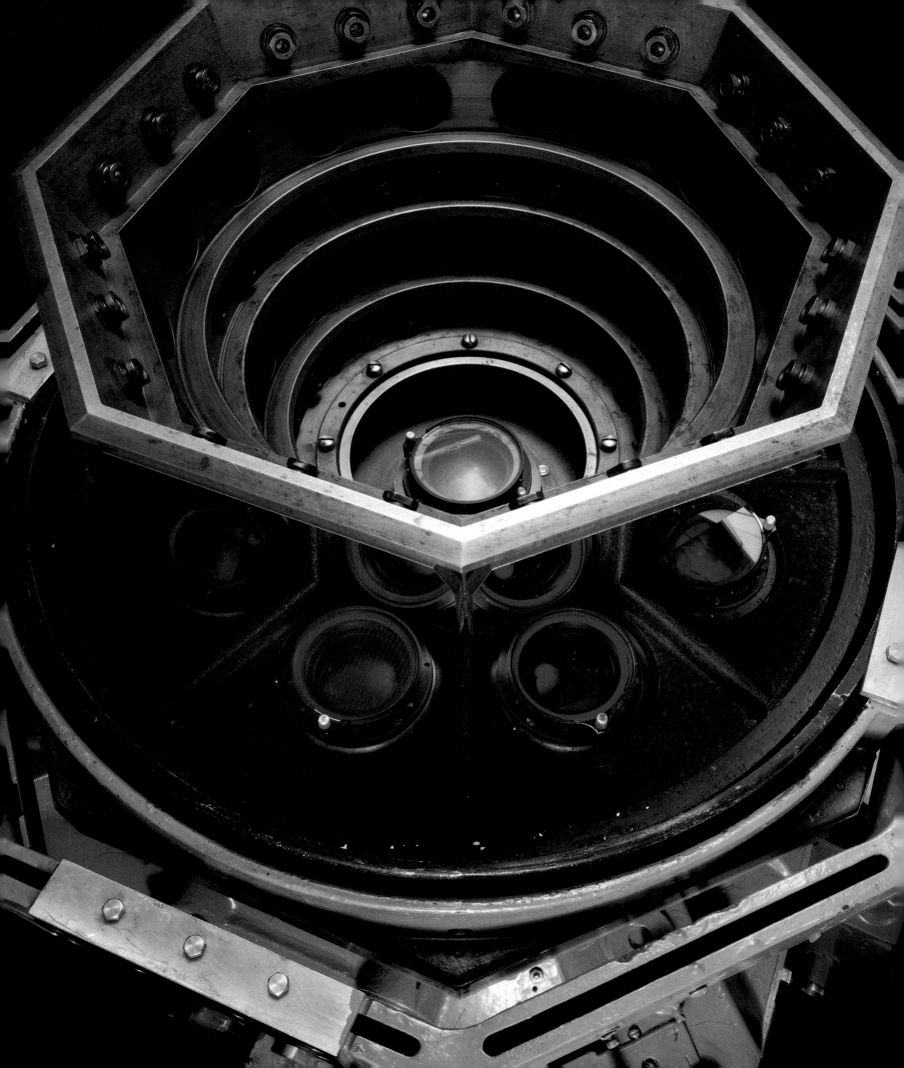

Above: *The Ermanox, a small camera introduced in 1924, has a fast lens and can make photographs in comparatively poor light. Because of these qualities, it was popular among pioneering photojournalists.*

Opposite: *This nine-lens aerial camera of 1935 was used by the U.S. Coast and Geodetic Survey. The central lens is directed vertically, while mirrors used in combination with the other eight lenses produce oblique views. The total field of view is 130°.*

Opposite: *The first dentist to use X-rays was Dr. C. Edmund Kells, in 1898. His office, recreated as it looked in 1905, had a large X-ray machine (right). Like many others working with radiation at the time, he had no idea that it could be dangerous. He died, ultimately, from X-ray exposure.*

Right: *This bacteriological laboratory is the one used by Dr. Simon Flexner and Frederick G. Novy, pioneer microbiologists, in 1905.*

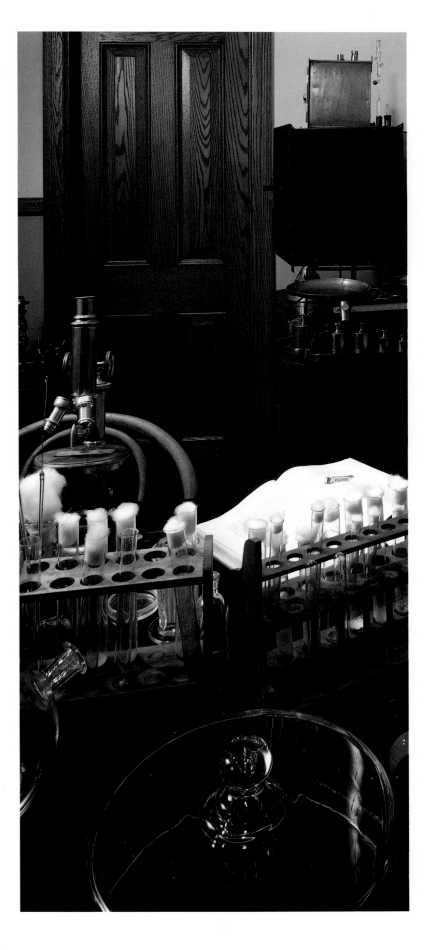

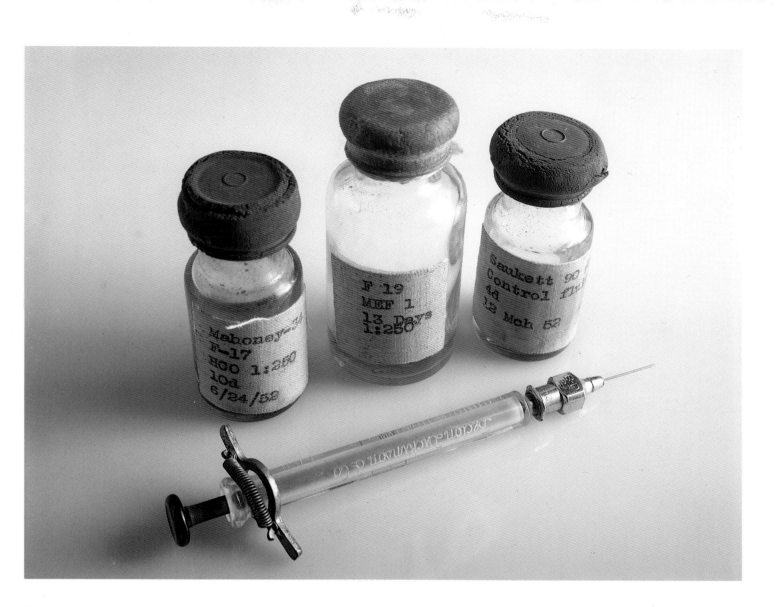

Two of the greatest—and most elegant—advances in medicine in this century are represented by the small and quite simple-looking objects here: the containers, opposite, *in which the first batches of experimental penicillin were sent to the U.S. Food and Drug Administration in the early 1940s, and the bottles and syringe,* above, *used by Dr. Jonas E. Salk in 1955 to vaccinate humans, for the first time, against polio. Sir Alexander Fleming, an English bacteriologist, discovered pencillin in 1928 by observing that colonies of* Staphylococcus aureus *failed to grow in the presence of a certain green mold,* Penicillium notatum. *The mold, he noted, produced some substance lethal to many of the common bacteria that infect human beings. Dr. Salk, experimenting with both live and dead polio viruses, developed his vaccine in 1954—and liberated humanity from a disease as old as history.*

451

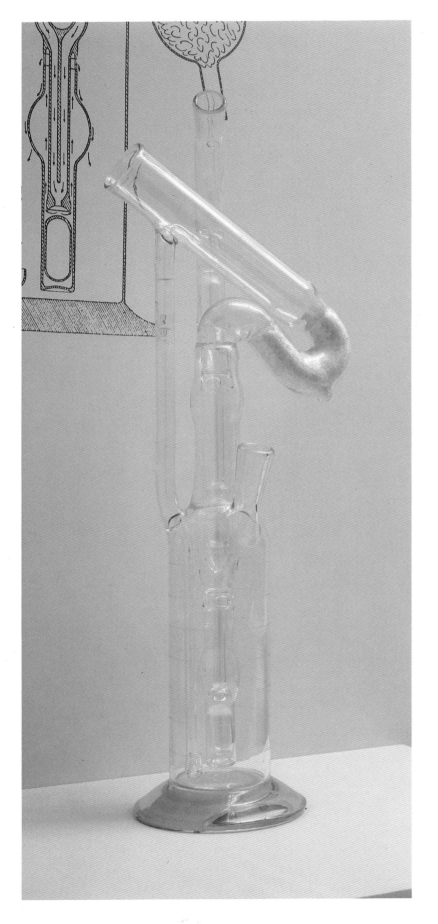

Left: *Designed in 1935 by aviator Charles A. Lindbergh and Nobel Prize winner Alexis Carrel at the Rockefeller Institute in New York City, this delicate glass pump enabled researchers to study living organs, such as kidneys or lungs. By means of pulsating pressure applied from the outside, nutrients were driven from the lower chamber through the blood vessels of the organ, which was placed in the slanting chamber at top. It could live in this environment almost indefinitely.*

Opposite: *This box, assembled in 1950 from a toy Erector set, is a section of a heart pump and a forerunner of the sophisticated heart-lung machines used in open-heart surgery today. It was built by William Sewall, Jr., a medical student at the time. This part of the device controlled the delivery of air pressure to the pump itself. Dr. Sewell used it successfully in experimental surgery on dogs.*

Befo
in su
had to
H. Gib
first sur
lungs app
Shown k
pump inver
Jr., while stil
Made from a
controlled the
and suction r
where al
sion

Opposite: *The Novy Formaldehyde Generator, invented by Dr. Frederick G. Novy of the University of Michigan in 1900, emits a fine spray of antiseptic to combat infection in hospital wards.*

Right: *Two inventions that made radio possible are the Fleming valve (above) and the DeForest audion (below). In 1904 Sir John Fleming invented his valve—actually the first vacuum tube that could detect wireless signals. Lee DeForest's 1906 audion, an improvement on Fleming's valve, permitted reception and amplification and, later, generation of radio waves, making long-distance telephone and radio communication practical, and earning its maker the title "father of the radio."*

In the early 1930s physicists were trying to understand the nature of the atom by splitting it apart. Researchers in Europe and the United States devised machines called accelerators that used electromagnetic forces to accelerate atomic particles to high velocities. Beams of these speeding particles were directed at a target, such as a piece of metal. The fragments of the bombarded atoms flew off into devices that measured their energy or velocity.

Above: *Ernest O. Lawrence of the University of California at Berkeley conceived the cyclotron in 1929. The cyclotron is an accelerator that as it impels a particle permits it to swing in an ever-widening spiral until it attains sufficient speed to be fired at a target. The model above was built by Lawrence in 1932 and attained an energy of six million volts.*

Above: *The synchrotron, built by Edwin M. McMillan between 1945 and 1949, took Lawrence's cyclotron idea several steps further. McMillan devised a different method for accelerating a particle and impelled it on a circle rather than a spiral. The danger sign refers to the synchrotron's 330 million volts—more than fifty times the energy of Lawrence's cyclotron.*

Left: *This television camera tube, made in the late 1930s, is based on the principle of storing a charge of electrons.*

As Edwin McMillan was working on his synchrotron, Luis Alvarez of Berkeley was building this linear accelerator, which fired a particle in a straight line. The section shown here is part of a forty-foot-long section—the first segment of a planned thousand-foot accelerator. This device was not completed because McMillan's synchrotron proved a cheaper way to reach very high energies. Nonetheless, linear accelerators are still being built today partly because the type of intense beam they produce has applications in cancer therapy. The sign at right, "BeV or Bust," recalls the physicists' goal in the 1940s of attaining a billion electron-volts of energy. Today the Fermi National Accelerator Laboratory near Chicago operates a 500 BeV synchrotron, and a 1000 BeV machine is under construction.

DANGER
HIGH VOLTAGE

BeV
or
BuST

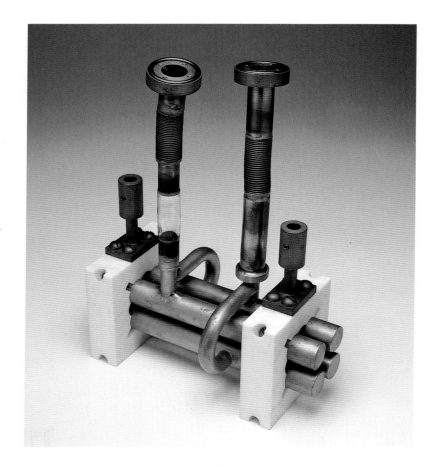

Left: *The first maser, which stands for "micro-wave amplification by stimulated emission of radiation," was invented by Charles Townes in 1954. The maser generates a radio signal of extreme purity. It led to the development in 1960 of an optical maser, better known as the laser, which emits a beam of light.*

Opposite: *In 1952 a twenty-six-year-old scientist named Donald Glaser invented a new device, similar to the cloud chamber, for tracking sub-atomic particles. The bubble chamber, as it is called, is filled with liquid hydrogen kept under pressure just below its boiling point. When the pressure is abruptly reduced, the passage of a cosmic ray or a particle from a smashed atom will cause the hydrogen to boil along the path of the particle. A flash of light illuminates the trail, which is then photographed. According to scientific legend, Glaser got the inspiration for the chamber from watching bubbles form in a bottle of beer. The chamber here was used at Brookhaven National Laboratory from 1963 to 1973.*

Left: *In order to test the idea, based on theories of Albert Einstein, that exploding stars emit waves of gravity, three scientists from the University of Maryland built this gravitational radiation antenna from 1959 to 1962. Joseph Webber, David M. Zipoy, and Robert L. Forward designed a solid, three-thousand-pound cylinder of aluminum freely suspended by a steel cable wrapped about its middle. In theory the cylinder would vibrate as gravity waves pass through it; in fact, exploding stars are too far from Earth to set off the device. However, the antenna is so sensitive that it detects infinitesimal fluctuations in its own length caused by the motion of its atoms—a phenomenon also described by Einstein.*

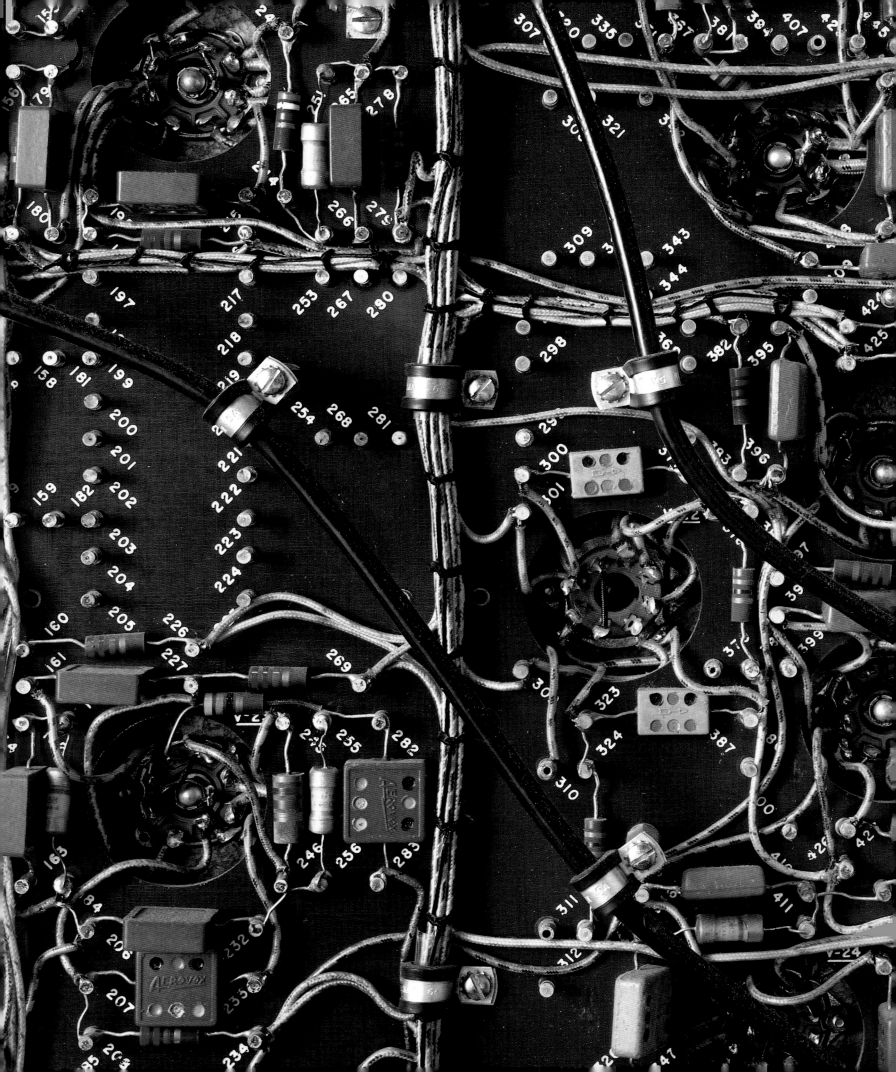

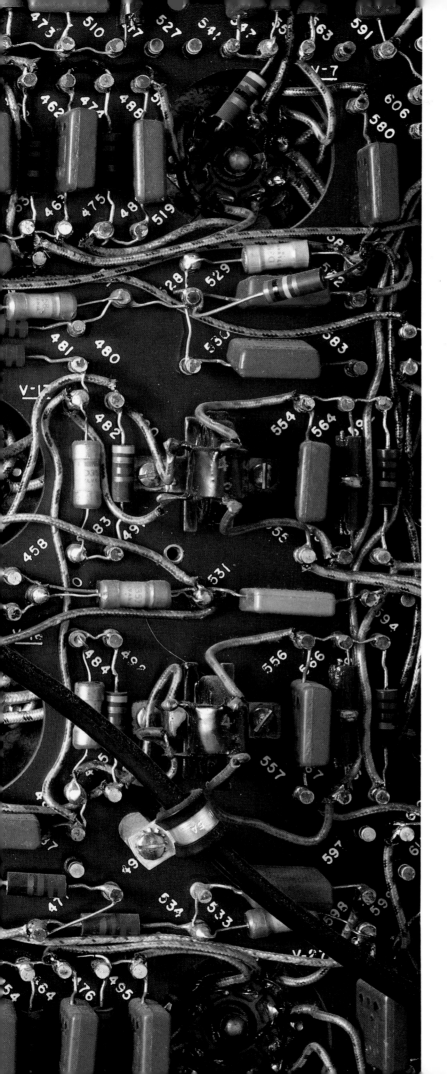

Wars are never without their unforeseen
technological results: computer science came out
of the military needs of World War II and the
Cold War after it. At left is a section of the
arithmetic element of the Project Whirlwind
computer, which was a milestone in its field.
Developed for the U.S. Navy at the
Massachusetts Institute of Technology in 1946,
Whirlwind was used in 1951 as part of the SAGE
air defense system on Cape Cod. Using radar
data, it could identify unfriendly aircraft
automatically, predict their courses, and direct
interceptor flights.

Opposite: *the* SEAC—*Standards Eastern Automatic Computer—was developed by the U.S. National Bureau of Standards. Completed in May, 1950, after two years of intensive work sponsored by the U.S. Air Force, it was almost obsolete by the time it went into service. (The* UNIVAC, *completed the next year, was a far more versatile machine.) Nevertheless* SEAC *ran for 70,254 hours between its completion and its retirement on October 20, 1964.*

Above: *Many inventive geniuses have worked to perfect the modern computer, but the name of John von Neumann, the Hungarian-born nuclear physicist and colleague of Albert Einstein at the Institute for Advanced Study in Princeton, will always occupy a prominent place. This computer, developed by Von Neumann and his associates at the Institute in 1952, incorporates a critical advance: it has the ability to store its own programs in an electronic memory.*

Preceding pages: *Wherever they came from, and whenever they arrived, immigrants to America have clung as best they could to the cuisine of their forefathers. Every city has its "foreign" restaurants, which by the 1930s advertised with neon signs. These come from five different cities and a variety of cultures.*

Left: *One of a legion of famous American players, Stanley Frank "The Man" Musial bats for the St. Louis Cardinals, his team from 1941 until 1963.*

Opposite: *For nostalgic evocativeness, this ticket booth from Yankee Stadium is on a par with any object in the Smithsonian. The original Yankee Stadium opened in the Bronx in 1923, one of many steel-and-concrete stadiums built across the land from 1910 onward, as baseball grew in commercial importance. Every season, thousands stood in line at this booth and bought tickets. Whether the fans sat in box seats or bleachers, the passion for baseball cut across all lines of class and sex.*

Below: *A baseball, signed by Mickey Mantle and Yogi Berra, and four baseball cards.*

470

Above: *The Baltimore Orioles souvenir cap at
left, typical of millions of such items, was bought
by a grandfather for his grandchild at the Baltimore Stadium in 1964. The child's glove, with felt
padding and a brass button, was used by its owner
and his son from 1913 until 1940. The baseball,
bought in 1938, has seen some hard wear but was
kept usable with a covering of electrician's tape.*

Opposite: *The memorabilia of over a century of
American sport are in this exhibit: Abraham Lincoln's handball (above the sneakers in the case at
lower right) is here along with Hank Aaron's
baseball socks (center top) and Muhammed Ali's
boxing gloves (narrow case, far right). In addition
there are Kyle Rote, Jr.'s soccer jersey ("Rote, 12"
at far left) and a bowling pin (right center, just
above Lincoln's handball) that belonged to Harry
Truman.*

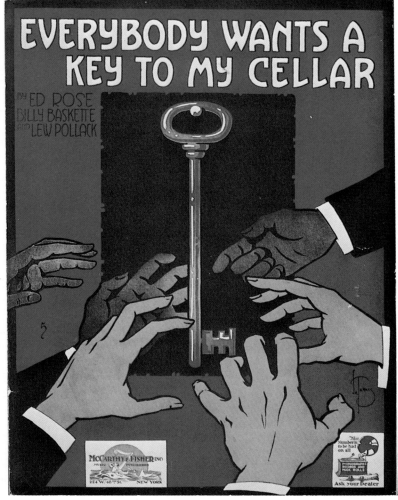

Above: *The "cellar" in question was filled not with peach preserves and dill pickles but booze. This ballad of the Prohibition era was made famous by Burt Williams.*

Left: *The juke box at center (Model 1015, manufactured by the Wurlitzer Company of Tonawanda, New York, in 1946) is in a class all its own: a bubbling kinetic sculpture and a shining icon of its decade, which is fondly remembered for bobby sox and crooners. Other mementos of American music and film are, from left to right, a poster for a Ronald Colman/Loretta Young film,* Clive of India; *Lester Young's saxophone; a bust of Enrico Caruso and one of his records; and various pieces of sheet music.*

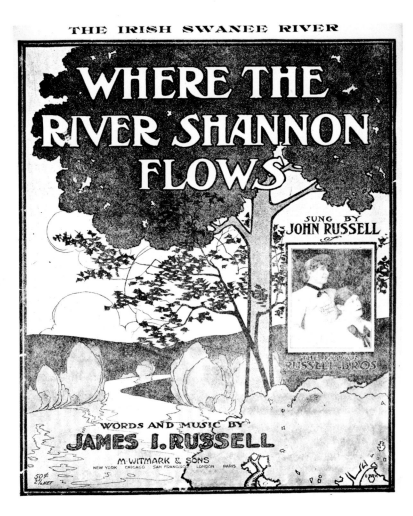

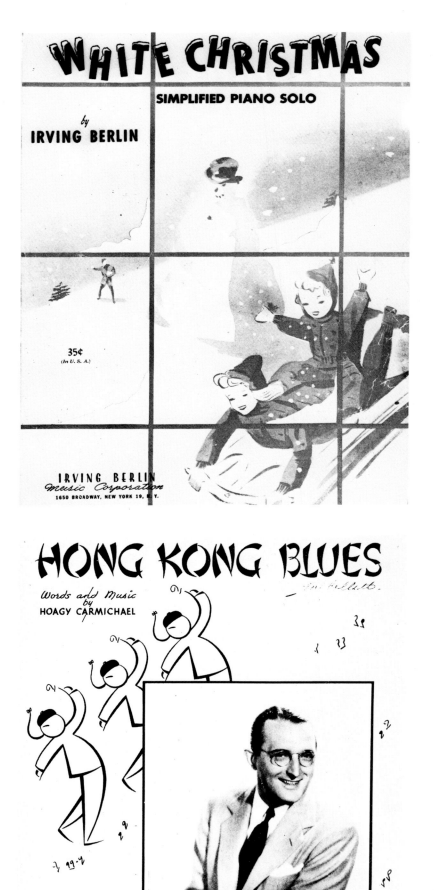

American popular music has always been truly of, by, and for the people. It is comprehensible, singable, accessible, and a vivid reflection of our multi-national character. Reading clockwise from above: a nostalgic Irish song of 1910 by James I. Russell; "White Christmas" by Irving Berlin, the most prolific of American popular composers; and "Hong Kong Blues," written by Hoagy Carmichel in 1939—one of hundreds of American songs with an exotic setting. The bandleader on the sheet music cover is the "Sentimental Gentleman of Swing," Tommy Dorsey.

476

In the 1930s, a form of social dance called jitter-bugging arose in the United States and swept the western world. Rooted in jazz and born in the honky-tonk, it evolved into a free-wheeling, if quite respectable, gyration, usually performed by teenagers to the music of swing bands. (At a famous Benny Goodman concert in Carnegie Hall, the audience rose and jitterbugged ecstatically in the aisles.) Reading clockwise, from bottom left: jitterbugging in London; in Clarksdale, Mississippi, in 1939; and at the Elks Club in Washington, D.C., in 1943—"the cleanest dance in town."

BUFFALO
BILL'S
WILD WEST

COMBINED
WITH
PAWNEE BILL'S
GREAT FAR EAST

"Arrow-head"
the
Belle of the Tribe

Left: *By the end of the nineteenth century, the American Indian had been completely (and often brutally) vanquished, and the "Wild West" had taken on all the pleasant contours of mythology. One of the most enduringly popular of all traveling spectacles was Buffalo Bill's Wild West— a kind of circus and rodeo. Buffalo Bill, whose real name was William F. Cody, was an army scout, buffalo hunter, and Pony Express rider who turned performer and impresario in the late 1870s. His show toured this country and Europe for many years, creating an image of America as the natural habitat of cowboys, Indians, gunfighters, and lariat-artists: an image that lingers on in our national legend even today.*

Opposite: *The Smart Set was a black theater troupe—"40 of 'em," as their poster says—that toured the East and Mid-west beginning about 1906. The comedian J. H. Dudley was their big drawing card, and their most famous offering was a three-act musical, "The Black Politician." The plot revolved around the mayoralty race in a hamlet called Marco, Georgia, with Dudley portraying a wheeler-dealer who shows the locals how the game is played. The show ran to splendid reviews in Rochester, Toledo, Fort Wayne, Boston, and Brooklyn, among other places. The Philadelphia* Inquirer *dubbed it "hilariously frolicksome."*

Above: *The Grand Street Theatre on New York's Lower East Side was the first to be built specifically for Yiddish theater, and its most famous manager and star was Jacob P. Adler, getting top billing here in a play called "The Broken Hearts," probably in 1908. Born in Odessa, Russia, in 1885, Adler emigrated to England and then the United States, earning himself an international reputation and the title, the "Bowery Garrick." He was, at the time of his death in 1926, the best known exponent of Yiddish theater in the world.*

Opposite: *Pat Maloney, a now obscure singer and comedian, was one of many purveyors of Irish wit on the American stage at the turn of the century.*

WITH YOU SOON!
PAT MALONEY

IN HIS
COMIC SONGS
AND
SAYINGS

Above: *Fanny Brice, born in Brooklyn in 1891 and was, beginning in 1910, one of the great stars of the Ziegfeld Follies. She specialized in Brooklyn dialect comedy, and turned her rather homely face into an asset. Though she had numerous plays and films to her credit, she probably was most widely known as radio's Baby Snooks.*

In the beginning American films, though regarded with high seriousness by critics today, were meant simply to entertain the broadest public as often as possible: scarcely an art form for the erudite. *Opposite, top, a family contemplates the offerings at a Manhattan cinema in 1915, which appear to be mostly in the thrills-and-chills genre. Opposite, bottom, again in Manhattan but this time in 1936, Charlie Chaplin brings 'em into the Lyric Theatre with music and sound. Like popular music, films often reflected the genius of recent immigrants, and film scores fed easily into the musical mainstream. Above,* "The Red Lantern," *a song from an Alla Nazimova film of the same title. (This Russian-born star played opposite Rudolph Valentino in* Camille, *among other famous roles.) Above, right, a song that took its savor from the enormous popularity of the Little Tramp.*

CHARLES BOYER
INGRID BERGMAN
JOSEPH COTTEN

Strange
drama
of a
captive
sweetheart!

M·G·M's
MELODRAMA

Gaslight

with
DAME MAY WHITTY   ANGELA LANSBURY   BARBARA EVEREST
SCREEN PLAY BY JOHN VAN DRUTEN, WALTER REISCH AND JOHN L. BALDERSTON BASED UPON THE PLAY BY PATRICK HAMILTON   A Metro-Goldwyn-Mayer PICTURE
DIRECTED BY GEORGE CUKOR   PRODUCED BY ARTHUR HORNBLOW, JR.

Opposite: Gaslight, *released by MGM in 1944 with three now legendary stars of the period, was a good example of the steamy (if perfectly virtuous) melodramas beloved by 1940s movie audiences. Such films were made delectable by the lavish expenditure not of production dollars but of acting talent and excellent cinematography.*

Above: *A yellow brick road and this pair of ruby slippers are the hallmarks of what may be one of the best Hollywood musical films ever made—The Wizard of Oz (1939). Judy Garland, as Dorothy, wore them on her journey to the Emerald City, where at length she absorbed the somewhat deflating intelligence that happiness is to be found more readily on a Kansas farm than in the land of magic.*

*P*uppets have been an enduring feature of American popular theater since the earliest times. Each generation has its own favorites, whether they are muppets cavorting effortlessly on the television screen or Punch and Judy on the back of a wagon. Among the most beloved of all puppets was one that was heard—mostly— rather than seen. Charlie McCarthy, opposite, a ventriloquist's dummy created by the late Edgar Bergen, rose to international fame in the 1940s on a half-hour, Sunday-evening radio show. Charlie, in evening clothes, was a wisecracking sophisticate. Next to him is Kermit the Frog, a green fleece hand-and-rod puppet designed by Jim Henson for television, and by now as familiar a character to millions of children as is Walter Cronkite to their elders. The marionette at right is Howdy Doody, the star of a television show that ran from 1947 to 1960. Right, top: *These two sturdy characters of 1865 are hand-carved of balsa wood and dressed in cotton.* Right, below: *Slugger Ryan, a rod puppet whose job is to tickle the ivories, began his career at Radio City Music Hall in New York City in the late 1930s. This Slugger, made of wood and cloth in 1979, was donated by puppeteer Bil Baird.*

*Arba, the Bicentennial Eagle, made by Ingrid
Crepeau in 1975, appeared in TV commercials for
the American Revolution Bicentennial Association.*

ACKNOWLEDGMENTS

Few books are ever the creation of one person. A book like this one, which tries to catch the flavor and represent the collection of a whole museum, is necessarily the work of a thousand hands. My thanks, therefore, go in many directions.

First to The National Museum of American History and the men and women who made it. I mean the inventors, tinkerers, carpenters, carvers, mechanics, embroiderers, experimenters, adventurers, crackpots, geniuses and dreamers (so many of them anonymous and unsung) who labored over the things—beautiful, heartening, astonishing things—now housed in the Museum.

Second, to the multitudes who visit the place every year and who, through their enthusiasm and appreciation, most truly create the Museum. In doing the research for this book I have dogged their steps, shamelessly eavesdropped on their conversations, watched their faces as they went through the collections.

Footsore and with my two daughters in tow, I am one member of this multitude—not an expert in any sense but an unabashed *amateur* of American history.

As the project began I had the invaluable assistance of Susan Ferris, a former colleague of mine on *Horizon* magazine. She helped me shape the material and did some of the basic research. At every stage I have been guided by the creative and managerial talents of my editor, Edith Pavese, whose name belongs on the spine of the book as much as mine.

Finally, I should like to thank the present staff of the Museum. Robert Harding of the Department of Education has been endlessly obliging—answering queries on an almost daily basis over the past year, and finding out whatever I needed to know. Josiah Hatch, Director of Public and Academic Programs, and his assistant, Meredith McMath, have offered cheerful and tireless help at each stage and without them the book would never have come to a conclusion.

Shirley Abbott

BIBLIOGRAPHY

Alcott, Louisa M. *Little Women*. New York: Collins, n.d.

American Heritage, eds. *The American Heritage Book of the Revolution*. New York, 1958.

Baker, Ray Stannard. *Woodrow Wilson, Life and Letters*. Vol. 7. New York: Doubleday Doran, 1939.

Barnett, Lincoln. "The Voice Heard Round the World." *American Heritage*, April 1965.

Beard, Charles and Mary. *The American Spirit*. New York: Macmillan, 1942.

————. *The Rise of American Civilization*. New York: Macmillan, 1964.

Beebe, Lucius, and Clegg, Charles. *Hear the Train Blow*. New York: Grosset and Dunlap, 1952.

Beecher, Catharine, and Stowe, Harriet Beecher. *The American Woman's Home*. Hartford, Conn.: Stowe-Day Foundation, 1975.

Benét, Stephen Vincent. *Western Star*. Toronto: Farrar and Rinehart, 1943.

Bernstein, Jeremy. *The Analytical Engine: Computers Past, Present and Future*. New York: Random House, 1964.

Billings, John D. *Hardtack and Coffee*. Boston: George M. Smith, 1887.

Billington, Ray Allen. "How the Frontier Shaped the American Character." *American Heritage*, April 1958.

Bode, Carl, ed. *American Life in the 1840s*. New York: Anchor Books, 1967.

Boorstin, Daniel J. *The Americans: The Colonial Experience*. New York: Random House, 1958.

————. *The Americans: The National Experience*. New York: Random House, 1965.

————. *The Americans: The Democratic Experience*. New York: Random House, 1973.

————. *The Exploring Spirit: America and the World, Then and Now*. New York: Random House, 1975.

————. *Portraits from The Americans: The Democratic Experience*. Washington, D.C.: Smithsonian Institution, 1975.

Botkin, B.A. *A Civil War Treasury of Tales, Legends, and Folklore*. New York: Random House, 1960.

Bradford, William. *Of Plymouth Plantation*. Edited by Samuel Eliot Morison. New York: Alfred A. Knopf, 1963.

Bridenbaugh, Carl. *Cities in Revolt*. New York: Alfred A. Knopf, 1955.

————. *Myths and Realities: Societies of the Colonial South*. New York: Atheneum, 1963.

Bronowski, J. *The Ascent of Man*. Boston: Little, Brown, 1973.

Burchard, John, and Bush-Brown, Albert. *The Architecture of America*. Boston: Little, Brown, Atlantic Monthly Press, 1961.

Byrd, William. *The Prose Works of William Byrd of Westover*. Edited by Louis B. Wright. Cambridge, Mass.: The Belknap Press of Harvard University, 1966.

Calder, Ritchie. *The Evolution of the Machine*. New York and Washington, D.C.: American Heritage and Smithsonian Institution, 1968.

Catt, Carrie Chapman, and Shuler, Nettie Rogers. *Woman Suffrage and Politics: The Inner Story of the Suffrage Movement*. New York: Charles Scribner's Sons, 1923.

Catton, Bruce, and American Heritage, eds. *American Heritage Picture History of the Civil War*. New York, 1960.

Catton, Bruce and William B. *The Bold and Magnificent Dream*. New York: Doubleday, 1978.

Clark, Ronald W. *Edison*. New York: G. P. Putnam's Sons, 1977.

Commager, Henry Steele. *The American Mind: An Interpretation of American Thought and Character Since the 1880s*. New Haven, Conn.: Yale University Press, 1950.

————, ed. *The Blue and the Gray*. Indianapolis: Bobbs-Merrill, 1950, 1973.

————, ed. *Documents of American History*. New York: Appleton-Century-Crofts, 1973.

Commager, Henry Steele, and Nevins, Allan. *The Heritage of America*. Boston: Little, Brown, 1949.

Conot, Robert. *A Streak of Luck: The Life and Legend of Thomas Alva Edison*. New York: Seaview Books, 1979.

Cooke, Alistair. *America*. New York: Alfred A. Knopf, 1973.

Coolidge, Olivia. *Women's Rights: The Suffrage Movement in America, 1848–1920*. New York: E.P. Dutton, 1966.

Cooper, Grace Rogers. *The Sewing Machine*. Washington, D.C.: Smithsonian Institution, 1976.

Cooper, James Fenimore. *The Leatherstocking Saga*. New York: Modern Library, 1966.

Cowan, Harrison J. *Time and Its Measurement*. Cleveland and New York: World Publishing, 1958.

Cummings, Richard D. *The American and His Food: A History of Food Habits*. New York: Arno Press, 1970.

Davidson, Marshall. *The American Heritage History of Notable American Houses*. New York, 1971.

————. *Life in America*. Boston: Houghton Mifflin, 1951.

Davis, Burke. *Jeb Stuart, The Last Cavalier*. New York: Rinehart, 1957.

Degler, Carl N. *Out of Our Past: The Forces That Shaped Modern America*. New York: Harper and Row, 1959.

Ellmann, Richard, ed. *New Oxford Book of American*

Verse. New York: Oxford University Press, 1976.

Evans, Christopher. *The Micro Millennium*. New York: Viking, 1979.

Finn, Bernard. "Edison." In *Dictionary of Scientific Biography* 4. New York: Charles Scribner's Sons, 1971.

Flexner, Eleanor. *Century of Struggle*. Cambridge, Mass.: The Belknap Press of Harvard University, 1959, 1975.

Florman, Samuel C. *The Existential Pleasures of Engineering*. New York: St. Martin's Press, 1976.

Foote, Shelby. *The Civil War, A Narrative*. New York: Random House, 1974.

Franklin, Benjamin. *Autobiography*. New York: Heritage Press, 1951.

Fry, Gladys-Marie. "Harriet Powers: Portrait of a Black Quilter." In *Missing Pieces: Georgia Folk Art 1770–1976* (exhibition catalog). n.d.

Gallagher, Robert. "I Was Arrested, Of Course" (interview with Alice Paul). *American Heritage*, February 1974.

Giedion, Sigfried. *Mechanization Takes Command*. New York: Oxford University Press, 1948.

Glaab, Charles, and Brown, A. T. *A History of Urban America*. New York: Macmillan, 1967.

Gluck, Sherna, ed. *From Parlor to Prison: Five American Suffragists Talk About Their Lives*. New York: Vintage Books, 1976.

Green, Constance M. *The Rise of Urban America*. New York: Harper and Row, 1965.

Greene, Lorenzo Johnston. *The Negro in Colonial New England*. New York: Atheneum, 1974.

Harrison, Molly. *The Kitchen in History*. New York: Charles Scribner's Sons, 1972.

Hellman, Geoffrey T. *The Smithsonian: Octopus on the Mall*. Philadelphia: J. B. Lippincott, 1967.

Hofstadter, Richard. "America as a Gun Culture." *American Heritage*, October 1970.

Holbrook, Stewart H. *The Story of American Railroads*. New York: Crown Publishers, 1947.

Irwin, Inez Haynes. *The Story of the Woman's Party*. New York: Harcourt, Brace, 1921.

Isham, Norman. *Early American Houses*. New York: Da Capo Press, 1967.

Jensen, Oliver. *The American Heritage History of Railroads in America*. New York, 1975.

Kammen, Michael. *People of Paradox*. New York: Alfred A. Knopf, 1972.

Karp, Walter. *The Smithsonian Institution*. New York and Washington, D.C.: American Heritage and Smithsonian Institution, n.d.

Kennett, Lee, and Anderson, James LaVerne. *The Gun in America: The Origins of a National Dilemma*. Westport, Conn.: Greenwood Press, 1975.

Kidwell, Claudia B., and Christman, Margaret C. *Suiting Everyone: The Democratization of Clothing in America*. Washington, D.C.: Smithsonian Institution, 1974.

Kimball, Fiske. *Domestic Architecture of the American Colonies and of the Early Republic*. New York: Dover Publications, 1922, 1966.

Kouwenhoven, John. *Made in America*. New York: Doubleday, 1948.

Kraus, George. *High Road to Promontory*. Palo Alto, Calif.: American West, 1969.

Lacour-Gayet, Robert. *Everyday Life in the United States Before the Civil War*. New York: Frederick Ungar, 1969.

Langdon, William C. *Everyday Things in American Life, 1776–1876*. New York: Charles Scribner's Sons, 1937–41.

Lerner, Gerda. *The Grimké Sisters from South Carolina*. New York: Schocken Books, 1971.

Ley, Sandra. *Fashion for Everyone: The Story of Ready to Wear*. New York: Charles Scribner's Sons, 1975.

Lindsay, Merrill. *The Kentucky Rifle*. New York: Arma Press, 1972.

Lomax, Alan. *Folk Songs of North America*. New York: Doubleday, 1960.

Lord, Francis A., and Yoseloff, Thomas. *Civil War Sutlers and Their Wares*. Cranbury, N.J.: A. S. Barnes, 1969.

Lynes, Russell. *The Domesticated Americans*. New York: Harper and Row, 1963.

Lyon, Peter. "Isaac Singer and His Wonderful Sewing Machine." *American Heritage*, October 1958.

Marzio, Peter C., ed. *A Nation of Nations*. New York and Washington, D.C.: Harper and Row and Smithsonian Institution, 1976.

McKelvey, Blake. *The City in American History*. London: Geo. Allen and Unwin, 1969.

Moreau de St. Méry's American Journey (1793–1798). New York: Doubleday, 1947.

Morison, Elting E. *From Know-how to Nowhere: The Development of American Technology*. New York: Basic Books, 1965.

Mumford, Lewis. *Roots of Contemporary American Architecture*. New York: Reinhold, 1952.

Pollard, H. B. C. *A History of Firearms*. New York: B. Franklin Press, 1973.

Potter, David M. *History and American Society*. New York: Oxford University Press, 1973.

———. *People of Plenty: Economic Abundance and the American Character*. Chicago: University of Chicago, 1954.

Risch, Erna. *Quartermaster Support of the Army; A History of the Corps 1775–1939*. Washington, D.C.: Quartermaster Historian's Office, Office of the Quartermaster General, 1962.

Root, Waverley, and de Rochemont, Richard. *Eating in America, A History*. New York: William Morrow, 1976.

Shields, Joseph, Jr. *From Flintlock to M1*. New York: Coward McCann, 1954.

Shurtleff, Harold R. *The Log Cabin Myth*. Cambridge, Mass.: Harvard University, 1939.

Sloane, Eric. *A Museum of Early American Tools.* New York: W. Funk, 1964.

Spruill, Julia Cherry. *Women's Life and Work in the Southern Colonies.* New York: W.W. Norton, 1972.

Stein, Leon, ed. *Out of the Sweatshop.* New York: Quadrangle/The New York Times Book Company, 1977.

Stern, Philip van Doren, ed. *Soldier Life in the Union and Confederate Armies.* Bloomington, Ind.: Indiana University, 1961.

Taylor, George R. *The Turner Thesis.* Lexington, Mass.: D.C. Heath, 1972.

Thomas, Shirley. *Computers, Their History, Present Application, and Future.* New York: Holt, Rinehart and Winston, 1965.

Thomason, John W., Jr. *Jeb Stuart.* New York: Charles Scribner's Sons, 1929.

Thomson, Peggy. *Museum People: Collectors and Keepers at the Smithsonian.* Englewood Cliffs, N.J.: Prentice-Hall, 1977.

Tocqueville, Alexis de. *Democracy in America.* Translated by George Lawrence; edited by J.P. Mayer and Max Lerner. New York: Harper and Row, 1966.

Twain, Mark. *The Complete Adventures of Tom Sawyer and Huckleberry Finn.* New York: Harper and Row, 1978.

United States Bureau of the Census. *The Social and Economic Status of the Black Population in the United States: An Historical View. 1790–1978.* Washington, D.C.: Current Population Reports, Special Studies, Series P-23, No. 80.

Van Doren, Carl. *Benjamin Franklin.* New York: Viking, 1938.

Wade, Richard C. *The Urban Frontier: The Rise of Western Cities, 1790–1830.* Cambridge, Mass.: Harvard University, 1971.

Waterman, Thomas T. *The Dwellings of Colonial America.* Chapel Hill, N.C.: University of North Carolina, 1950.

Weisberger, Bernard. *The American Heritage History of the American People.* New York, 1970.

Wheeler, Gervase. *Homes for the People.* New York: Charles Scribner's Sons, 1855.

White, John H., Jr. *A History of the American Locomotive: Its Development, 1830–1880.* New York: Dover Publications, 1979.

Wiley, Bell Irwin. *The Life of Billy Yank.* Indianapolis: Bobbs-Merrill, 1952.

Wills, Garry. *Inventing America.* New York: Vintage Books, 1979.

Woodmason, Charles. *The Carolina Backcountry on the Eve of the Revolution.* Chapel Hill, N.C.: University of North Carolina, 1953.

INDEX

CREDITS

Grateful acknowledgment is made for permission to quote from the following works:
The American Heritage History of Railroads in America © 1975 American Heritage Publishing Company, Inc. *Benjamin Franklin* by Carl Van Doren © 1938 by Carl Van Doren, renewed 1966 by Ann Van Doren Ross, Margaret Van Doren Bevans, and Barbara Van Doren Klaw. Reprinted by permission of Viking-Penguin, Inc. *The Bold and Magnificent Dream* by Bruce and William Catton, published by Doubleday & Company, Inc. *The Domesticated Americans* by Russell Lynes © 1957, 1963 by Russell Lynes. Published by Harper & Row. *Inventing America: Jefferson's Declaration of Independence* by Garry Wills, published by Doubleday & Company, Inc. *Soldier Life in the Union and Confederate Armies* by Philip Van Doren Stern, published by the Indiana University Press.

All color photographs were taken by Michael Freeman and Robert Golden except for the following:
Lee Boltin: pages 380, 382, 383 top and bottom, 386 top, 387, 388, 389.
Bart Gorin: pages 470 bottom, 485 top.
John Lynch: pages 438–9.